Praise for *Can't Take It with You*

"Lewis Cullman is one of this nation's major and most generous philanthropists. Here he combines a fascinating autobiography of a life in finance with a powerful exposé of how the business of giving works, including some tips for all of us on how to leverage our money to enlarge our largess."
—Walter Cronkite

"Lewis Cullman has woven a rich and seamless fabric from the varied strands of his business, philanthropic, and personal life. Every chapter is filled with wonderful insights and amusing anecdotes that illuminate a life that has been very well lived. This book has been written with an honesty and candor that should serve as a model for others."
—David Rockefeller

"An extraordinary look at the accomplishments of a pioneer in finance. Cullman has approached his role as a philanthropist with vigor and presents a powerful argument for reform among private foundations."
—George Soros
Chairman, Soros Fund Management

"I was so enjoyably exhausted after reading the book—I can only imagine living the life! It seems there is no good cause that Lewis has not supported, no good business opportunity that Lewis has missed, and no fun that Lewis has not had."
—Agnes Gund
President Emerita,
The Museum of Modern Art

"Now I know that venture capitalism and horse trading are almost as much fun as looking for new species in the Amazon. This book is exceptionally well written. The prose is evocative, vibrant, and inspirational."
—Edward O. Wilson
Professor Emeritus, Harvard University
Honorary Curator in Entomology,
Harvard's Museum of Comparative Zoology

"A fun read...an insider's story."
—John S. Reed
Interim Chairman and CEO,
New York Stock Exchange

CAN'T TAKE IT WITH YOU

CAN'T TAKE IT WITH YOU

The Art of Making and Giving Money

LEWIS B. CULLMAN

WILEY

JOHN WILEY & SONS, INC.

Published by John Wiley & Sons, Inc., Hoboken, New Jersey.
Published simultaneously in Canada.

For general information on our other products and services, or technical support, please
contact our Customer Care Department within the United States at 800-762-2974, outside
the United States at 317-572-3993 or fax 317-572-4002.

Wiley also publishes its books in a variety of electronic formats. Some content that appears
in print may not be available in electronic books.

For more information about Wiley products, visit our web site at www.wiley.com.

Library of Congress Cataloging-in-Publication Data

Cullman, Lewis B., 1919–
   Can't take it with you : the art of making and giving money / Lewis B.
Cullman.
      p. cm.
     ISBN 0-471-65763-8 (cloth : alk. paper)
  1. Cullman, Lewis B., 1919– 2. Businessmen—United States—Biography.
3. Philanthropists—United States—Biography. I. Title: Can't take it with you.
II. Title.
HC102.5.C85 A3 2004
332.63′27′092—dc22

                                     2003023866

Printed in the United States of America

10 9 8 7 6 5 4 3 2 1

To Dorothy

CONTENTS

FOREWORD

Readers of Lewis Cullman's wonderfully engaging memoirs will find themselves in the company of a master storyteller who weaves at least five different themes into the narrative of his life.

There is, to begin with, the *bildingsroman*-like tale of the young Lewis breaking free from the seemingly preordained fate of a life in the family tobacco business prescribed for him by his father.

Next, there is the story of a pioneering entrepreneur who, through a combination of superb analytical ability and exquisite bargaining skills, helps to create the leveraged buyout. Lewis's first success in this area validated his ability to be a substantial player in business independently of his father. It also created the network of friends and business associates who were to help him string together a series of deals that, when described by Lewis, make for compelling reading.

A third tale is the deep satisfaction Lewis Cullman finally found not just in buying and selling off companies but, rather, in taking one from a small-scale operation grossing $15 million a year and building it into the dominant force in the U.S. calendar market, with annual revenues of $500 million. This, of course, is the story of Keith Clark, later known as the At-A-Glance Group, through which Lewis helped transform the economic landscape of Western New York State by providing employment for some 1,400 people and giving the At-A-Glance workforce, not to mention the community of Sidney, New York, the best childcare facility that I have ever seen.

The wealth that At-A-Glance produced put Lewis and his wife, Dorothy, in a position to follow the dictates of his mother, who taught him the value of philanthropy. She stressed the pleasure of giving money away during one's lifetime, rather than simply bequeathing it after death. The story of how Lewis and Dorothy set out to give, to date, $100 million to organizations that they care about is one of the most fascinating aspects of this book. The Cullmans are engaged philanthropists; they take an active role in the affairs of the cultural and educational endeavors they support. Their generosity is magnificent, but they are also ingenious in the ways that they make their gifts both take institutions in new directions and leverage other gifts as well. Lewis's descriptions of his support of Chess-in-the-Schools, The New York Public Library, The American Museum of Natural History, The Museum of Modern Art, The New York Botanical Garden, The Metropolitan Museum of Art, and many others make for the most instructive reading in this volume, one that all individuals, wealthy or not, should find inspiring.

Finally, there is a fifth story to be found in these memorable pages, and that is the telling of a life that, for all its successes, has had its fair share of both domestic heartache and, in his marriage to Dorothy, happiness. Mr. Cullman's emotional honesty in these sections is every bit as compelling as his descriptions of the art of deal making.

Throughout all of these five story threads there runs a single unifying theme: "Success is simply often a matter of opening yourself up to opportunity," as Lewis puts it with typical cogency. Lewis Cullman had the good sense to open himself up to opportunity throughout his life, and that strategy brought him a lot: the happiness of being a meteorologist, despite his father's disapproval; the success of being one of America's first venture capitalists; the satisfaction in building Keith Clark into one of the best managed companies in the country; the joy of substantial, enlightened philanthropy; and the satisfaction of a long and happy marriage.

There are lessons for all readers in the life story of this exemplary American. We are grateful to Lewis Cullman for sharing it with us.

—Paul LeClerc

President, The New York Public Library

PREFACE

A few years back I was congratulating my friend Bob Menschel on the publication of his book, *Markets, Mobs, & Mayhem*, when he suggested I write a memoir of my own life and career. A book? The idea struck me as crazy at first. I had sold my company and retired from the business world in 1999 at the tender age of 80, but I had done so only in order to have more resources and time to devote to what had become an all-consuming passion for my wife, Dorothy, and me: giving our money away to worthy causes, in ways that it might do the most good. Now, I was up to my ears in charitable organizations and boards. Where was I going to find the time to write a memoir?

The more I pondered a book, though, the more I thought it might just make sense. For one thing, I had a running start—a kind of personal memory bank just waiting for me up at Columbia University. I had been interviewed three times by the school's Oral History Research Office, in 1978, 1988, and again in 1998. Events grown murky to me were captured in those transcripts in great detail: the ins and outs of the deals I had been involved in, the fine points of the personalities I had dealt with, my school years and wartime service—in all, over 600 pages of invaluable resource.

I also owned a moment in history that I consider well worth recounting. Four decades ago, I swallowed a whale. With only a thousand dollars of our own at stake, Herb Weiner and I engineered the purchase of a $62.4-million corporation. We thought of it as a "boot strap" deal back in those days, but the press eventually came up with a fancier term: leveraged buyout. Ours was the first LBO on record, and the LBO would go on to revolutionize the world of finance, for good and for ill.

Beyond that, I had been intimately involved in the business world for 50 years, a half century of the greatest growth any economy has probably ever seen. Through my family, I reached back hundreds of years into the history of New York City and the Jewish experience in America. How many people can brag that the murder of their great-great grandfather remains one of New York's most infamous unsolved crimes? Or that another ancestor wrote the stirring words inscribed on the Statue of Liberty? I can. All that seemed worth telling, too.

One of the advantages of making it into one's mid-80s with all one's marbles in place (*more or less*, as my office staff would be quick to add) is the perspective gained and the humility taught. I would like to write that I plotted that first LBO to a scientific fare-thee-well, but the truth is that we made it up by the seat of our pants. Instinct, not science, was the modus operandi at the time, and it's still vital today. So is plain luck and serendipity. A genius, I sometimes think, is just someone who managed to stumble around all the pitfalls.

The final motivation for writing this book has been money, but not in the usual sense. I think people who have been given the opportunity to earn great riches have an iron-clad obligation to give back in equal measure, and I hope this book—and Dorothy's and my example—will encourage others to do as we have done. So much of the vast wealth of America is tied up in sterile private foundations that exist primarily for their own self-perpetuation. It's time to end that, for the good of us all. That's my crusade.

Most of all, I hope readers will have as much fun reading this book as I have had living the life I've written about. Enjoy.

—Lewis B. Cullman
New York City

ACKNOWLEDGMENTS

Like my life, this memoir has been a collaborative effort. I'm grateful to a host of mentors who are no longer around to hear my thanks: Cecil Driver, my senior advisor at Yale; Andy Scharps, who took me under his wing at Wertheim & Co.; Herb Weiner; and many, many others. The late Louis Starr—a Hotchkiss schoolmate, neighbor, and cofounder of the oral history program at Columbia University—helped arrange the interviews that preserved so much of the raw material of my life.

Special thanks to Bob Menschel for making the suggestion that led to this book and to his editor, Howard Means, who helped put the transcript of the interviews into an orderly memoir. Jeanne Glasser, at John Wiley & Sons, saw the book through to publication with grace and care. Selma S. Foer, Susan Mui, and Denise Peppas assisted me in a hundred ways, large and small.

Bob Bernstein and Peter Osnos gave generously of their time and expertise as did my niece, Kathy Talalay, and Peter Galassi and his staff at the Department of Photography of the Museum of Modern Art. Many thanks to them and to all the others who read the manuscript and made constructive suggestions: Judith Bruce, Ward B. Chamberlin, Jr., Walter Cronkite, Gerry Edelman, James Gara, Agnes Gund, Marley Kaplan, Ruth Kaplan, Jerry Kohlberg, Arthur Levitt, Bob Lenzner, Glenn Lowry, Mike Margitich, Susan Martin, Marty Packouz, Marnie Pillsbury, John Reed, Herbert M. Sandler, Bob Silvers, Eliot Spitzer, Marjorie Talalay, Billie and Larry Tisch, Michael Vachon, John Weinberg, and E.O. Wilson. This memoir rests on all their shoulders.

ONE

DEAL ME IN

Every life has a turning point, a moment when what you will be begins to break away from what you were. Mine came on a sunny day in June 1963 as Herb Weiner and I were having lunch at the Wall Street Club, on the sixtieth floor of the Chase Manhattan Plaza, at Pine and William streets. Designed by Gordon Bunshaft of Skidmore Owings & Merrill, the Chase Manhattan building had been completed only two years earlier, and the Wall Street Club was its crown: high-ceilinged, with sweeping views in all directions from a wall of windows. Most important for this story, the club was just around the corner from my office at 120 Broadway.

Herb Weiner didn't cut a great figure—he was short and dark haired, with a mottled complexion. Sadly, he didn't have that much longer left to him either. Within a decade of our lunch, still in his forties, Herb would be dead of what was then known as galloping leukemia. But Herb was a brilliant tax accountant and tax lawyer—as smart a man as I have known, with some of the most expressive gestures I've ever seen. Herb's hands were a kind of running commentary on everything he had to say, and believe me, Herb liked to talk.

The subject of our lunch that day was a fund I had started not long before with a group of primarily Canadian investors. To get around the glacial procedures of the Securities and Exchange Commission, we had incorporated the fund north of the border as The Incubation Group, Ltd., but its focus was purely American. Our goal was to invest in unrecognized stocks—ones with strong fundamentals but little-to-no market charisma, a "sleepers fund" you might call it today. We figured we could buy the securities at a deep discount and wait for the investing herd to discover their virtues.

Herb wasn't with the fund, but we had worked together for several years at Cullman Bros., Inc., the family tobacco business then headed up by my father, Joseph Cullman Jr. Herb left to rejoin Touche Niven (later Touche Ross) about the same time I went out on my own. Both of us had had it with the slow pace of life at an old-line, in-bred company. As I'll get into later, I also had family dynamics to contend with. But I made it a point to stay in touch with Herb because I valued his advice, his analyses, and above all, his original way of looking at the world of finance and investments.

That's what we were doing over lunch at the Wall Street Club: running over Incubation's holdings, tossing around possible additions and subtractions. I was eating a salad, picking apart some long-forgotten outfit's profit and loss statement, when Herb held up one of those expressive hands and stopped me cold.

"You know," he said, "you're making a great mistake."

"What do you mean?" I asked. I was startled.

"Instead of investing in these securities, why don't you buy the companies?"

I remember my response exactly: "Well, that's very interesting. How do we do that?" I had nothing against the idea in principle, but there was the little matter of means to get around. I wasn't from a poor family, but I wasn't sitting on tens of millions of dollars of ready cash either, and Incubation didn't specialize in tiny companies. Buying any of our holdings was going to take some serious money.

Herb's answer was as enigmatic as anything I ever knew him to say: "I have a brother-in-law named Abe Kaminsky, up in Troy, who has this computer…."

That was the moment, really, when the light first went on for me, the moment when I began to glimpse how you could buy a company by mobilizing its own resources. The real-estate people had been doing the same thing for years—leveraging deals based on physical assets such as buildings and land. Talking with Herb, I had a hunch that we might be able to do the same thing using nothing more than a company's earning capacity. We called it a "bootstrap" operation in those early days. The term "leveraged buyout" wouldn't come into common usage for another decade or so, and it would be longer than that before Jerry Kohlberg, Henry Kravis, and others would make the term famous. KKR, the firm Kohlberg and Kravis helped found, along with George Roberts, would even carry the leveraged buyout to its illogical extreme when it paid the staggering sum of $25 billion for RJR Nabisco, then the largest buyout in Wall Street history; but back in 1963, Kohlberg and Kravis were still toiling away at Bear Stearns.

Herb and I were the ones who built the model that the LBO rose from—the ones who first applied the ancient principles of leverage to the complex world of modern finance. Of necessity, we did it entirely on the fly, making it up almost every inch of the way. Within 15 months of our lunch at the Wall Street Club, with a grand total of $1,000 of our own money at stake, Herb and I would engineer the purchase of a business with a market value of $62.4 million.

If only it had been as easy as that makes it sound.

⋖◆⋗

Abe Kaminsky turned out to be no slouch in the brain department himself. Abe was a professor at Rensselaer Polytechnic Institute in upstate New York. I no longer remember what he taught, but his job gave him access to one of those room-sized computers seen in old photos: vacuum tubes, trips and switches every which way, punch cards, the whole nine yards.

Herb and I briefed Abe on our luncheon conversation. Then Abe took the securities I already had in Incubation, entered in their numbers, cross-referenced them with a bunch of criteria we thought would make sense for an acquisition, and sent the computer to work. What would seem like days later to a modern laptop user, the trusty RPI machine kicked out the results, ranked according to the greatest probability of pulling off a successful acquisition. Ironically, or maybe not so, this cutting-edge technology of 1963 had selected as its top pick a company that made its money killing rats and other pests: Orkin Exterminating Company of Atlanta, Georgia.

Otto Orkin probably deserves a book of his own. His parents emigrated with their six children from Latvia to the United States in 1891, when Otto was five years old. He was still in his single digits when he was assigned the chore of controlling rats on the farm the family settled on, near Slatington, Pennsylvania, in the eastern part of the state, northwest of Allentown. By 12, Otto was spreading arsenic in places where rodents liked to gather. Two years later, all of 14 years old, he borrowed 50 cents from his dad, bought his first load of bulk powdered arsenic, and began mixing and selling his poisons door to door.

Teased by locals who called him "the Rat Man," Orkin appropriated the name for his business and started spreading out along the eastern seaboard, working south all the time. By 1909, still in his early twenties, he had saved up $25,000, then a princely sum. Based in Richmond, Virginia, Otto Orkin and the Rat Man Co. began to expand into other pests: bed bugs, carpenter ants, cockroaches. (Generally speaking, cockroaches get bigger the further south you go. In Florida, where they're known as Palmetto bugs and get as big as a toddler's fist, they actually fly!)

Diversification worked. Twenty years later, Otto Orkin was headquartered in Atlanta, with more than a dozen offices in eight states. In 1937, he celebrated surviving the Great Depression by renaming his business Orkin Exterminating Company, Inc. The Rat Man had gone upscale.

Otto Orkin gets credited with many innovations in pest control. He was among the first in the business to begin using DDT, after the military had tested it during World War II. As early as 1950, when television was still in its infancy, he began running ads featuring the "Orkin Man," a corporate logo that over a half century would grow from a cartoon sprayer to a muscle-bound Master of the Pest Control

Universe. Otto was a showman, too. Around 1950, he marked the expansion of his Atlanta headquarters by having the mayor scissor through a ceremonial ribbon of mousetraps. But his greatest innovation had to do with the very nature of the business itself.

Early on in the formation of his company, Otto Orkin did some elementary market research that showed customers didn't think his rat poison was very good. The Rat Man knew his arsenic compounds killed rats as well as anything available, so he questioned his sample group further and learned the real problem was that people didn't know how to use the poison he was providing them. That led to his breakthrough realization: Instead of just selling chemicals, he should be selling a service—rodenticide and application rolled into one—and that's how his business evolved and why it succeeded so well while myriad other small pest-control outfits fell by the wayside.

By 1960, Otto Orkin was nearing his mid-seventies and was ready to step back from a prolific work life that had started in the previous century. He had eight more years remaining—he would die in 1968—but he had begun to cede control of the company to his sons, Sanford and Billy, and son-in-law Perry Kaye. (Sanford and Billy's sister, Bernice, got a share of the pie, too.) The Orkin children showed no reluctance at grabbing the reins. First, they bought out their father. Then in 1961, with the founder gone from the picture, they took the company public, offering up 360,000 shares, or 15 percent of the company, at $24 a share.

Initially, at least, all this maneuvering seemed brilliant. Orkin Exterminating caught the crest of a rapidly accelerating market and rode it to what must have seemed dizzying heights. By late 1961, Orkin stock was selling at $30, up 25 percent from its initial price and almost 50 percent from its low for the year. Because the Orkins held 2.04 million shares of the company, they figured their 85 percent of the business must be worth in excess of $60 million. Then reality set in.

At the peak of the 1961 market, the Dow Jones Industrial Average stood at 735 with a price-earnings ratio greater than 20, and stocks yielded more than bonds. In short, the market was a bubble, waiting to burst. The bear market that followed—fed by the lethal combination of inflation and stagflation—troughed in 1962 with the DJIA at 536, down more than a quarter in less than a year. Orkin Exterminating did not escape the carnage. It bottomed out along with the market at $18 a share, which by the same series of calculations they had used earlier, put the family's share at slightly over $36 million, down a hefty $24 million or so.

Mind you, Orkin Exterminating was still an absolutely delightful business. The company was doing about $37 million a year in revenues and earning $6.7 million pre-tax. It had $10 million in excess cash, virtually no inventory other than some chemicals and applicators, and almost no receivables because the route man would pick up cash on the kitchen table when he came to squirt the poison around. That's why we had added it to Incubation. The share price didn't affect any of that. But having once felt richer than the facts merited, the Orkin clan suddenly felt poorer than they really were. That's the nature of money: It fools you equally on both the high and low ends.

Abe Kaminsky's computer was right. The company had glowing fundamentals, and its owners were motivated sellers, looking for ways to get their money out of a business they had no desire to run. Herb Weiner and I had to sell them the solution. Then we had to figure out how to pull it off with almost no money of our own.

———✦———

Our first trip to Atlanta, in early October 1963, did not start propitiously. We told the cab driver to take us to the address we had copied down from an old annual report. Turns out, that was the former headquarters. Just after going public, Orkin had moved to a very fancy, almost extravagant building, which was part of a new office park. When we finally found the place, we were led into Perry Kaye's office, and then Perry brought in his brothers-in-law Sanford and Billy. I was in my early forties then, but among this group, that seemed almost ancient. None of the three was out of his twenties. Billy, in fact, might have been half my age.

Sanford, it turned out, was the dandy of the triumvirate, and maybe the playboy. He had a fondness for suits hand-tailored in Manhattan—we took to kidding him about it as the negotiations went along. As I was later to learn, Sanford also was not inclined to a long work day. He and Billy both had offices with rear doors that opened up to the business park. Sanford liked to come to the building and check with the receptionists at the front desk to see if any business was pending; then if none was (and that seemed to be the rule), he would head out the back exit of his office and take off for the golf course.

Whether Billy headed for the golf course most days himself, I never figured out. He was simply too young, and mostly too silent, to get much of a bead on. Perry Kaye, clearly, was the brains of the outfit—the only one, in fact, who seemed to do a damn thing actually related to the business—so it was Perry on whom Herb and I concentrated.

Our strategy, basically, was to tell the Orkins what they didn't want to hear, then come back with something that would be much more interesting to them. First and foremost, what they didn't want to hear was that the company should be paying dividends; so that's where I started.

"Look," I explained, "what you've got here is an unregulated utility. I mean, a pest-control service really isn't much different than an electric company or a phone company. People subscribe to the service. They take it month after month. They pay month after month and so on. Now, normally utilities are dividend-paying stocks. People expect that. They buy the stocks because of the yield. So if you want to boost the share price and take your money out of the company, why don't you start paying dividends?"

It was a sensible enough suggestion for someone in my position to make. I was representing an institutional investor in the company; Orkin had excess cash lying all over the place; and announcing a dividend would almost certainly juice the share price, which was then lingering in the low, low twenties. But Herb and I also knew full well that the very idea of a dividend would give the Orkin family conniption fits. They owned 85 percent of the company—paying dividends would be like taking money out of their own pockets. And the dividends the family got on their own 2-million-plus shares would be subject to a top federal personal tax bracket that was then set at 91 percent on taxable income over $400,000, a ridiculous rate.

Perry, Sanford, and Billy didn't disappoint. By word and expression, they made it clear that they would rather remove their own appendix without aid of anesthesia than pay a dividend. That brought me to the second part of my spiel.

"Well," I said, "if that's the case, why not take your money out on a capital-gains basis at 25 percent?"

"What do you mean by that?" Perry asked, I think only half rhetorically. Our dividends gambit seemed to have unmoored their expectations.

"I mean that I'll buy the business from you."

"What do you want to pay?" If Perry was shocked, he didn't show it.

"Well," I said, "the market is around 20, 21. I don't know. Should we pay more? No, maybe that's right. I'll bid you the market."

"That's not enough," he snapped back.

"Okay, I made a bona fide bid. Now it's your turn."

"Do you want a serious offer?"

"I didn't come down here to kid around with you. Of course, I want a serious offer."

They all looked up at me, and I could see they knew what Perry was about to say. This much, at least, they had rehearsed.

"$26 a share," he said after a suitable pause.

"Do you have a room where we can talk this over?" I asked.

As I mentioned earlier, Orkin Exterminating was a wonderful business—an almost trouble-free cash cow. Herb and I figured it was worth at least $25 a share, and perhaps as much as $30. The brothers had hung a pitch over the center of the plate, right in our sweet spot, but the last thing we wanted was to let them know that. Looking part nonplussed, part puzzled, Herb and I stalked off to the room we had been assigned. Behind closed doors, we told jokes and whatever else we could think of to pass the time. After about twenty minutes, we figured our anguish was evident; so we joined back up with the Orkin contingent.

"We're going to buy Orkin for $26 a share, but that's just to set the price," I told Perry. "We don't want the stock. We're buying the assets." The point was important: Liability conveys with the stock, and even back in those less litigious times, we wanted nothing to do with that. Orkin, after all, dealt in poisons.

I can't remember whether I expected the assets requirement to be a stumbling block or not, but it wasn't. On behalf of all three of them, Perry readily assented; so we shook hands and agreed to meet again in a week or so, and Herb and I headed home to New York. Sanford and Billy both looked like the cat that had swallowed the canary as we said goodbye, and well they should have. The Orkin family stood to gross over $53 million on the deal, not bad for people who had fled Eastern Europe two generations earlier. Herb and I were pretty pleased, too, except for one item. We had just agreed to purchase a pest-control company for $62.4 million. Now, we had to find the money. Details. Details.

The cast of characters had grown by the time we reconvened in Atlanta. Herb Weiner was both a lawyer and accountant, but he was primarily a money guy. I'd never before done anything like this in my life. Clearly, we needed someone to help us with the negotiations, and Jim Cherry seemed to be just the guy.

Jim was a senior partner with one of the old-line "white shoe" New York law firms, Hayes St. John. More important, he could sit around a table for hours, taking in all the fine points, never getting excited about anything, and never giving anything away. (Jim was an insomniac. Maybe he was just too tired to react half the time, but it worked!) He was also tried and true: Herb had done a previous deal with him. As it happened, Hayes St. John and I both had offices at 120 Broadway; so I popped in on Jim Cherry one day and told him about the deal we were trying to put together, and next thing we knew Jim was on the plane with us, heading back to Atlanta.

Perry Kaye had beefed up his side, too. Al Garber was a partner in the accounting firm that did the auditing for Orkin Exterminating. I'd met him two years earlier when he dropped in to see me at my office at 120 Broadway, not long after the company's public offering. He knew, of course, that I had picked up some shares for Incubation, but I think he also had done his homework and was aware that the Cullman family generally was pretty active in the investment community. Al never told me exactly why he had come to see me, and never said in so many words that the Orkins were interested in getting their money out of the business, but I suspect that if I had suggested we head uptown to see my brother Joe, who was then CEO of Philip Morris, Garber would have been out on the street hailing a cab in a New York minute.

I didn't, of course, and at that time I certainly wasn't prepared to try to take on a deal like this on my own. But I hadn't been terribly surprised when Abe Kaminsky's computer picked out Orkin Exterminating as a company that might be ripe for selling. And I wasn't surprised either to see Al Garber sitting with Sanford and Billy Orkin and Perry Kaye when Herb, Jim, and I walked into the room for our second meeting.

The Orkin clan had laid on a lawyer as well: Allan Post of the local firm of Hansel, Post, Brandon, & Dorsey. Allan had a wonderful Southern accent—he could make the phrase "earnest money" last a good five seconds—and indeed earnest money seemed to be very much on Perry's and the brothers' minds.

The meeting began on a high note, with a lot of chit-chat back and forth—some of it social, some business—intermixed with a large list of questions about small details. Gentlemanly lawyer that he was, Allan Post especially seemed determined to treat the meeting as if it were all a prelude to a good round of golf, but there was an undertone of expectation that got harder to ignore as the hour moved on.

Finally, Perry looked up from contemplating his desktop, unable to stand it any longer, and asked the question that everyone had been avoiding: "Where's the money?"

Rather than take him seriously—and since our purchase money at that point was almost purely theoretical—I used the moment to try to break the underlying tension.

"Gee, I'm sorry, Perry," I said. "I brought the wrong checkbook."

Happily, that did lighten things up, and we got down to real issues. Orkin was still expecting to report earnings of $1.30 a share on October 31, just a few weeks away. Perry Kaye had used that figure at our earlier meeting to justify his asking price of $26 a share—20 times earnings. At this get-together, we reaffirmed our willingness to buy on that basis and began to lay out some schedules for what would happen when. At the end of the meeting, we all parted with a civil round of handshakes and smiles. Progress had been made. Our team seemed to be a good one. But earnest money had been called for, and we had nothing to show. Obviously, that situation could last only so long. We needed to put up or shut up. It was time to get serious about inventing the LBO.

≈≈◆◆≈≈

Assembling the financing for the Orkin purchase began with a bang. When we got back to New York, Herb suggested we approach the Prudential Insurance Company. I initially vetoed the idea, not for business reasons but because of a possible conflict of interest. My uncle, Howard Cullman, was on the Prudential board at the time. Not only would the Pru be bending over backwards to avoid the appearance of favoritism, but the board really couldn't approve any loan to us so long as Uncle Howard sat on it. The way I saw it, we would be handicapped from the get-go. Herb, though, argued that at least initially we would be contacting the Pru at the executive level, not the board. Besides, Uncle Howard's term was about to expire. By the time the loan got to the board for approval, he would be gone and any conflict of interest would vanish with him.

I reluctantly agreed, and Herb called Ray Charles, who headed up Pru's Bond Department, and told him that he was a partner in Touche Niven and that he was involved in a financial transaction the Prudential might want to have a look at. The next thing I knew, Herb and I were meeting with Ray Charles and two of his top people, Frank Childreth and Brad Thayer, at the Prudential headquarters in Newark, New Jersey. We told them what the deal was, explained why we thought Orkin was a good buy, and without batting an eyelash, Ray said he would recommend a loan of $37.5 million against the purchase.

One overture and we were better than half way there. This is easy, I remember thinking. I should have started doing this years ago. Then things got interesting.

For one thing, the Prudential loan might have made us feel a lot better, but it didn't do much to allay the cold feet down in Atlanta. Our half-full cup was still half empty as far as Perry and the Orkin boys were concerned. And not without reason. The loan the Pru was giving us was basically risk-free from the lender's point of view. Orkin had great numbers, and the business practically ran itself. What's more, we would be paying a little under six percent to the Pru for the privilege of using its almost riskless money. Uncle Howard or no Uncle Howard, *not* giving us the loan would have been a dereliction of duty. But buying a business was a lot like bidding at auction. On a percentage basis, the total price is likely to rise only incrementally in the final few minutes, but that's where all the excitement lies. We were headed into the same territory.

It was about this time that Herb suggested approaching someone with almost as much money as the Prudential and no shareholders to account to: the du Pont family. Our point of entry would be George Weymouth, a very pleasant, back-slapping kind of guy who had grown up in Wilmington, Delaware, home to generations of du Ponts. George was then chairman of Laird & Co., an investment banking firm he had founded and organized. Most important, he had had the good sense to marry the beautifully named Dulcenia Ophelia Payne du Pont. Known as Dio, she was one of the owners of Bohemia Stables, owner of Kelso, who back in 1962 was just rounding into form as one of the great thoroughbred racers of all time. I was hoping Dio's husband had a nose for the finish line, too.

Herb had done a fair amount of tax work for George and knew he liked to bring deals to the du Pont family. We thought this would be a good one for him to latch on to, but George didn't offer his services for free. Herb, Jim Cherry, and I had set up a shell corporation we called Kinro to handle the Orkin purchase. ("Kinro" is simply an anagram of Orkin.) The initial split was 40-40-20, with Jim getting the smaller share as the last man in. Standard accounting practices and principles didn't allow Herb to be an owner of record; so his position in Kinro was represented by Abe Kaminsky, the brother-in-law computer genius who had put us on to Orkin in the first place.

Bringing George Weymouth on board, Herb estimated, was going to cost us half the deal. I didn't see that we had a lot of choice—we had to move forward or we would lose the Orkin family's waning confidence in our capacity to pull this off. But I saw a lot of advantages, too. The du Pont name had been golden since the early 1800s when Eleuthère Irénée du Pont began producing his famous black gunpowder on the banks of the Brandywine River, at Wilmington. If we could bring the du Ponts on board, the Orkins and Perry Kaye could no longer doubt that we were serious suitors. I also felt fairly certain that if the du Ponts put their imprimatur on the deal, my own family might want to come in as well. Basically, I could present them an opportunity that already bore the Good Housekeeping Seal of Approval.

By then, we had closed to within theoretically $10 million of our goal. The Pru had already upped its participation to $37.5 million on a straight loan basis when Ray Charles suggested the company would go in for an extra $2.5 million—or $40 million total—if we gave it a kicker. From our point of view, Prudential would have been justified in asking for a percentage of the deal several million dollars earlier. Besides, beggars can't be choosers; so we suggested a kicker of 19 percent. The figure had no special logic although Herb did point out that we wouldn't be able to consolidate Kinro and Orkin for tax purposes if a third party owned 20 percent or more of either company. At that point, consolidation was the furthest thing from our minds, but we needed a reason to hang our hat on. And it worked: Ray Charles bought the explanation lock, stock, and barrel.

The Pru also approved of our taking $2.4 million out of the Orkin till, about a quarter of the company's excess cash. We were going to ask the Orkin family and Perry Kaye to take back $10 million in seller's notes. That brought the running total to $52.4 million. Add on $5 million from the du Ponts and another $5 million from the Cullmans, and we were home free.

To stack the odds entirely in our favor, Herb and I had the bright idea of inviting Sanford and Billy Orkin and Perry Kaye up to Wilmington to put the finishing touches on the package. George Weymouth volunteered the Wilmington Club, a venerable downtown men's institution, for the venue. George also arranged for his brother-in-law, Pierre Samuel du Pont IV, to chair the meeting. Later a governor of Delaware and still later a contender for the Republican presidential nomination—in 1988, when he never seriously threatened the first George Bush—"Pete" du Pont was both the bait in the trap and, so it seemed, a near guarantee of the family's participation. The best laid plans of mice and men, as the saying goes, do sometimes go astray.

The weather, we had no control over. It was snowing in Atlanta on the day in February 1964 when the Orkin contingent was scheduled to fly to Wilmington. Instead of arriving rested after a few hours of air time, they all caught a sleepless sleeper train that ground its way north through Charlotte, Washington, and Baltimore. Sanford, Billy, and Perry showed up bleary eyed at the Wilmington Club, ready for bear.

The lecture hall we were meeting in—a very fancy room, but far larger than our needs—didn't do much to warm things up.

Turned out, we had no control over Pete du Pont either. In preparation for the meeting, I had written our honorary chairman a script that I called an *aide-memoir*. The name was a joke—a reference to the du Pont family's French roots—but the purpose of the script was completely serious. Apart from impressing Otto the Rat Man's offspring with our Wilmington connections, we had two hurdles to clear at the meeting, and I wanted them both presented just right. The first was the $10 million in seller's notes we wanted the Orkin family members to take back—a show of good faith on their part that I didn't foresee any problems with. (And indeed there were none.) The second hurdle was considerably more tricky.

As mentioned earlier, Perry Kaye had justified the asking price of $26 a share as being twenty times earnings that were expected to be announced October 31. That date had come and gone, and actual earnings had been about a nickel lower than projected. Logic seemed to dictate that we should pay less for the company as a result; so we all sat down in the lecture room of the Wilmington Club, and Pete du Pont read his *aide-memoir* letter perfectly, breezing through the seller's notes and making reference to the reduced earnings before dropping the purchase price accordingly.

That's when Perry Kaye spoke up. "Mr. du Pont, this is not the deal that I negotiated with Mr. Cullman."

Herb, Jim, and I were ready to jump in at this point, argue our case hard, and see where the chips fell, but Pete du Pont would have none of it.

"Well, what was the deal?" he asked Perry.

"About two-and-a-half million more," someone told him, maybe Sanford, and that was all Pierre Samuel du Pont IV needed to hear.

Looking as though he was exercising the divine right of kings, old Pete held his hand up and delivered the verdict: "Well, we're not going to fight over $2 million or so."

He didn't dig his heels in at all, and he didn't give us a chance to dig ours in either. That was it, and it was awful. Pete du Pont just gave the money away—and it wasn't even his to give. I should have realized at that moment that he would make his name in politics.

So much for the Grand Wilmington Strategy. The only thing that seemed to impress the Orkin contingent deeply about the adventure was Pete du Pont's ready generosity. Even George Weymouth hadn't come through. As likable as he was, he didn't really cut much mustard with the du Ponts. He had been typecast in the family as the brother-in-law who kept bringing in all these oddball deals. There would be no $5 million from their side, and without their participation, I had no intention of approaching my own family for another $5 million. We were still in the backstretch, $10 million from the finish line. What's more, it was the critical $10 million—the equity in the deal, the real money.

To his credit, I suppose, George Weymouth was tremendously bothered by his failure to deliver the du Pont family. His pride was wounded: He had assured us when we first brought him into the deal that there would be no problem. I think he also could see dollars flying out of his bank account. George knew what a good opportunity this was, and like us, he knew it was all in danger of slipping away.

As for me, I had just about written George off when he called one day with what he seemed to think was very good news.

"Lewis," he said, "I was out to dinner last night and met with Wayne Rollins of Rollins Broadcasting. I told him about the Orkin deal, and he says he wants to put up $10 million."

"Gee," I said, "That's very interesting. Where's Wayne going to get $10 million?"

"Oh, he's going to borrow it from the Chase bank."

"Borrow it!" I said, feigning disbelief. "Who ever heard of borrowing money like that?"

I was certain this was just more hot air being blown our way, but I figured, what the heck, I'll play along so George doesn't get his feelings hurt. So I said to him, "Look, George, I'd love to talk to Wayne, but why don't you have him get me a letter of commitment from Chase first?"

The very next morning, I arrived at my office and found a letter from an officer of Chase waiting on my desk: "We are prepared to lend Rollins Broadcasting, Inc. $10 million to complete the purchase of Orkin Exterminating Co." To be honest, you could have knocked me over with a two-dollar bill.

In his own way, Wayne Rollins is almost as interesting as Otto Orkin. Like the Rat Man, Rollins was born dirt poor in 1912 on a farm in northwest Georgia. He made it through the Depression by working 70-hour weeks in a textile mill. Then in 1948, he formed a business partnership with his brother, John, in Radford, Virginia. John ran an auto dealership, while Wayne picked up a small community radio station on which his brother could advertise. The formula was repeated time and again, focusing mostly on African-American communities. In 1956, Wayne was ready to take on the television industry. Four years later, in 1960, Rollins Broadcasting, then headquartered in Wilmington, Delaware, went public. And it was all upwards from there. When O. Wayne Rollins died in 1991 at age 79, he was worth almost a billion dollars, a patron saint of Emory University, and a pillar of the Atlanta philanthropic community.

The gifts and the money, though, were all for later, as was the burnished reputation. This was early 1964, and Wall Street didn't have that high an opinion of Wayne Rollins and his broadcasting company. It was an open secret on the Street that the underwriting for the public offering, through New York Securities, had been extremely shaky. Beyond that, Rollins simply was a very, very crafty guy—great for a magic show, maybe, but not necessarily what you're looking for in an investment partner.

Just as difficult, bringing Rollins Broadcasting in was going to change the mechanics of the deal. The Prudential had come aboard with the assumption that it was making a loan to a group of private investors, not a hybrid of individuals and a publicly traded company. Jim, Herb, and I would need to do our own renegotiating, too. Our intent had been to give 80 percent of equity to the first person who put up the $10 million to complete the purchase. We (now, with George Weymouth included) wanted to keep 20 percent for ourselves, for prepackaging everything. Truth told, I was looking forward to being part owner of a highly successful exterminating company. Why not? The place was printing money. I wasn't anywhere near as excited about having a minority position in one of Wayne Rollins' side enterprises.

Still, that letter from Chase was the brightest star in our heaven, and maybe the only way to finally complete the deal. What's more, Rollins Broadcasting was on its way to the best year in its short, shaky history. For the quarter that ended July 31, 1964, revenues would soar 53 percent over the same quarter the previous year, and net earnings would climb 16 percent. After wallowing in the low- to mid-teens ever since the 1961 market break, Rollins' stock had begun to follow suit.

Those signs, at least, looked positive; so we took Wayne over to Newark to meet with Ray Charles and his team at Prudential. Not surprisingly, Ray wanted more—warrants on ten percent of Rollins Broadcasting, as it turned out, to go with the interest and kicker we had already agreed to. Wayne Rollins fought the warrants tooth and nail but finally had to give in. He wanted Orkin as much as we did.

Then it was our turn to negotiate.

"You know, Wayne," I can remember saying, "I don't really think I want to own 20 percent of a subsidiary of Rollins Broadcasting because what am I going to do with 20 percent? I'd have to register with the S.E.C., all those kinds of things. Don't you think it would make more sense if we established at the outset what the 20 percent should be worth and then you could evidence that in Rollins stock?"

To me, the numbers seemed obvious. Twenty percent of the $10 million that was the hard money in the deal, after all the debt instruments and obligations to the sellers (and shareholders) were accounted for, amounted to $2 million. Because Rollins Broadcasting was then selling around $20 a share, I figured Wayne was into us for 100,000 shares of his company. Naturally, Wayne did the math differently; he wasn't going to give us a share more than 50,000. Nothing ever seemed to be entirely straight with him. I was determined to stand pat even if the deal collapsed—or at least act as if I would. George Weymouth was ready to cave without putting up even the semblance of a fight. That's where we left matters: with the battle lines drawn and no resolution in sight.

I recall driving up to New Hampshire in the midst of all this. My wife, Dorothy, and I were heading up to the Holderness School in Plymouth, New Hampshire, to pick up my son, Duncan, for the start of spring vacation. Along the way, I stopped at some country hotel and called George. Practically the first words out of his mouth were that we should accept Wayne Rollins' proposal of 50,000 shares.

"George," I told him, "it's no deal."

"Oh, we've got to, absolutely," he went on. Then he started to scream and yell at me: You're going to do this. You've got to do that. He was raving and ranting. He almost threw the phone down, he was so mad.

"Well," I said when he was through, "sorry, but that's it. You just pick up the phone, call Wayne, and tell him if that's the way it is, the whole deal is off." With that, I hung up, and Dorothy and I went on to pick up Duncan.

George and I had a series of such phone conversations, including one in early June when I called him from a Broadway theater during intermission, but eventually he came up with an interesting proposal to save the deal. He had managed to squeeze only another 5,000 shares out of Wayne, a piddling amount, but instead of taking the 50 percent of the 55,000 shares due him, George was going to claim only 20,000 shares. That left 35,000 so-called Cullman shares, less than the 50,000 I thought we were owed but up significantly from the 25,000 we would have gotten without putting up a fight.

That wasn't the end of it entirely. For one thing, our attorney and minority partner Jim Cherry got the smell of money and started demanding a bigger piece of the pie for his professional services. I think he believed the deal would never work out. Once he saw it coming to completion, he was damned if he wasn't going to skim all the crumbs off the table he could possibly get. We gave him the crumbs he wanted, but that was the last time he ever worked for me. George Weymouth had clearly gotten his own whiff of the money, too. Without ever telling us, he had bought 100,000 shares of Rollins Broadcasting. He'd also helped Wayne as a guarantor on the Chase loan. No wonder he was so desperate to close the deal.

Herb and I also had been holding out for a $600,000 fee to be paid us for negotiating the sale—basically one percent of the purchase price. Naturally, we were looking for more money, but we also wanted to make a case for the Internal Revenue Service that we had been paid on a commission basis for our services. Between George's bumbling and Jim Cherry's greed, the fee ended up being $300,000, and Herb and I got less than half of that.

Money, though, does that to people, and eventually we got everything straightened out. In June 1964, we announced that Rollins was buying Orkin. I particularly liked the way *BusinessWeek* began its account of the purchase, in its July 11, 1964, issue:

In the modern pace of American finance, examples of business Jonahs swallowing whales are a lot more frequent than before. But every so often a deal comes along that still truly captures the imagination...

<hr />

In truth, there were no losers in the Orkin deal. Wayne Rollins picked up the exterminating company he would use to build the service-industry giant, Rollins Inc., that would almost make him a billionaire. Ray Charles and Prudential got their interest, their kicker, and warrants to purchase 115,000 shares of Rollins Broadcasting for 10 years at $22 a share—a sweet deal all around, especially given that Rollins stock had soared to $61.50 a share when the sale officially closed on September 1, 1964. The Orkin family, including sister Bernice, got its money out of the business with minimal tax liability, and the Orkin shareholders got a handsome premium on the stock. As for me, I got to field test a way of turning a small investment into a lot of buying power, and of course, I made a bundle in the bargain.

In all, Kinro had put $1,000 at stake—$400 each from Herb and me, $200 from Jim Cherry—and we had to give up half our equity to get George Weymouth involved. By the time we dotted the final "i" and exchanged 100 percent of the capital stock of Kinro for 55,000 shares of Rollins Broadcasting, my original $400 investment had grown more than 2,500 times, to $1.1 million. (Remember, this was before CEOs routinely pulled down seven-figure salaries and huge stock options for losing market share. A million was still a million in the late summer of 1964.)

It might have been a day or two after the last papers were signed when Dorothy turned to me and said, "That's a heckuva deal. What are you going to do for an encore?" I wasn't exactly certain, but justified or not, I had the feeling that Wall Street looked at this thing as a fluke— something I'd lucked into—and that had begun to bug me. Finally, I said, "Damn it all, Dorothy, I'm going to go out and do this thing again, right away. I'm not going to stop."

I now had some serious money to play with, and I was learning how to use it. Not bad for a guy who always thought he'd be a weatherman.

TWO

MARCHING TO NEW HAVEN

In 1939, my maternal grandmother, Frances Nathan Wolff, published her memoirs under the title *Four Generations*. Near the end, she included a family tree that folds out to three pages. At the very top is Daniel Robles de Fonesca, a Sephardic Jew whose ancestors had fled Spain for the Netherlands after Ferdinand and Isabella expelled the Jews in 1492, just as Christopher Columbus set sail for the New World. (Sephardic, from the Hebrew *Sepharad*, meaning Spain, refers to the Jews of the Iberian peninsula, including Portugal.) In time, the Robles family would emigrate to Essequibo, later known as Dutch Guyana, on the northern horn of South America, where Daniel would be born and take as his wife Sarah Levy. Daniel and Sarah had two sons, Jacob and Samuel, who married two sisters, who gave birth respectively to two girls and two boys, and so the tale begins.

Descending and widening as it goes, the family tree runs through von Honigs and the first Wolff (Moses ben Wolff, descended from a Prague rabbi); Cappés, Levys, and de Costas; Tobiases, Hendricks, Nathans, and Mays, all the while tracing a winding route through Europe and on to the New World. At length, the tree gets to my parents' generation—Frances Wolff married Joseph Cullman Jr.—and then to my own. Stretching out on to the third fold-out page are Frances and Joseph's offspring: my oldest sibling, also Frances, called Nan; then my three older brothers, Joseph 3rd, W. Arthur, and Edgar M., named for Dad's good friend Edgar Meyer, who went down with the *Titanic*. Finally, all the way on the extreme right of the tree, there I am: Lewis B., for Benjamin.

My siblings were all married by then. Their spouses are listed below their names. Nan even had a child, Frances Jacobs. But I'm out on the end of the limb all alone, the youngest child, the only unmarried one in 1939, and the first of us all to come into this world not in someone's home but in a hospital. In some ways, the placement is not a bad metaphor for my childhood and early years.

⬥

I was born with some formidable blood in my veins. From my mother's side came all those well-traveled Sephardim. Unlike the Robles, Simeon ben Honig's ancestors sought refuge from the Inquisition in Austria. By the eighteenth century, Simeon had become a wealthy enough merchant to lend a significant sum of money to the Austrian empress to help finance the war with Prussia. Simeon was rewarded with a monopoly over the tobacco trade and eventually given the title Baron von Honigstein. His son, Aaron Cappé, won a civil appointment to the royal palace and might have spent his mature years employed there had he not become involved in an affair with a courtier and been forced to skedaddle out of the country. The idea had been for Aaron and a cousin, the same Moses ben Wolff, to lie low with a relative in Holland until the scandal blew over, but while they were there, the French Revolution broke out, and the two young men decided to flee the continent as well. They shipped off to the Dutch West Indies, where they set themselves up in trade and intermarried with other Sephardic exiles.

In 1773, another of my maternal ancestors, Simon Nathan, was run out of Jamaica by its British masters for selling the American colonies banned items such as rope, canvas, and gunpowder. (Being run out of places is a theme in all Jewish generational tales, but my ancestors at least found some novel reasons for expulsion.) Landing in New Orleans, Simon wended his way north to Virginia, where he stayed long enough to loan the new state $52,000, for which he received the personal thanks of Gov. Thomas Jefferson. In Philadelphia, Simon married Grace Seixas, and the two of them finally settled in New York, establishing the Nathans there. Other strains of my mother's ancestry had settled in New York, then still New Amsterdam, as early as 1655, right at its dawn.

It was in the generation before my grandmother where the size of her extended family started to get seriously out of control. By the best count, Granny Wolff was one of one hundred first cousins. Thanks to their prolific mothers and fathers, I sometimes think I must be related to every other Jew in Manhattan. One cousin founded Barnard College. Another, Benjamin Seixas, was a founder of the New York Stock Exchange. (Although I have no documentation to prove it, I also must be related to Vic Seixas, one of the dominant professional tennis players of the 1950s.)

Yet another cousin married the New York state jurist Albert Cardozo and gave birth to Benjamin Nathan Cardozo, the second Jew—after Louis Brandeis—to serve on the U.S. Supreme Court. Cousin Robert Nathan was among the most popular poets and novelists of the 1930s and 1940s and a highly successful screenwriter on the side. Cousin Emma Lazarus wrote the poem that is inscribed in her memory on the Statue of Liberty, the one that ends with those famous lines:

> *... Give me your tired, your poor,*
> *Your huddled masses yearning to breathe free,*
> *The wretched refuse of your teeming shore.*
> *Send these, the homeless, tempest-tost to me,*
> *I lift my lamp beside the golden door!*

None of my forebears came to a more colorful end than Granny Wolff's father, Benjamin Nathan. The headline on page one of the July 30, 1870, *New York Times* tells the story more dramatically than I possibly can:

HORRIBLE MURDER

•

Benjamin Nathan, the Broker,
Assassinated in His Own House

•

His Body Found Bathed in Blood and
Terribly Mutilated

•

Shocking Details

Benjamin Nathan, my maternal great-grandfather, had been a vice president of the New York Stock Exchange, "fifty-six years and seven months old," the *Times* informed its readers, "almost without an enemy...in the very prime of life...one of the most prominent, wealthy, public-spirited and best beloved of our Jewish citizens." Among the many institutions Benjamin Nathan had supported was Mt. Sinai Hospital—the *Times* called him "almost the creator" of the hospital—but the estimated half million dollars he had given away during his lifetime (about $6.4 million in current dollars) "reached and lightened the loads of men of all creeds and lineages."

He had left his wife and six of his eight children, including my grandmother, at the family's summer home in Morristown, New Jersey, and come into the city alone on July 29, 1870, to offer prayers at synagogue for his own mother on the anniversary of her death. His intent had been to spend the night at his mansion at 12 West Twenty-third Street, "one of the most elegant and spacious of the private residences of the City," and then return to New Jersey. Before midnight, his son, Frederick, a 26-year-old broker, came to wish him goodnight. At some point later, another son, 24-year-old Washington—"a young man of pleasure," as the *Times* would later describe him—also returned home and presumably stopped to speak with his father before heading to bed. By morning, Benjamin Nathan was dead, bashed six times in the head, his right hand crushed. Because he had been found on the second floor, near the house safe, police suspected a burglar. The *Times* account, three columns wide across the front page, even included a hand-drawn floor plan of the second floor of the house. For days afterwards, crowds formed on Twenty-third Street to view the murder scene.

The Stock Exchange immediately posted a $10,000 reward for "the arrest and conviction of the murderer or murderers of Mr. Benjamin Nathan." The city and the dead man's family supplemented the reward to raise it to $47,000—more than $600,000 in current dollars, a small fortune—but no one was ever brought to trial for the murder, much less convicted of it. The police suspected the house-keeper's son, a Civil War veteran and general handyman for the Nathans, but could never develop a case. The newspapers and society seemed to have been more suspicious of my great-great uncle Washington, who discovered the body. In a less than flattering obituary after his own death in 1892, at age 44, the *Times* noted that Washington had "chosen evil associations and...started upon a wild course from which his father's pleadings could not turn him." In 1879, Washington made the newspaper's front page on his own, when an enraged woman shot him twice at point blank range while he was visiting the hotel room of a well-known actress. One of the bullets lodged in his jaw muscles and was never removed.

In any event, Benjamin Nathan's murder remains one of New York City's great unsolved crimes, enshrined along with Lizzie Borden in *Studies in Murder*, Edmund Pearson's best-selling 1924 account of seven notable American homicides. (Supreme Court Justice Cardozo and I both got our "Benjamins" from the famous victim—surely the only thing we have in common!)

My grandmother was thirteen when her father was bludgeoned to death. Until then, she had nothing but pleasant memories of the family home. As a toddler, she had held her toys up to the nursery window so they could be admired by the little boy who lived next door: Willie Morse, son of Samuel F. B., the telegraph inventor. Later, she would play in a nearby park with Edith Cooper, whose grandfather had founded Cooper Union. For quieter moments, there was the family art collection to contemplate. When Granny Wolff's own mother died in 1879, seventy-seven of the paintings were sold off for the grand sum of $39,217, including two works by William Adolphe Bouguereau that collectively brought in almost $10,000. (In recent years, pop singer Michael Jackson paid $1.3 million at auction for two of Bouguereau's oils, and actor Sylvester Stallone sold another for $2.6 million.) After Benjamin Nathan's murder, though, the family vacated the Twenty-third Street mansion, never to return again.

They settled first at the Albemarle Hotel at Twenty-fifth Street and Fifth Avenue, then rented a house at Fifth Avenue and Forty-sixth Street before buying a place further up Fifth Avenue, between Fifty-fourth and Fifty-fifth Streets. It was there in 1877 that my grandmother married Julius Wolff. She had turned 20 only a few months earlier; he was seven years her senior, already established with Wolff Brothers, a family investment business on Wall Street. Their fourth child and second daughter—Frances, my mother—was born six and a half years later.

In 1899, just as the century was about to turn, Frances Wolff and Joseph Cullman Jr. met for the first time at Frothingham Dancing School, one-flight up on Fifty-ninth Street between Fifth and Sixth Avenues. She was 16; he, 17 and headed for Yale University. Although the attraction between the two was immediate, the prospects for any permanent union were poor. The Cullmans were Ashkenazi Jews of German origin. For the Sephardic Wolffs, marrying an Ashkenazi violated the old Jewish caste system. The Cullman Seniors had their concerns, too. Polio had left Mother with a weak arm and leg. Dad's family worried that a less than healthy wife would produce frail grandchildren. But the New World meant new ways, and my father was already the bulldog he would be for the rest of his life—and not just metaphorically. Muscular, barrel-chested, and a little over five feet six inches tall, he came to literally resemble a bulldog as his jowls sagged in later years. (When Mother told her sister, Emily, she was engaged to my father, Emily famously responded, "But he's so short!") The two were married in 1906. Finally in 1919, at the tail end of five children, I came along.

———◆◆———

If the Cullmans have less colorful roots than my mother's side of the family, it wasn't for lack of trying. My great-grandfather Ferdinand Kullmann and his brother, Heinrich, were wine merchants in the German river town of Bingen-am-Rhein, entitled to use the imperial coat of arms on their label because they sold to the emperor himself. Ferdinand also had what proved to be an unfortunate appetite for liberal politics. For a while during the revolutionary spring and summer of 1848, it looked as if he and other like-minded Germans were going to get their way. Conservative local governments fell one after another, replaced by sympathetic ministers. On May 18, a national assembly met in Frankfurt to draft a constitution and create the architecture of a new, united Germany that would draw on the lessons of the young republics in France and America. The counterrevolution arrived that fall with a vengeance. By year's end, disheartened liberals—"Forty-Eighters" as they became known—were fleeing Germany in droves. Ferdinand Kullmann and his wife, Eva, were among them. They left behind the great bulk of a sizable estate.

At Ellis Island, Ferdinand anglicized the family name to Cullman, then settled briefly in the new town of Hoboken, across the Hudson River from Lower Manhattan, before taking up more permanent residence on Seventh Street, between Greenwich Village and Chinatown. Small, gentle, and handsome, sweet natured to one and all, Ferdinand proved to be not much of a provider in his new homeland. Inevitably, he tried selling wines, a field he was well versed in, but Americans then had little taste for the product. On the side, he made and sold cigars, a more profitable endeavor in general but something for which he apparently had no talent whatsoever. My great-grandmother Eva once suggested that her husband's cigars had wounded more Union soldiers than the entire Confederate army ever managed to shoot. When times got hard for the family, Heinrich Kullmann, who had remained in Germany and prospered, would send a bank draft, but Ferdinand at least had introduced the Cullman family to the tobacco trade, however ineptly. His oldest son, Joseph, would take it from there.

Joe Cullman, my grandfather, was a few days shy of his fifteenth birthday when he first reported for work at Egbert Dills & Company, Tobacco Merchants, at 175 Water Street, part of a two-block-square area of dockside merchants known as Burling Slip on the bottom tip of Manhattan. The year was 1869. When he died in 1938, Joe Senior had spent 69 years in and around those docks. He had long ago taken over the Egbert Dills business and brought in his own brother, Jacob, as his partner. By then, the business was known as Cullman Bros., and it was run by my father, Joe, Jr., universally known among his colleagues as "Mr. Junior."

To supplement the tobacco leaf it imported and bought domestically, Cullman Bros. had set up a farming operation of some 3,000 acres in the Connecticut River Valley to grow the delicate shade tobacco favored for cigar wrappers. (Troy Donahue and Connie Stevens fall into each other's arms in a shaded Connecticut tobacco field in the 1961 film *Parrish*.) Probably because the farm was Dad's idea, my grandfather opposed it, but Mr. Junior prevailed, as he did in most matters. Rather than drive up to check on the business, he would take a sleeper train up to Springfield, Massachusetts, where his car would be dropped off and hauled into Hartford. Dad liked to travel in style.

As Cullman Bros. grew, the accumulated surplus got invested in securities; and as the surplus portfolio grew, the family's attention to the stock market multiplied accordingly. In 1926, with the market beginning the long upward sweep that would come to an abrupt end three years later, my father was told to get in on the action directly. The advice came via a phone call from Paul Adler of the old investment firm of Adler, Coleman, and the story was told around the family table for years thereafter.

"Joe," Paul Adler said to my father, "there's a seat available on the New York Stock Exchange. You've got to buy it. It's a license to steal."

"How much is it?" Dad asked in return.

"$500,000."

"$500,000! That's ridiculous, but I'll make you a bid at $50,000 a year GTC [good till canceled], and we'll confirm it every year with a drink." And so he did.

A decade later, in 1936, Paul Adler called with the news: "Guess what? You bought a seat."

In truth, the NYSE seat—held under an entity known as Cullman Brothers, as opposed to Cullman Bros., Inc.—never made much of a dent in anyone's life. More than anything else, it was proof that the Cullmans had arrived: The American dream had been delivered. Prosperity was ours. But it had been a daring stroke more than four decades earlier, in 1890, when money was still tight and "Mr. Junior" was only eight years old, that made all the difference.

—◈—

In 1883, Joe Senior started taking annual trips to Holland to bid at auction on tobacco from two Dutch colonies, Sumatra and Java. (The year 1883 proved to be an auspicious one for both colonies: Krakatoa, which sat between them in the Sunda Strait, exploded out of existence on August 27, the largest volcanic eruption in recorded history.) Sumatra tobacco, particularly, was considered a quality wrapper leaf, and it generally sold for well below the Cuban competition. For seven years, Joe Senior sharpened his skills at the auctions and slowly built back up a business that had fallen into disarray with Egbert Dills' illness and death in 1882. Often, Joe Senior's wife and son—my Grandmother Zillah and my dad—would tag along. When business was done, they would visit family members in Frankfurt and elsewhere in Germany. In 1890, though, an Ohio congressman named William McKinley put a stop to the party.

Succumbing to the arguments of American farmers and manufacturers and with an eye to his successful 1896 run for the presidency, McKinley pushed through Congress the highest protective tariffs in the nation's history, raising rates an average of 49.5 percent on a whole host of commodities, including imported tobacco. (The McKinley Tariff, as it became known, also banned imports produced by forced labor, proof that some political arguments never go away.) For Joe Senior and his business, the tariff posed a clear threat, but it also opened a tiny window of great opportunity, and my grandfather decided to jump through it.

With the deadline fast approaching for imposing the new tariffs, Joe Senior set sail for Amsterdam, where he bid on and bought hundreds of thousands of pounds of choice Sumatra leaf. To hold the purchase, he deposited a large chunk of money that he had borrowed from his father-in-law, Louis Stix (the "Louis" I'm named for, despite the different spellings). Then, while his purchase was crawling across the Atlantic by freighter, Joe Senior raced back ahead on a fast steamer to find the $3 million necessary to complete the deal.

In a scene enshrined in the mythology of the Cullman family, my grandfather went to see Moses Taylor Pyne, president of the National City Bank, who told him that it was, alas, against the law for any bank to loan an individual more than $500,000. (At the time, the total capital of the bank stood at just about $5 million.) As Joe Senior stared ruin in the face, Moses Pyne added a rider: "But the law says only that my bank cannot loan you more than half a million. It doesn't say *I* can't."

The freighter had docked 36 hours before the McKinley tariff was set to go in effect. With half a million from National City and $2.5 million from its president, Joe Senior completed the sale and offloaded his tobacco with mere hours to spare. Suddenly, he was sitting on a huge stockpile of first-rate cigar wrapper purchased far cheaper than his competitors would be able to buy it for years to come. For Joe Senior's family, it was the turning point—the stepping stone out of a gritty entrepreneurialism into upper middle class society.

Joe Senior's son would go into the business with him, but he would go to Yale first, marry into the elegant Wolffs and Nathans, and begin rubbing elbows with the Cardozos and other new cousins known to society. The family houses would improve, too, from the house on Fourteenth Street where Joe Senior and Zillah first set up shop, to 39 West Seventy-first Street, where they moved in 1895, and to the brownstone at 46 West Sixty-ninth Street, half a block west of Central Park, which Joe Senior gave my parents as a wedding present and where my siblings and I grew up. There were summer houses, too: a big fieldstone place in Far Rockaway, out on Long Island, that my parents settled on when they were still engaged, and a cabin in Connecticut that eventually grew into the family compound. Typically, Dad came into possession of the cabin, which we called Cedar Lodge, by a combination of rash decision making and sheer big-heartedness.

The Crash of 1929 wasn't the only Wall Street disaster of the decade. In the immediate aftermath of World War I, the Dow Jones Industrial Average ballooned by 51 percent, only to go diving over the edge on November 3, 1919. By the time the DJIA bottomed out nearly two years later on August 24, 1921, it had given up nearly all its post-war gain, plunging from a high of 119.62 to a low of 63.9. The average was just about at its nadir when Otto "Mike" Goldsmith, a partner in what would eventually become the Paul Weiss law firm, stopped by to see my father. That story, too, is part of the family mythology.

"Joe," lamented Mike Goldsmith, "this crash has ruined me. I'm totally wiped out, destroyed."

"Calm down," Dad told him. "Don't you have any assets at all?"

"Well, yeah, there's a log cabin up in North Stamford."

"How much is it worth?"

"Maybe $25,000," Mike answered.

"Fine. I'll buy it sight unseen."

And so the Cullmans became Connecticut country gentry. Sort of. Mike Goldsmith, in fact, wasn't kidding. His sole asset was a log cabin, nothing more, and the unkempt acreage that came with it. And back then, before Stamford became an international corporate address, the cabin was completely in the boonies—so completely that my mother refused to even go look at it. Two years of cajoling finally got her to make the trip, by which time the place had been fixed up and enlarged.

In 1927, my grandfather Joe added his own touch to Cedar Lodge: the gift of a huge swimming pool, shaped roughly like the continent of Africa, with a waterfall and rocks, all done up to look almost like a natural pond. Throw in a stable and a few horses and a tennis court, and pretty soon the property was starting to get the feel of a private resort. I remember hack riding with Dad, long days of tennis (my brother, Joe, would eventually be instrumental in launching women's professional tennis), and family dinners in the summer that always seemed to include a table's worth of cousins.

You would think that having been born into and raised in such a family, and having enjoyed to such a large extent the fruits of its success, I would have wanted to be a part of the engine that made it all happen. Tobacco should have been second nature to me, and that portfolio of securities not far behind. Yet, almost from the beginning, I seem to have had no taste for either.

⸺◆⸺

I no longer can recall whether I was six or seven, or maybe even eight, but I remember the exchange exactly.

"What do you want for Christmas?" my parents asked me.

"A subscription to the New York City Daily Weather Map," I answered without blinking an eye.

"Fine, and what else?" This was in the middle of the Roaring Twenties. Everyone was flush, and the subscription I had asked for cost the magnificent sum of $6 a year. Odd as my parents must have thought the request, I'm sure they figured I was just at the top of my list.

"Nothing," I said. "That will be sufficient."

In truth, I had had my heart set for a long time on that map—a single printed sheet that showed a fully drawn map of the United

States, crisscrossed by wind direction arrows and superimposed with high and low pressure zones. I can't remember anymore where or when I got hooked on weather although I do know that I loved snow as a very young boy and was always fascinated with where it might have come from: this magical stuff that drifted down from the sky and changed the look and texture of everything. I recall scribbling on some underpass in Central Park "Have it snow!" As I got older, I loved the idea of being able to digest all the weather information I could get my hands on, even given the primitive state of the science, and coming up with a forecast that would tell your next-door neighbor whether he needed to carry an umbrella to work that day. To have an idea before anyone else did what the skies were likely to do, what the temperature would be, whether it would be blustery or mild was almost godlike.

I did get my *Daily Weather Map*, and I pored over it as faithfully as any junior scholar until I had a pretty fair introductory grasp of meteorology, but a dozen years would pass before I dared to tell anyone of authority that what I really wanted in life was to become a weatherman. In the meantime, there were my father's plans for us, and that included the schools he chose for us. (His plans, I should add, certainly *did not* include a son who tried to make his living predicting sunshine or storms.)

My mother is really the one who raised us. Dad liked to make pronouncements, but the daily stuff of life from making sure we had enough clothes on before we went outside to telling us about the birds and the bees was all her territory. I can remember one memorable afternoon when Mother attempted to walk my older brother Arthur through a very state-of-the-art introduction to sex called *Growing Up*. At some point, the guide instructed her to turn to the tutee and ask if he had any questions.

"Why, yes I do," Arthur answered. Naturally, all the rest of us put our ears on high alert.

"And what would that be?" You could hear the trepidation in my mother's voice.

"I've always wondered how they make paper." And thus Arthur presaged his future career as an academic.

Despite such minor setbacks, Mother soldiered on, generally with good humor. (Trying to teach four sons about sex would test a saint.) To us and to her, there was never any question that she was just filling in the gaps between important matters. In the selection of schools, as in all the other elements of our childhood that my father considered critical to our upbringing, his word was law.

My sister, Nan, had her own track laid out for her, but we boys marched off in lockstep to each new place Mr. Junior pointed us toward. First came Collegiate School, the nation's oldest independent school, founded by the Dutch Reformed Church in 1628 to educate the children of what was then the colony of New Amsterdam. (Boston Latin, the nation's oldest public school, was founded seven years later, a year before Harvard began.) First located at the very southern end of Manhattan, Collegiate had long since moved to 260 West Seventy-eighth Street, only a dozen blocks or so from our home on Sixty-ninth Street. In those days before Manhattan parents battled tooth and nail to get their children into private schools, Collegiate was almost a neighborhood school for us kids.

At age 11 I was sent off to the Fessenden School in West Newton, Massachusetts, along with my brother Edgar, older by a year. Begun in 1903, Fessenden was then and still is a boarding school for boys from first through ninth grades. If I was at all daunted by the idea of leaving home before I was even a teenager, my concerns must have been allayed by having Edgar along. Somewhere along the way, I had jumped a grade at Collegiate. He and I were classmates, or thought we would be.

We had barely unpacked our suitcases at Fessenden when the powers that be decided it wouldn't do for Edgar and me to be in the same class. The choice was either to kick him up a year or kick me back one, and the answer seemed obvious. My mother burst into tears as she berated old Mr. Fessenden, the school founder, for scarring my poor psyche, but both my father and the school had spoken, and the decision stuck. In fact, as things turned out, the new arrangement worked just fine. Although I was back with my chronological class, I had already studied and mastered most of what was put before us that year. Basically, I went on an academic glide path that first month at Fessenden and stayed on it for all three years there. For the most part, I couldn't have been happier. I can't say the same thing about the next stop on Dad's academic line-up.

The Hotchkiss School in Lakeville, Connecticut, was part of the second wave of New England boarding schools. The Philips Academies at Andover, Massachusetts, and Exeter, New Hampshire, had been launched in the 1780s. Although it wouldn't make much of a splash until the mid-twentieth century, Deerfield Academy dated back to 1797. Hotchkiss didn't come along until 1891, founded by Maria Harrison Bissell Hotchkiss for the express purpose of preparing boys who were to enroll at Yale University.

Indeed, it was the Yale connection that had gotten this whole train rolling in the first place. My father was determined that his first son and namesake, Joseph 3rd, would follow him to New Haven. The surest way to gain admission, he was told, was through Hotchkiss. When Joe proved unqualified, Dad went looking for the school that best would prepare him for Hotchkiss, which brought him to the door of the Fessenden School. The rest of us boys figured he must have gotten a quantity discount at both places because we followed right along.

Like most New England boarding schools of the time, Hotchkiss was built around the concept of rugged, manly Christianity. Living conditions were Spartan; trips home, rare. You arrived on campus in September and weren't allowed to leave the school again until Christmas vacation. There was a Hotchkiss way to do everything. The Headmaster, George Van Santvorrd—or the Duke, as we boys not always lovingly called him—was not to be doubted. (Dad, at least, had prepared me for that!) And woe be to the boy who wouldn't do things and see things and believe things the Duke's way. Naturally, I set out to do exactly that. Two stories should suffice.

It was typical of Hotchkiss that every boy was expected to play fervently a game called touchball—basically, one-hand touch football—that had been devised by the school's athletic director, Otto Monahan. And it was typical, too, that when I collided with a teammate and split my front tooth just before Thanksgiving my lower-mid year there, the Headmaster refused to let me go back to New York to have it fixed.

"But I need to go over Thanksgiving," I told him with as much earnestness as I could muster. "Otherwise, I'll have to miss classes, and I don't want *that* to happen."

"No dentist is going to see you on Thanksgiving anyway," the Duke responded as he waved me out the door. "Christmas break will be time enough."

Bingo! He'd given me all the opening I needed. I rushed to a phone and called my mother.

"Find a dentist in New York who will see me on Thanksgiving and call me back," I begged her. When she did, I marched proudly back into the Duke's office and told him that I had a dental appointment lined up and was ready to go.

I could tell that he was ready to concede he had lost a battle, but he had no intention of losing the war.

"Fine," he said, looking me straight in the eye, "but if we catch you at the Yale–Princeton game, you'll be expelled."

I wanted to assure him that doing so was the furthest thing from my mind, but I thought maybe I had pressed my luck—and my dissembling skills—far enough. In fact, it had occurred to me that escaping the confines of Hotchkiss for a long weekend and rooting for Yale at Palmer Stadium in Princeton on a beautiful late fall afternoon might be the perfect solace for my ruined front tooth. (After all, weren't we being prepped for Yale?)

I'm not sure how the Duke knew, but Yale games were a huge deal in our household. My father rarely missed one anywhere. He had six tickets on the 50-yard-line of the Yale Bowl in the top row of the lower section so that my mother, who never entirely recovered from polio, wouldn't have trouble reaching the seats. We would park next door in the yard of a gravestone maker and picnic beforehand among the waiting tombstones. Dad didn't miss many away games either: Cornell meant another sleeper car, this time to Ithaca. Princeton was only an hour away, but while the rest of my family was settling into Palmer Stadium, I was home, listening on the radio.

To this day, I wonder why I wasn't there in person. I missed seeing one of the most exciting Yale–Princeton games in years. I remember the final score being something like 26–23 in favor of the Elis, including a memorable play in which Yale's star end Larry Kelly "accidentally" kicked a loose ball forty or fifty yards downfield, then raced after it and fell on it. The refs let the play stand, but Princeton wasn't amused. More important almost than the score, the stadium was packed that day. The odds of anyone's actually catching me in attendance must have been one in a thousand or more.

My final year at the school, when I got the chance to disrupt the stifling decorum of the Hotchkiss dining hall, I was less cowed by the Duke in particular and by the whole spirit of intimidation that the school seemed to run by in those days. Or maybe I was just a bigger wise guy. The occasion was my brother Arthur's wedding. (He had sorted out the birds and the bees on his own by then.) Because I couldn't go down to New York to be fitted for the cutaway I was expected to wear as an usher, the tailors sent an outfit up for me to try on. I was modeling it for a few of my pals when one of them said, "I dare you to wear this thing to dinner tonight." Now, really, who could resist a challenge like that?

My dinner cutaway caused plenty of excitement as we ate, but it was at the end of the meal when things rose to a fever pitch. The tradition was for students to exit the dining hall by classes, with the seniors going first. This time, instead of rising to leave en masse, my classmates stayed in their seats, clapping as I made a grand exit all on my own. By the time I got to the door, the applause had turned to hooting and hollering.

The Duke was not amused. Never in the history of Hotchkiss had the dignity of the dining room been so disturbed, he assured me when we reconvened in his office.

"I don't know what you mean," I said to him.

"You're supposed to dress with propriety!"

"Well, what could be more proper than a cutaway, sir?" I answered with my best deadpan. Amazingly, he didn't toss me out the door and off the campus on the spot.

There were worse moments with the Duke, none so bad as the time he confronted me over my role as business manager of the school paper, the Hotchkiss *Record*. The job basically consisted of selling advertising to local merchants. I had taken it over from none other than Henry Ford II, whose famous name had helped open plenty of doors that otherwise would have remained closed, including the door to the ad department of his father's automobile company. Even so, I managed to outsell him. Before long, our ad revenues were so far over budget that the editorial staff took to kidding me about what I was doing with all the excess money. As happens in such schools, the kidding worked its way to the administration's ears, by which time the joke had become a rumor and I had become its villain.

"It's been brought to my attention that you're pocketing some of the revenues of the *Record*," the Duke told me one day when I had once again been summoned to his inner office. This time I didn't have to feign shock.

"What are you saying?" I replied, completely taken aback. "That's got to be a joke!"

I can hear him now: "It's not a joke, I assure you, Cullman. I don't accept that as a joke at all."

I went immediately to the *Record* editor and explained to him that all the kidding had gotten out of hand. He went to see the Headmaster and clear up any misunderstanding, and like so many other run-ins I had at the school, this one ultimately came to nothing. But it left the worst taste of them all, one that obviously lingers still.

It's one of those benign tricks of memory, I suppose, that the virulent anti-Semitism of Hotchkiss back then keeps slipping out of my mind. There were years when we Cullmans alone made up the Jewish quorum of the school, and as with all minorities, our status made us vulnerable. I can remember attending a reunion with Dorothy in the 1970s or 1980s when one of my classmates, by then a Princeton professor, walked up to me and said, "I don't see why in the world you ever come back to these reunions after what we did to you."

"What did you do?" I asked him, completely baffled.

"Don't you remember? That night they were showing *The House of Rothschild*, we locked you up in your room."

I did remember, once he said it, but whatever my reaction then, I had stuffed that recollection in the attic for 30 or more years.

Yet I did learn to study at Hotchkiss. The Latin and physics programs were both first-rate, and my Greek teacher was excellent. Greek seemed to me less a matter of a well-tuned ear and more one of logic and objective math skills, and I had plenty to offer in both those fields. And, of course, the Hotchkiss School did prepare us for Yale, just as it was supposed to, and helped make certain we were admitted, just as my father intended for us to be. Where we actually went to college, as Dad was quick to remind us, was our choice entirely, but if we chose any destination other than New Haven, we would be paying our own way through.

⟫⟪

In 1996, as secretary of the Yale Class of 1941, I helped raise $20 million to commemorate our fifty-fifth reunion. The majority of that was money I donated myself toward the restoration of Branford

College, the decaying Georgian masterpiece that was my home for four years in New Haven. Thirty years earlier, when we were all still in our mid-forties, I also headed up the fundraising for our twenty-fifth reunion. That time, we raised $655,000, a record amount back then.

In the more than 60 years since my graduation, I've served on more Yale committees of one sort or another than I dare remember, most of them quite happily. Kingman Brewster, the university's president during the troubled years of the Vietnam War and the civil-rights revolution, was my classmate way back when. Not long ago, Rick Levin, who became the university president in 1993, and I played chess against each other on the freshman common, using kids from New Haven schools as living chess pieces. (At the time we were raising money for Chess-in-the-Schools, a favorite cause. More about that later.) Yale is as much a part of my being as almost anything else I can think of, and yet if I had to do it all over again, and if I knew then what I know now, I probably would have gone to college somewhere else.

Not that I didn't have fun at Yale. After my four years at Hotchkiss School, I felt as if I'd been sprung from a monastery to which I had been involuntarily committed. I started skiing while I was in college, on weekends only, but that was the beginning of a lifelong passion. By the time my four years were up in New Haven, I think I could have found my way in my sleep to Northampton, Poughkeepsie, and New London. I was starting to know the Smith and Vassar and Connecticut College campuses almost as well as I knew my own.

There were great summer trips, too. In 1939, after we had completed our sophomore year, Walter Gips and I set out in a 1936 Buick for the West Coast, including Banff and Lake Louise in the Canadian Rockies: 70 days, 10,000 miles, all on a combined budget of $10 a day for gas, car, lodging, food, everything. Many nights we slept under the stars, or in the car. When we had to buy lodging, it was invariably short on elegance. In one place we ended up sharing a double bed, not my regular style. To make up for the days when we could barely afford to eat, Walter and I would pull up to some resort hotel where the wealthy had repaired with their college-age daughters, change clothes, scrub ourselves up to a fare-thee-well, and saunter in as if we owned the place—or at least were paying guests. Not only did we get free food out of our con game; we also were able to provide the bored summering coeds with a little fresh entertainment.

I remember stopping at the elegant Hotel Del Monte, in Monterey, California. Built in the 1880s by the Southern Pacific Railroad, it had been the sight of the first golf course west of the Mississippi River. Despite several devastating fires over the years, the hotel was still about as luxurious as things got in that part of the country. After an hour or more of tennis, we sauntered into high tea and ate our way through an entire plate of sandwiches washed down with six cups of tea each. "Oh, we played an awfully long set of tennis," we would moan every time the waiters looked at us, trying to ascertain why they didn't recall our faces from breakfast that morning. I'm not sure Walter and I had eaten a square meal between us in the prior week. A few weeks later we were at the elegant old Broadmoor in Colorado Springs, Colorado, wolfing down more tea sandwiches and anything else we could lay our hands on. The trip would have worked out perfectly if the Buick hadn't given up the ghost in York, Pennsylvania, five hours from home, forcing us to complete the journey by train. The following summer, I pretty much repeated the trip with another Yale friend, Jim Rothschild, but this time in my own Lincoln Zephyr.

The late 1930s were still hard times for a lot of people. Europe was falling apart. The Japanese had gone into China. I was mostly insulated from all that: Cullman Bros. was doing just fine. I had wonderful teachers at Yale, great courses. It sounds decades ahead of its time, but there was a numbers theory class there that I enjoyed quite a lot. I also made friends I've stayed in touch with for more than 60 years. But there were too many ghosts around the campus, the lingering (and sometimes not so lingering) traces of too many Cullmans. Dad was

Class of 1904; his brother, Class of 1913. My oldest brother, Joe, graduated in 1935, Arthur followed in 1937, and Edgar in 1940. And most of us didn't just walk away from the school after we graduated. I remember a rumor going around back when Rick Levin became Yale president that he had been elected in the offices of Cullman Bros. It's sheer bunk as far I know, but I can understand how such a rumor would get started.

Try as I might, I found it hard to be myself in such a place, hard to discover who I really was and what my real interests were. Not only was I walking in so many family footsteps; like my brothers, I had my father's expectations hanging over me, which was the second and maybe deeper reason we had all been marched through Fessenden, Hotchkiss, and the Old Blue. Grampa Cullman had died early in my college career. Mr. Junior was running the show now, and Mr. Junior meant for his sons to be the next generation of Cullman Bros., or die trying. Not that I had any real alternatives to offer up.

Mind you, I had kept up my interest in meteorology all along. At Yale, I would wander down to the New Haven station of the U.S. Weather Bureau, pore over the weather maps, and have a nice chat with the local guys. I always found it very satisfying, a nice break from the routines of college life, but I never was able to envision meteorology as anything more than a hobby until my senior year in college. I had majored in government, and like all Yale seniors, I was required to produce a thesis in my field, in consultation with my senior adviser, Cecil Driver, the head of the government department.

"What are you going to write about?" Cecil asked me, reasonably enough, during our first meeting at Timothy Dwight College, where he was master.

"I haven't a clue," was all I could answer.

"Well," he went on, "what are you interested in?"

"Do you mean what about government interests me?"

"No," he said. "Just anything. What really interests you?"

Until that moment, I think, I had never felt secure enough to tell anyone, other than my parents early on, about my interest in meteorology. It just seemed too embarrassing. But something about Cecil Driver encouraged me to honesty that afternoon. He had disarmed me with his questions, and I spilled the beans. The weather fascinates me, I told him.

"That's wonderful!" he said when I was through. Cecil went on to suggest that I write my thesis on the U.S. Weather Bureau, which I did. Far more to the point, he was the first adult to show any enthusiasm over my interest in meteorology; the first to treat it as a serious academic subject, not just some lingering fascination from childhood; the first to make me think that maybe this could be more vocation than avocation. One teacher really can make all the difference.

I still had no idea how I was going to crawl out from under Dad's assumptions about my future, but at least I could begin to see some daylight in the distance. And then World War II came along and provided me with all the cover I needed.

THREE

WEATHERING THE WAR

Not long ago, Gerald Edelman, the director of the Neurosciences Institute in La Jolla, California, was explaining to me that most scientific discoveries are serendipitous: Researchers stumble upon them while searching for something else.

"Do you know what the definition of serendipity is?" Gerry asked when he was through. "It's when you go looking for a needle in the haystack and find the farmer's daughter."

That's what happened to me. I was looking for some way out from under my father's expectation that I would join Cullman Bros. and begin learning the tobacco business—a *real* needle in the haystack, as far as I was concerned—and I found Cecil Driver, Athelstan F. Spilhaus, and the United States Navy. To me, no farmer's daughter could have been more beautiful. Of course, Germany and Japan also helped out.

World War II was already raging in Europe when I graduated from Yale in the spring of 1941. The Pacific theater was nearing a boil, too, but I can't lay claim to any great patriotic fervor at the time. Like a lot of my classmates, I had joined the Naval Reserve at Yale—the Navy, after all, was the "gentlemen's service"—only to drop out when some mandatory weekend drill interfered with a party I had wanted to attend. It did occur to me, though, that the military was going to need meteorologists and that this might be a chance for me to turn my avocation into a vocation, at least for the duration of the war.

About the same time, I stumbled across a graduate program at the Massachusetts Institute of Technology that seemed just right for the purpose so I polished up my senior thesis on the U.S. Weather Bureau and sent it off to Cambridge, hoping MIT would be so dazzled by my insights into the bureaucracy of weather that it would ignore my almost total lack of training in math, physics, and other relevant disciplines. Alas, MIT didn't, but just as I was beginning to despair, my older brother Joe, who had already signed up with the Naval Reserve, sailed to the rescue.

From his posting in Washington, D.C., Joe heard that the Navy was launching a program to train meteorologists for the war effort through the New York University College of Engineering. I followed up on Joe's information with some calls of my own and soon found myself at NYU being interviewed for admission by none other than Athelstan F. Spilhaus, one of the most interesting men I've ever run across.

Today, Spilhaus is known mostly by geophysicists for having invented the bathythermograph, which measures the temperature of the ocean depths and has been used for everything from mapping sea beds to hunting submarines. For several decades after World War II, though, Athelstan Frederick Spilhaus was perhaps the leading popular visionary among American scientists.

Born in South Africa, Spilhaus came to the United States in 1931 and quickly established himself as an extraordinary out-of-the-box thinker. Spilhaus conceived of a new world built around cities with state of the art communication and waste management systems, and much more. He set the population of his cities at 50,000 people, the optimum number for a participatory democracy. Beyond 50,000 citizens, he argued, people began to feel lost and powerless. Some of his cities actually got constructed, in Europe. Others—the ones that were to float at sea or even be built under water—didn't. He was an advocate of global birth control and proposed creating ski slopes by covering towering mounds of discarded automobiles.

At the University of Minnesota, where Spilhaus ran the Institute of Technology from 1949 to 1967, he pioneered the idea of connecting buildings with covered skyways and underground tunnels to protect against the frigid winters of the northern plains. He also oversaw a popular comic strip, "Our New Age," that explained the wonders of the scientific future to over 5 million readers every Sunday, and he put together the American science exhibit at the 1962 Seattle World's Fair. (The site is now the Pacific Science Center, just under the famous Space Needle.) He had a wonderful practical side, too. I went to see him one day and found him puzzling over some problem; so I asked what was up.

"I'm trying to figure out another kind of cable I can use for my bathythermograph that will break more often. They're not losing enough of them!"

Although Spilhaus didn't become a U.S. citizen until 1946, five years after I met him, he was named America's first ambassador to UNESCO in 1954.

Like Cecil Driver, Athelstan Spilhaus didn't think I was deranged when I told him how interested I was in meteorology. Nor did he seem to find it particularly odd that I had taken so few courses to prepare for the field. Instead, when the interview came to an end, he said to me, "You want to take this program?"

"Yes," I answered.

"Show up Monday." And so I did.

Until then, I had always thought of education as a process of accretion: You learned a little each course, each year, each school—sometimes more, sometimes less, depending on the quality of the instruction—but in time it all got piled together until you could consider yourself a competently intelligent adult. At NYU, I came to understand how much the intersection of interest, opportunity, and just the right moment can accelerate the learning curve exponentially.

I was far from the most prepared or able student in the program. There were math and physics majors to contend with, from schools every bit the equal of Yale. Most of the eighty people in the program were also basically under contract to one of the armed services, mostly the Navy. They were competing against each other for future slots in what was bound to be a fairly limited meteorological corps. I had every expectation that I would end up in the military, too, but although I had been given a provisional Navy ranking as an "aviation specialist probationary," I had signed up for the NYU program as a straight civilian, through the back door and paying my own way. If anyone was more motivated than I, though, I would still be surprised.

In truth, I can't think of a period of my life that I enjoyed more. The NYU engineering school was up in the Bronx. At first, I commuted by car from our summer home in North Stamford. I always liked it out there, and in those days the drive into the Bronx took half an hour to 45 minutes at the worst. But the work was too interesting, too all-consuming to waste time on transportation. While I was at Yale, my parents had bought an apartment at 910 Park Avenue, near Eightieth Street. I thought about moving there—at that point it was still unoccupied—but that would have meant doing my own cleaning and cooking; so I took a dorm room at the engineering school instead and worked until very late every night.

I remember looking forward to every single class. Maybe because I had bottled up my interest in meteorology for so long, my appetite for learning about it was absolutely voracious. Consequently, I was able to learn all the math and physics and other sciences I needed with a speed that never would have been possible in some other venue. Speed turned out to be important, too. On December 7, the Japanese air force bombed Pearl Harbor, and what was supposed to be a two year program became, for me, a six-month course of study. Under the new wartime pressures, the thesis requirement for a degree was waived for the top ten students in our class. As I was among them, I suddenly found myself an active duty Navy ensign, with orders to report to the Lakehurst Naval Air Station on the central coast of New Jersey.

Everyone knew about Lakehurst back then. On May 6, 1937, the German passenger zeppelin, *Hindenburg*, the pride of the fleet, heralded as still further proof of Nazi technological prowess, burst into flames while attempting a mooring at the Lakehurst Naval Air Station.

At more than 800 feet long, the *Hindenburg* was the largest aircraft ever to fly, yet by modern standards, the loss of life was minimal: Only 36 people died in the conflagration. But the film footage of the 34 seconds it took for the *Hindenburg* to burn and crash to the ground remains riveting to this day, and the radio broadcast by a horrified Herb Morrison of WLS in Chicago—actually a tape being made for later rebroadcast—is unforgettable:

> It's burst into flames.... Get out of the way, please, oh, my, this is terrible, oh, my, get out of the way, please! It is burning, burst into flames and is falling on the mooring mast and all the folks we...this is one of the worst catastrophes in the world!...Oh, it's four or five hundred feet into the sky, it's a terrific crash ladies and gentlemen...oh, the humanity and all the passengers!

For rigid airships like the *Hindenburg*, the Lakehurst crash was the end of the line. None would be built again. The nonrigid, lighter-than-air ships, or blimps, were the wave of the future. (The word "blimp," by the way, was born on December 5, 1915, at Capel Air Station south of London when a Royal Naval Air Service lieutenant flicked his finger against the side of the airship and described the ensuing sound as *blimp*.) By the start of the 1930s, Goodyear Tire and Rubber—the same people who would later make the TV-blimp a standard at American sports championships—was crisscrossing the country with a small fleet of airships to advertise the company's wares. The Navy noticed and began experimenting with the basic Goodyear model at Lakehurst in 1931. When war broke out a decade later, Congress authorized Goodyear to build 200 of the blimps for military purposes and designated Lakehurst on the East Coast and the naval air station at Moffett Field, California, as the principal centers for the blimp fleets. (One hundred sixty-eight of the "K series" blimps, as they were designated, actually got made before war's end.)

A little smaller than a football field at 253 feet long and 60 feet wide, powered by twin 425 horsepower engines, and manned by crews of a dozen or more, the K-ships crept along at a top speed of maybe 100 miles an hour, but they could stay aloft for 60 hours at a time, which made them extraordinarily useful for search-and-rescue missions, photo reconnaissance, and especially escorting convoys. Using what was known as MAD, magnetic air detection, the blimps scanned below the surface of the ocean for submarines. They also carried primitive depth charges, just about enough explosive to turn a canoe over, but the blimps weren't meant to be combat-worthy. As soon as they spotted a sub, they radioed in its coordinates and left the kill up to heavier-than-air planes. Of the roughly 89,000 U.S. ships that crossed the Atlantic and Pacific under airship escort during World War II, not one was sunk by enemy fire. Amazingly, only one blimp was lost—No. K-74, shot down by a surfaced German U-boat in the North Sea.

Our job at Lakehurst was to provide sufficient weather information to launch the airships successfully and to bring them back in when they came home. We tried to do just that, and we succeeded most of the time. But the place was a zoo, and I arrived knowing next to nothing about Navy procedures.

Lakehurst ran under a dual command structure. The station itself, to which I was assigned, had its own commanding officer. So did the squadron that flew the blimps. The plan might have made sense if there was any chance of our working at cross-purposes or if there had been a great divergence in our ultimate ends. As it was, we had two bosses barking (sometimes conflicting) orders, even though we all worked and lived together and pursued a common goal.

My own immediate boss, a Navy old-timer named Kellerman, knew very little about meteorology, but that didn't stop him from trying to forecast wind speed and direction every 15 minutes during morning take-offs. Predicting the wind in 2- to 3-hour increments is hard enough—then and now—but my guess is that Kellerman had been ordered by some commander who knew even less about the weather than he did to produce predictions on the quarter hour and he had lacked either the sense or the fortitude to tell the brass that it just couldn't be done.

Kellerman and I alternated taking the early trick. I remember coming down one morning when it was his turn on duty and finding the hanger doors wide open even though the wind was howling at maybe 40 knots with big black clouds streaming overhead, just waiting to bust open. Why the heck did they let those airships out, I wondered; so I walked over, picked up the forecast form that the blimp people had been relying on, and there was the answer: "Southeast 5, gusts to 7; southeast 7, gusts to 9, with a little bit of escalation," and so it went every 15 minutes for the entire 90-minute take-off period. Just as I was checking the anemometer to find out what the wind was really doing—40, gusting to 60, out of the northeast—Kellerman came roaring in.

"Cullman, why the hell weren't you here earlier?" he shouted. "I could have blamed this goddamn thing on your inexperience!" At least he had a sense of humor.

The Navy showed it had its own sense of humor by insisting that aerological officers such as myself take free-balloon rides so we would have a better feel for what our blimp crews were facing. (A blimp is really just a free balloon with motors.) We would pile into the basket, the ground crew would let loose the mooring ropes, and away we'd go, suspended under a huge bag of highly volatile hydrogen. In time, the Navy would switch over to the more stable and expensive helium, but not until the *Hindenburg* exploded.

To go up, we would break open a sand bag and begin trickling sand out through our fingers. To come down, we'd vent gas. The balloons were remarkably sensitive to the most minute adjustments. To hold ourselves at an even altitude, we would drag a hawser, maybe fifty feet of big ship's rope, on the ground below us, which posed no problems as long as the wind was light or we were flying above some remote stretch of sand. Sometimes we would be careening along at ten knots or so; and our trailing hawser would knock over a chimney, or punch a hole in a barn, or scare a brood of hens so badly that they wouldn't lay eggs for a week thereafter. If things really got slow, we would call down to the people in the fields below us, as if the Creator himself were summoning them from on high. When it was time to land, we'd simply "rip" the bag, the hydrogen would go flying out, and down to the ground we would thump. That wonderful military acronym "snafu"—situation normal, all fouled up—is said to have been coined just about the time I was at the Lakehurst Naval Air Station. It's no surprise.

I might well have remained at Lakehurst for much of the war, caught in the mess with Kellerman and all the rest, knocking over chimneys left and right, if I hadn't gotten to know the commanding officer of the squadron there. Although I wasn't under his authority, he would frequently pop in and ask me what I thought the weather was going to do. One day, five months after I had arrived at Lakehurst, he showed up at the door with a different message:

"You know," he said to me, "we're going to open up a new naval air station, in South Weymouth, outside of Boston. You want to go?"

"When do we leave?" I asked.

"How about tomorrow? You want to fly up with me tomorrow? You'll be in charge up there."

Thus it came to pass that a still-wet-behind-the-ears Navy ensign who a year earlier had expected to be dragged kicking and screaming into the tobacco business (and who was prepared to enlist to avoid that!) ended up instead starting his own weather shop from scratch, performing a public good while doing something he loved. Isn't war grand?

⎯⎯●◄⎯⎯

I feel guilty saying this because I was so far from the front and all its dangers, but if wartime service can be delightful, my time at the South Weymouth Naval Air Station was just that. I arrived there in May 1942 and didn't leave until the fall of 1944. Along the way, I gleaned more practical knowledge about the weather than a classroom could ever teach, got a first-rate technical education, had the first glimmers of how I might try to make a peacetime profession out of this, and met and married a lovely woman. For a while, I also became the fair-haired boy of the commandant of the First Naval District. As so many things do in the military, that came about more by fluke than anything else.

Constructed in a great hurry at the start of the war on a large swath of unused marshland, the South Weymouth Naval Air Station would eventually have two hangars: a metal one, followed by a huge wooden one—almost a thousand feet wide, two hundred feet high, and covering eight acres—that was for a time the world's largest such structure without a center support. The doors alone weighed 250 tons apiece and opened on railroad tracks. To discourage heavier-than-air craft from landing, the two hangars were placed at right angles to each other, with a narrow slot in between for a runway, hard enough to hit in good weather and even worse in a storm. (We were blimp people, after all.) But all that was in the future when I first arrived at South Weymouth. Back then, in its earliest days, the naval air station consisted of nothing more than an administration building, a bachelor officers quarters, some barracks for the enlisted men, and a few houses for key officers. The blimp—there was only one then—was simply moored on the field. And the aerological department, my end of the operation, was tiny: one aerographer's mate, one aerologist (I), and just enough equipment to do our job.

One afternoon, the petty officer and I were jawing away when we heard doors slamming around and scrambled topside for a look. The anemometer pole was bent over at a 45-degree angle—a bad sign. Worse, we were in the middle of a very big, very black, very turbulent cloud. When it cleared away, the blimp that was moored was gone, disappeared into the woods. A tornado had ripped through South Weymouth and carried our airship away with it.

Not more than a week later, I was looking at the weather map when I noticed what seemed to be the same configuration of circumstances barreling down on us. We had a new blimp from Lakehurst moored by then; so I sounded a general alarm and headed to the top of the administration building to monitor the weather situation. We had all available hands—maybe 40 officers and enlisted men—out in the field, holding on to the lines, when the storm came roaring in. Did the wind blow quite as hard as it had the week before? I don't think so, although the men out there had to hang on to those lines for dear life. Was it even a tornado? Not really. But we did save the blimp.

The next morning when the commandant of the First Naval District checked in by phone, he reported that the same storm had torn through the Naval Air Station Squantum—a heavier-than-air base ten miles away—and flipped 50 planes into Squantum Bay, a massive loss. I wasn't on duty when the call came in, but here's how the remainder of the conversation was relayed to me:

"How'd you make out at South Weymouth?" the commandant asked after he had delivered the Squantum news.

"No problem," said whoever answered.

"No problem? How come?"

"Well, our man forecasted it, this blow."

I had in a way, but if I hadn't had the previous week's storm to go on, I wouldn't have been so prepared to act, and anyone could have figured that out. Never mind. As far as the commandant was concerned, I was a weatherman extraordinaire. At least for a while, I could do no wrong!

Some of the most enjoyable times I spent at South Weymouth were at the nearby Blue Hill Observatory. The oldest continuously operating weather observatory in the United States, Blue Hill got its start in 1885 when a recent MIT graduate with the very proper New England name of Abbott Lawrence Rotch spent $3,500 of his family's money to build his own small stone observatory on top of a hill near his parents' summer home in East Milton, Massachusetts. Rotch soon became a world renowned meteorologist, and his observatory followed suit, augmented by three expansions until it came to resemble a castle watchtower on a hill. In 1906, Rotch was named the first professor of meteorology at Harvard University. With his untimely death from a ruptured appendix six years later, at age 50, his observatory was bequeathed to Harvard, which administered it until 1971, when its care ultimately was taken over by a group of private preservationists.

The 1930s and 1940s, when I came to know Blue Hill, were its golden years. Under the leadership of Charles Brooks, the observatory amassed a library of 25,000 volumes and became the headquarters of the American Meteorological Society. The war effort had pulled in some of the best people in the field, but those who weren't in uniform were likely to be at Blue Hill—either because of age or because they were involved in vital research—and for two years, I had the run of them. Just as I had done with the U.S. Weather Bureau outpost in New Haven a few years earlier, I would wander in and see who wanted to chat and what I could learn, but this candy store was so much bigger. And I had something valuable to bring to the table myself.

Like everything else, weather information was classified and carefully monitored during the war. At the South Weymouth Naval Air Station, I could get all the data I wanted from the Navy, but at Blue Hill, the meteorologists were starving for information; so I struck a deal with them.

"Look," I told them, "I'll break Navy regulations and carry classified weather data in my head up to you because I have complete faith that you won't misuse it. In return, I want full cooperation from you."

To my mind, it was completely a win-win situation. The meteorologists at Blue Hill weren't going to transmit weather data to the enemy, and they had the skill and the equipment to enhance greatly my own capacity to forecast the weather. In fact, a great relationship ensued—for the Naval Air Station and for my own education. I remember one time when I was tracking a cloud with a nephoscope: a round black mirror surrounded by a brass ring with compass points and a little stylus that plotted the cloud's true direction. This particular cloud looked unusually threatening; so I called Blue Hill and asked them to spot it, and by triangulating our readings, we were able to determine that the top of the cloud was on the order of 60,000 feet—extraordinarily high and a classic precursor to a bad hail storm. We took what precautions we could at South Weymouth, and the next day we got word that Stoughton, Massachusetts, not far southwest of us, had been pelted with hailstones the size of baseballs.

If this had been only about intellectual satisfaction and stimulation, the Blue Hill connection would have been reward enough, but thanks to it, I also was able to help save the Navy—and the country— a bundle of money.

To those who have never lived there, hurricanes in New England might seem an unlikely occurrence. They are rarer, certainly, than in the Caribbean, but when a hurricane does make it to the northeastern states without exhausting itself farther to the south, it tends to be a dilly. The one the old-timers still talk about was the Great New England Hurricane of late September 1938. Rain poured down on the region even before the storm made landfall at Suffolk County on Long Island and soon after at Milford, Connecticut. Parts of the Connecticut River Valley got as much as 17 inches before the storm moved on. At Hartford, the Connecticut River crested at 19 feet above flood stage. The accompanying winds were some of the highest ever logged on the East Coast. Blue Hill Observatory recorded sustained winds of 121 miles per hour, with gusts topping out at 186 miles per hour. The storm surge devastated the shores of Narragansett Bay. Downtown Providence, Rhode Island, found itself submerged under a storm tide of almost twenty feet. Throughout southern New England, nearly 9,000 homes and other buildings were destroyed by the hurricane, along with 2,600 boats; the storm was catastrophic for the New England fishing fleet. In all, an estimated 680 people lost their lives.

Memories of the Great Hurricane were still fresh six years later, in mid-September of 1944, when a new hurricane slammed into the New Jersey coast, took a sharp right hand turn, and started north; but this time there was a military machine to protect. I'd spotted the storm veering our way early on and put out a general alert for the First Naval District. For those of us at South Weymouth, there wasn't really much to do except bring the blimps into the hangar, tie them down, close those massive doors, and hope the building wouldn't blow away. But as the storm neared, we got a call from the naval air station at Quonset Point, Rhode Island, requesting permission to bring their planes up to South Weymouth and store them in our lighter-than-air hangar. The storing part was no problem: We just untied the lines and let the blimps float up to the top of the hangar so the planes could park underneath them. Once we did that, we had space enough to store a small air force under our roof. Getting the planes down on that little slot of a runway in near-hurricane conditions was a good deal trickier.

For the most part, blimps don't care what the ceiling is. They just keep dropping down until they get below the weather and can see where they are. When our blimps at South Weymouth got lost over land, they would descend until they found a highway, then follow the road markers home. High wind is what makes life hell for blimp pilots. Heavier-than-air planes are the opposite. As long as they don't get caught in some kind of wind shear or micro-downburst, they can survive quite high winds, but back then the pilots who were bringing the planes from Quonset Point needed a ceiling of at least 600 feet or they weren't allowed to land. Blue Hill was 600 feet above sea level; so I called my friends there and said, "I need a ceiling observation every 15 minutes because I have these planes coming in," and with their help, we were able to bring all the planes from Quonset Point in safely and cram them into the hangar before the full force of the hurricane bore down on us. And a serious hurricane it definitely was. A Class 3 storm like the one in 1938, the "Great Atlantic Hurricane," as it became known, killed 390 people, most of them at sea and many of whom were naval personnel.

It's hard to affix a price tag, but I would guess that by working with Blue Hill and by having the meteorologists up there on my side, I saved the Navy somewhere on the order of $4 million in damaged or destroyed aircraft, not to mention the potential human cost in lost or injured pilots and crews. And it all went back to the fact that early on at South Weymouth, I had broken the rules and started sharing classified data with the observatory. Naturally, this being the military in wartime, I was rewarded for my stellar performance by being shipped off to Africa.

————◆◆————

By the summer of 1944, airships operating out of South Weymouth had logged some 25,000 hours in antisubmarine patrols over the North Atlantic, the equivalent of nearly eight years of continuous flight by our one relatively little naval air station. I even got to fly in one of them, a bumpy, unpleasant ride over the Gulf of Maine. The blimps would continue to patrol U.S. waters until the very end of the war. Indeed, a German U-boat was sunk east of Long Island in a combined attack by surface ships and lighter-than-air craft operating out of Lakehurst on May 6, 1945, two days before the Nazis surrendered. But with the invasion of Europe under way, the call went out for U.S. blimps to begin running antisubmarine patrols across the Straits of Gibraltar and elsewhere in the western Mediterranean. The question was whether to fly the airships over or send the envelopes by cargo plane for inflation abroad. Strangely enough, the Navy tried to do the simplest thing first.

On August 15, 1944, Allied forces launched "Operation Dragoon" with attacks on Marseilles and Toulon on the south coast of France. Toulon was captured on August 28. By early September, American forces had pushed into the interior of Provence and recaptured from the Germans (who had taken it from the French) a rigid airship base at Cuers that dated back to the 1920s. We soon sent the uninflated envelope to Cuers, to be blown up on location, the first test of the new system. Then we turned our attention to the Great Atlantic Hurricane that was bearing down on the East Coast. Not long after the storm abated, we got our report card back from France: "Erection failed," the cable read memorably, "Fly them over." And so we did, using my forecasts. I followed in person, a month or so later, strapped into the seat of a DC-4 that picked its way across the Atlantic by way of Gander Field in Newfoundland and the Azores, but I wasn't headed to Provence.

My orders were for another lighter-than-air base, the new naval air station at Port Lyautey, halfway between Casablanca and Tangier on the Atlantic coast of French Morocco, and I was far from the only meteorologist so assigned. A weather forecast doesn't necessarily improve because ten people are making it, but that seemed to be the Navy's logic. Simply put, there were way too many of us.

At Port Lyautey, I found myself one of 13 officers and 60 enlisted men assigned to do the work that could have been done by maybe two officers and four men. The shifts were superb if you had a taste for doing nothing—8 hours on, 96 hours off. The weather wasn't that bad, either. Prevailing westerlies brought in cool ocean air most of the time, unless a sirocco was blowing dry, hot air in from the east. Eggs were plentiful in our part of Africa. Across the strait, the Brits on Gibraltar were starving for eggs but had excess gin. Trading one for the other just seemed natural, and kept us handsomely supplied with fortified spirits. I even had a Jeep at my disposal and used it to explore Fez and other exotic locales, but if I was going to take a few months off to see the world, a Navy station in French Morocco wasn't my ideal destination. One day I had just returned from the map room to my quonset hut when a courier showed up with the news that the admiral was coming in and wanted a special forecast. The request was ridiculous: We had already made a forecast, and the weather is the same for an admiral or seaman second class. But I was so bored by then that I almost welcomed the idiocy.

Eventually, we moved across the Mediterranean to Cuers. The wine was better there, but there wasn't any more to do. At South Weymouth, almost every day seemed to bring some new tidbit of knowledge about meteorology, especially if I managed to wander up to Blue Hill. Here, we spent our days watching the war wind down and arguing over what part of the military system was the least efficient. Foolishness. Complete foolishness.

Finally, in the late summer of 1945, I flew back to the States on another DC-4 and wound my way down to Norfolk, Virginia, where I separated out of the Navy as a lieutenant senior grade. It was time to figure out how to make a civilian living out of this weather business—for me and my wife.

⟫━◆━⟪

I arrived at the South Weymouth Naval Air Station on the twenty-fifth of May, 1942, and first saw Thais MacBride a month or two later. She was from Hingham, Massachusetts, 20 minutes or so away, but her family owned the local Stetson Shoe Company, one of a number of shoe factories that had accounted for about 75 percent of employment in South Weymouth before the war. As part of the neighborhood gentry, Thais was regularly invited to parties at the naval air station Officers Club, and that's where we met.

Both of us had arrived that evening with someone else, as I remember, but I had apparently gone out of my way to include in the festivities a girl who wasn't having much fun—a wallflower, as we used to call them—and Thais had observed that and taken my gallantry as a sign of good character. Soon we were dating, and very soon after that, on December 19, 1942, we were married at the Congregational church in Hingham.

All those Sephardic ancestors of mine, I imagine, would have been appalled at my marrying a Protestant. My great-grandmother Emily Nathan, widow of the murdered Benjamin, even included a clause in her will providing that no benefits from her estate should go to any heir who married outside the faith. (The clause seems to have been inserted to spite her son, Washington, who had married as I did, and it was no mean threat. The *New York Times* estimated the value of her estate to be as high as $1.5 million at her death, about $26.5 million in current dollars.) Never notable for its religious zeal, my immediate family seemed mostly unfazed by the arrangement, even though I was the last of the five siblings to marry and the first to take a non-Jewish spouse. Thais's family, a rock-ribbed New England clan through and through, wasn't so sanguine. Although the subject was never brought up directly, her parents clearly had trouble getting comfortable with the idea of our marriage.

I might have let their disapproval bother me more if I hadn't felt half the time as though I had fallen through a rabbit hole, but I just couldn't help it. Thais was beautiful, I was doing work I loved, and we were living like kings and queens. Thanks to my rank as an ensign and high-blown status as head of the aerological department, we qualified to move into a brand new three-bedroom house on the station, complete with a crew of enlisted men to look after the grounds and a part-time maid service. In the *carpe diem* spirit that wartime always seems to foster, we entertained frequently and were entertained almost as often.

When the bubble finally burst on South Weymouth and I was sent off to French Morocco, Thais went to live with my family in New York City. Soon I was getting a steady stream of letters from home telling me that my wife was literally wasting away: twenty pounds, thirty pounds, maybe more, and this off a frame that wasn't carrying a lot of extra weight at its prime. By the time I got back to the States late in 1945, the doctors had given Thais a clean bill of physical health, and she had even begun to gain back some of what she had lost. The neurosis or depression or whatever it was that had brought on her wasting illness was an augur of worse things to come, far worse really, but the future is a tale poorly read, and I was anxious to get on with the present. Thais and I bought a house in Hingham, near her parents, and before I knew it, I was the co-owner and head forecaster of Weather Advisors, Inc.

In the Navy, I had seen first-hand how accurate forecasting could save a government entity money, even lives. Municipalities, I figured, faced much the same set of circumstances. They had an infrastructure and capital investment to protect against the ravages of weather, and they needed to be prepared to deliver services in a timely fashion when a storm hit and after it passed through. So that's where I began trying to market Weather Advisors, Inc., but not just at the town hall. I figured that if I could convince the people on the front lines of dealing with weather that I had something to offer them, I would be better than halfway home.

For months on end, I crisscrossed Massachusetts, east to west, north to south, searching out the guys who were oiling the back roads or fixing the sewer pipes. Whenever I found one, I'd stop, introduce myself, and begin talking about my weather service. The resistance, of course, was enormous: You could just see that "Who is this nut?" look creeping across their faces, but I didn't let that stop me.

"Listen," I'd say, "when you hear the Weather Bureau's forecast that it's going to snow tonight, what do you do?"

"We tell the men to be down at the barn at one o'clock."

"Fine," I would go on, "but let me point something out to you. You're making a forecast on top of the Weather Bureau's forecast. How do you know the men should be at the barn at one o'clock, instead of two or three?"

"Oh, well, if they say 'snow tonight,' there's probably going to be enough on the ground by one o'clock to get started with the plowing."

"That's my point," I'd wind up. "We'll take that responsibility off your hands. We'll tell you not just when it's going to snow, but we'll call and tell you when there will be enough snow to plow. We're not out to change the Weather Bureau's forecast, but we can tailor-make it for you, and save you and your men a lot of time and the city a lot of money."

Just as I would later learn on the fly how to purchase a company by leveraging its own assets, so I was now learning as I went how to sell an intangible. (And that, too, would prove useful when Herb Weiner and I first walked in the door of Orkin Exterminating.) When you set out to peddle a weather service, you have no samples in your bag. You're selling yourself first, then adding to that a concept of what you want to do for someone, which means you have to appeal to the imagination almost as much as to the rational side. Standing out there on some hot, dusty summer road north of Athol toward the Berkshire Mountains, I would have to get a crusty, sweaty superintendent of streets to imagine a day 60 degrees colder, with snow beginning to pile up on the streets. Then I'd have to get him thinking about my call and how it could ease his life, and finally I needed him to convince his bosses to subscribe to the service I was offering.

On top of that was the problem of pricing. I was looking to make a profit, but how do you price an intangible service that offers the same quality and quantity of information to municipalities with widely varying needs and capacities to pay? Boston clearly had far more resources than Athol; it also had more roads to plow and thus stood to save more from the timely application of our service. But how were we going to translate those differences into a pricing schedule that would be generally perceived as fair and that the market could bear?

My partner in Weather Advisors, Parker Chick, had an interest in meteorology, but Parker was also maybe 15 years my senior and had been a bond salesman; so I thought he would be a useful and steadying influence on the business side of the operation. With Parker's help, we dreamed up this ingenious system of pricing that factored in per capita income, street mileage, population, and a whole host of other variables that ultimately justified our charging one place $200 a year and another $10,000. I ran the system by one of my old Yale friends, the same Walter Gips that I had traveled out west with a decade earlier. Walter had graduated from Harvard Business School and was working there as a research assistant, and he turned our jury-rigged system into a case study of pricing and services that became a standard part of the curriculum. For years afterwards, I kept running into people who remembered my name from that study.

If anything, accurate communication proved even tougher than fair pricing. Like rumors, weather forecasts seem to grow in intensity and fade in accuracy the more they are repeated. I'd call up a superintendent of streets and tell him the forecast. The next day, I would check in with him to see how everything had gone, and he would start complaining and then read me back a forecast that bore no resemblance to the one I had first phoned in. Obviously, we needed to tamp down the human element so I devised a forecast form that consisted of something like 500 possibilities, each with a little check box next to it. Number one probably said "Snow." Next came "Starting at," with separate numbered check boxes for all 24 hours, and on it went. I copyrighted the form, then had it printed up in pads, and sent multiple pads out free to everyone to whom we were reporting—one for the office, one for the bedside table or wherever they were likely to answer the phone.

Now, when a storm or some other major weather event was brewing, we could call up our clients, tell them to grab the pad, and then start dictating the weather forecast: "1, 3, 63, 167, 268, 422." Not only did we make sure they got the forecast exactly as we meant it, but they could call someone else and pass the same numbers along without skewing the information in the process. The pads, in fact, became the only real tangible in the whole business.

We had no real model to go on, but amazingly enough, Weather Advisors, Inc., began to show signs of success. By the time I was able to step back long enough from simultaneously selling the product and making the forecasts, we had signed up forty cities and towns in Massachusetts and even had begun to branch into the private sector as the official meteorologists to Northeast Airlines. Our offices improved as our client list did: from a nondescript Boston hole-in-the-wall for a very brief period to a tiny private airport at Norwood, Massachusetts, to Logan Airport, once we had signed up Northeast Airlines.

My mother, I'm sure, was pleased. Whatever she thought about the wisdom of the undertaking, she always wanted her children to be happy, and I couldn't help but feel pleased with what I was creating. Dad, by contrast, withheld his approval on just about every front. He never understood why I didn't move back to New York after the war, and he certainly couldn't figure out why I would want to go into the weather business. Weather forecasting? There was no real money in it even if you *were* successful! But he was more than baffled when Thais and I adopted our son. As far as my father was concerned, a life that seemed to be having trouble finding any traction was now in danger of skidding off the highway.

—❖—

Duncan Cullman was born October 3, 1947, to a single mother and a father unknown. (His birth certificate, when I finally obtained it, listed his name as "Male Perry." In one of those wild coincidences that keep life interesting, his place of birth was Cullman, Alabama.) Somehow, some way, his mother had shown up in South Weymouth, gone into labor, and presented herself at the local hospital. There, she had come to the attention of a doctor who knew Thais and I were looking to adopt. When the new mother said she wanted to give her child up for adoption, the doctor contacted us, and Duncan came to live with us about five weeks later, in early November. The official adoption wouldn't take place for another six months or so, but that was largely a technicality. Thais and I had been approved for adoption and had brought Duncan into our house, and as far as we were concerned, we were parents from that day forward, with all the obligations that entailed.

Our first real test came shortly after he had moved in. No matter what we fed him, Duncan simply couldn't keep any food down. By the time we finally found a doctor who could tell us what was happening, he had fallen below his birth weight. The condition—known as pyloric stenosis—isn't all that uncommon, but to new parents it can be frightening in the extreme. The muscle around the pylorus, where the stomach narrows at the beginning of the small intestine, is simply too large. It pinches the pylorus so much that the food a child takes in has no exit. Instead, it comes right back up, first as small baby "spit ups" and later, as the baby ages, as projectile vomiting. Happily, a surgeon at Children's Hospital in Boston took care of Duncan's problem with relative ease and no long-term effects, but I think the struggle we went through in those early months as parents made me stew all the more at Dad's attitude.

I vividly remember a meeting he and I had in Hartford during those troubling months. I was there on business for Weather Advisors; he had come up from New York to check on the tobacco farms. It seemed a good chance to try again to explain our motivation—Thais and I had been told we couldn't have children of our own—and talk through the problem, but calm discussions were never my father's long suit, especially when he was agitated over something.

"You should have waited to have one of your own," he told me, even though he knew about our medical diagnosis. At the heart of his objection seemed to be his strong feeling about "blood relations," but maybe even deeper than that was a resentment that he wasn't in control. Mr. Junior had contemplated many things for his sons. He'd set a course for us from Collegiate School forward. He had never imagined that I wouldn't go into the tobacco business or that I would present him with a grandchild who bore no genetic link to him, and what Dad hadn't contemplated in advance, he always had trouble wrapping his mind around. That's the best interpretation I could put on it, but none of that took the sting out of his words, or made me less angry at his attitude. (I should add that my father did eventually execute a special provision to include Duncan in his will, but as we never talked about the matter, I don't know whether that meant he had accepted his adopted grandson or was simply biting the bullet.)

As strained as relations were with my father—and as much as I resisted the idea accordingly—I was slowly coming around to his point of view about the weather forecasting business. Yes, it was possible to build a successful firm: I'd shown that. But, no, it might not be possible to achieve the sort of financial security that I thought I should be able to provide for a wife and, thus far, a sickly son.

There had been some particular difficulties. To resolve a falling out between Parker Chick and me, I let him buy me out of Weather

Advisors, then immediately launched a competing company, Cullman Weather Service, with an NYU classmate named Walter Untermeyer. But the real problem wasn't partnerships or business plans. I had no doubt that I could out sell and out hustle any similar private forecasting service. The problem was the playing field: It wasn't anywhere near even. On the one side were a very few for-profit firms like our outfits, trying to carve out a business, and on the other was the U.S. Weather Bureau, acting like the 800-pound gorilla of meteorology. More and more frequently when I showed up in some new town trying to sell our service, I would hear something like, "Well, that sounds great, but let us check with the Weather Bureau." Then lo and behold, the next day my contact would call back with news that the Bureau had agreed to do just as we had been proposing.

To me, the Weather Bureau was using U.S. taxpayer dollars to restrain competition, a raw deal all the way around; so I arranged to testify before a Senate subcommittee chaired by Senator Joe Ball of Minnesota against the bureau's 1948 federal budget appropriation. My argument was a classic free-market one dolled up with a little flag waving. Meteorologists had proven their worth in the recent war, and they would prove their worth again, but unless meteorology grew into a worthwhile profession, with a reasonable chance of earning a well-paid living in the private sector, even students who had a bent in that direction were going to look elsewhere, and the opportunity to make a good living would happen only if and when the Weather Bureau stopped using public funds to go nose-to-nose with private entrepreneurs. As in any other business, competition in weather forecasting was good. It spawned research and sharpened practices. Give us little guys a chance to get a foot inside the tent, and everyone would win.

That's what I intended to say, and indeed that's what I submitted as advance testimony. (My Uncle Howard, who had experience in these matters, told me that my ideas would be taken more seriously if committee members and their staffs had a chance to study them ahead of time.) But between my preparing the testimony and delivering it,

Francis Reicheldorfer, the chief of the Weather Bureau, met with some of my fellow private forecasters and promised to create a clear line of demarcation between private meteorology and the government. Could I soft-pedal my testimony, my colleagues asked, now that the bureau had come around to our way of thinking? I told them I didn't believe it for a second—bureaucracies *never* willingly cede power—and I was right as rain on that one. But I did pull my punches before the subcommittee, so much so that the members probably left wondering why I had asked to speak in the first place.

By then, too, I had pretty much decided to lay one last bet on weather forecasting. New York City was the ultimate jackpot: the biggest city with the greatest resources, the most need and the most to pay. I had Garden City out on Long Island in the portfolio. Hartford had signed up, too, as had others. A business that had seemed to be stuck in Massachusetts when it was Weather Advisors had taken on a regional cast as Cullman Weather Service and, I hoped, was headed toward a national profile. If I could land the contract to provide private forecasting for New York, not only would I have a broad and steady revenue stream; I could also use New York's cachet to go after the other major cities.

That was the upside scenario. If New York said no, I would consider myself grateful for all I had learned and lucky for the fun I'd had along the way, but I was getting out. So I came down to New York and made my pitch to the Department of Sanitation, complete with charts, statistics, and glowing testimonials from the *Hartford Courant* and elsewhere about our sterling forecasts and all that could be gained from them. Not long thereafter, when I met up with my brother Joe somewhere around Grand Central Station, I could tell in an instant by his gentle manner and kind solicitations that he had heard about my efforts and that the City of New York in its infinite wisdom was about to say no. I'm not sure to this day if Joe thought I needed a shoulder to cry on, but he was always very well plugged in.

My father got into the act a few days later, suggesting I pay a visit to his good friend Arthur J. Cohen, known as Tommy. (None of Dad's friends seemed to go by their given names.) Tommy Cohen didn't have a job to offer me, but he did pass on some words of wisdom that would shape the rest of my life: "Look," I remember him telling me, "my only advice to you is don't in any way give up your independence."

About the same time, Dad asked me if I didn't want to learn the banking business at the elbow of another of his good friends, Maurice Wertheim. Because I didn't have a better plan in mind, I turned in the key to the offices of the Cullman Weather Service, which effectively disbanded the business; packed up Thais and Duncan and moved us south to New York; and in June 1948, reported for work as a very untrained trainee at Wertheim & Co. Tommy Cohen's independence would have to wait, but his advice would always be there, like a lingering melody.

FOUR

"YOU JUST MIGHT MEET SOMEONE"

Maurice Wertheim was one of the leading figures of New York in the 1930s and 1940s. He had served as head of the American Jewish Committee during the critical years from 1941–1943 and had been one of five Jews who met with Franklin Roosevelt in 1942 to try to warn him of the Holocaust—the only such meeting Roosevelt is ever known to have attended. Wertheim was an arts patron and philanthropist as well: The 1953 show "French Paintings Since 1870 from the Maurice Wertheim Collection" was among the first private assemblages ever displayed at the National Gallery of Art in Washington, D.C. (The paintings—twenty-six Impressionist and Post-Impressionist works, including works by Cezanne, Degas, Manet, Monet, Gaugin, Van Gogh, Pissaro, Picasso, Renoir, Seurat, and Toulouse-Latrec—were left to the Fogg Art Museum at Harvard, Wertheim's alma mater.) He was a founder of the New York Theater Guild and had also donated to the federal government 1,800 acres of land in Suffolk County, New York, the core of what is now the Wertheim National Wildlife Refuge. Just for good measure, he had been publisher of *The Nation* for several years during the Great Depression.

He had married well, too. Cecile Wertheim was the granddaughter of Henry Morgenthau, Sr., who had served as ambassador to Turkey in the years leading up to World War I, and niece to Henry Morgenthau, Jr., FDR's long-time Treasury secretary and the architect of the famous 1944 Bretton Woods conference that brought 41 nations together to plan post-war economic policy. Barbara Wertheim Tuchman, one of Maurice and Cecile's three daughters, would go on to win Pulitzer

Prizes for her study of World War I, *The Guns of August*, and for *Stillwell and the American Experience in China, 1911–1945*.

I knew all about Maurice Wertheim, of course. He and my father were great friends. They had both started out in the tobacco business—Wertheim had been vice president and secretary of the United Cigar Manufacturing Company from 1907 to 1913, just as my father was picking up land in the Connecticut River Valley and expanding Cullman Bros. from tobacco middlemen to tobacco growers. The Wertheims' house at 43 West Seventieth Street was a block from the four-story brownstone where we had all grown up. Like my parents, they had a Connecticut country place as well, an estate in Cos Cob, a short drive from North Stamford. Dad was also a regular at Maurice Wertheim's fishing camp in Quebec, and he and my mother liked to pack off in the dead of winter to the Wertheims' seaside house at Varadero, in Cuba.

Maurice Wertheim left the tobacco business for investment banking in 1915 and opened his own firm a dozen years later, in 1927, at 120 Broadway, where I would later have my own office. Investment banking is what had made his fortune, but until the day in 1948 that I walked through the door at Wertheim & Co. to begin my training, I had assumed that it was a commercial bank. Imagine my surprise when I didn't see any teller windows or loan officers tucked tactfully off to the side. Investment banking? Who ever heard of that?

Sensibly, and because I probably would have been dangerous anywhere else, I was assigned to the research department and told to learn how to analyze securities and read balance sheets. Both might as well have been in Greek initially, but maybe because I had been analyzing weather data continually since 1941, I mastered the two skills without much difficulty and easily passed the exam allowing me to become a registered representative, fully entitled to sell stocks and bonds. Peddling securities, which was what I was expected to be doing once I had completed my basic training, proved a good deal more frustrating. I didn't mind selling—I had been doing that continuously, too, ever since we launched Weather Advisors. I just didn't see the point of selling the securities they wanted me to push.

I would sit there day after day at my desk, looking at the papers in front of me and listening to the people around me, and I would find myself wondering: Buy GM? Buy GE? Buy AT&T? What are these people talking about? Why is someone going to do this? What's the underlying reason, and what was I possibly going to say to someone to convince him to part with his money on such an uncertain prospect of fair return? After maybe the five-hundredth time of asking myself what the hell this business was all about, I figured that I had better find some way to make the job interesting; so I began drifting away from what Wertheim & Co. had hired me to do and finding things there that I wanted to do.

As I always seemed to do wherever I was, I started talking with people and seeing what I could learn from them. Andy Scharps had come over to Wertheim from Manufacturers Trust Company, where he had been an officer, and gone to work directly for Maurice Wertheim. That meant he spent his time on deals because whatever the rest of us at Wertheim & Co. might exhaust our days doing, the guy who signed our paychecks was a deal man. I can remember to this day Andy's telling me one of the boss's favorite sayings: "I like to shoot one or two ducks a year, and that's enough. To heck with the rest of the time." Even then, it made a lot of sense to me.

Andy was maybe 15 years older than I, but we had a great chemistry between us. Perhaps he even saw himself as my mentor; certainly, I was an eager student. From what I know, he was always behind the scenes during Maurice Wertheim's deals. He might have sat at the table occasionally, but only as a silent participant. Still, Andy seemed to have a natural instinct for the art of negotiation. Or maybe he was just a good poker player.

"You've got to remember that when you go to the negotiating table and you've shot your last argument, it shows up in your eyes, and you're dead," he once told me. "There's only one way to solve that problem: Always leave the table with at least one or two arguments up your sleeve that you haven't used. And the only way to do that is to do more homework than the other side."

I never forgot that. A dozen years later, when Herb Weiner and I were preparing for our first trip to Atlanta, Andy Scharps might as well have been sitting right beside me, urging me to do my homework and reminding me to never, ever give up my last argument.

———⟩•⟨———

Just about the time I was getting a graduate MBA education from Andy Scharps—and as a precursor, I suppose, of my future career—I began tripping over deals that I thought Wertheim & Co. should be interested in. I was on the train one morning, riding into work, when I ran into a guy named Buck Ewing, who had been in my brother Joe's class at Yale, six years in front of me, and was then at Morgan Stanley. Buck, it turned out, had a special interest in oil companies, especially the Franco Wyoming Oil Company, which sounded to me like a spaghetti concern but was in fact a very rare and wild bird.

Franco Wyoming was a Delaware corporation that owned property, presumably oil-producing, in the United States: That was the "Wyoming" part of the name although it also had large tracts of land in Texas and elsewhere. Its shares, though, were traded on the Paris Bourse: hence, "Franco." But the business was a lot more complicated even than the name. Three men—a Frenchman, an Englishman, and Carl Pforzheimer, who was a founder of the American Stock Exchange and had made a fortune trading Standard Oil way back when—had set up a shell corporation called the Franco Wyoming Securities Corporation. Through the shell, the three principals took all the registered shares of Franco Wyoming Oil owned by French holders and, in effect, transferred the shares to themselves as nominees. Then the securities corporation issued bearer shares against those registered shares so they could be traded in France. Just to make certain no one could penetrate their control, Pforzheimer and his partners had built in another unique provision that allowed them to vote any of the bearer shares of shareholders who did not request a proxy. The primary benefit of all this maneuvering seemed to be that the Three Musketeers got to vote practically all the stock of the oil company at every meeting, always to their best advantage.

Buck Ewing had looked into the Franco Wyoming situation just deeply enough to know something was going on; so he set up an account with Wertheim & Co, with the approval of his own higher ups at Morgan Stanley, and asked me to begin picking up some shares in it. That, I did. (I was, after all, supposed to be a securities salesman, even if I was having trouble acting like one.) I even found out that the guy on the foreign trading desk we used was running his own little shell game, changing his quote depending on whether you were a buyer or a seller. I went in to see him one day with a sell ticket on top and a buy ticket hidden beneath it, and said, "How's Franco?" Figuring I wanted to sell, he gave me a quote half a tick below market; so I pulled out my buy order and said, "Here, I want to pick up 500 shares." He was furious, needless to say, but I'd caught him in his own act.

Mostly, though, I began to read up on Franco Wyoming: everything I could find, all the challenges that had been brought against its singular control structure in the Delaware chancery courts, and how none of them had managed to crack the triumvirate. The more I learned, the more I became convinced that here was an opportunity just waiting for Wertheim & Co. There were huge underlying assets that weren't being reflected in the share price because the three de facto (certainly not de jure) owners had been treating the company like a private playpen. Finally, I went to the Wertheim partners.

"You know, I think this is something that the firm ought to do," I told them.

"What do you mean?"

"Well, I think we could probably find a way to offer the bearer shareholders in France some kind of an award, or tell the banks that we'll pay them a certain amount, something to smoke out these three guys. Let's throw the bastards out."

Clearly, I didn't know exactly what route would work best, and I was nothing but a junior salesman at the time, but if Maurice

Wertheim had still been in charge, I suspect he might have been interested all the same. It didn't take a genius to see the potential in Franco Wyoming, and the fight promised to be a dilly. Wertheim had died, though—of a heart attack, at age 64 out at his Cos Cob estate. In his place as senior partner was his good friend and estate coexecutor, Joe Klingenstein. My father always referred to Joe as "the friendly undertaker," and the friendly undertaker had no interest whatsoever in my deal or in investment banking generally. He was a trader: He liked to buy and sell securities, period.

I tried for a little while longer to find someone at the firm who shared my interest in taking on Franco Wyoming, to no avail. I even tried to get some other firms involved, with no more luck; so I finally dropped the idea. A dozen years later, in 1964, just as we were winding up the Orkin deal, Lazard Frères & Co. came swooping down on Franco Wyoming just as I had proposed doing. Suits flew around the Paris courts. The New York newspapers grew rich off the advertising war the two waged against each other. In April, Lazard tendered an offer to purchase 820,000 shares of Franco Wyoming—about two-thirds of its outstanding stock—at $55 a share, considerably higher than what the stock had been trading for on the Bourse over the previous five years. Franco Wyoming countered with a letter to shareholders, contending that the company's investments alone were worth $40 a share. Add in U.S. oil and gas properties and French shipping operations, the letter said, and the real value of the stock was more than $80 a share. By mid-May, the fight was all over, and Lazard Frères, having picked up the company for maybe seventy cents on the dollar, had made an absolute bundle.

I suppose I should have been discouraged by the Franco Wyoming experience. Instead, I seem to have gotten the taste of deal-making in my mouth and couldn't get it out. If one doesn't work, I decided, let's try another one; so I went looking again. This time, I came upon a company almost as interesting as Franco Wyoming and two and a half centuries older.

In 1668, two intrepid entrepreneurs named Sieur de Groseilliers and Pierre-Esprit Radisson set sail from London on a pair of ships, the *Eaglet* and the *Nonsuch*, bound for the Hudson Bay, where they hoped to trade with the Cree Indian tribe for beaver pelts. The *Eaglet* was forced by a storm to turn back before it crossed the ocean, but 15 months after sailing out of the Thames, the *Nonsuch* sailed back in loaded with furs and without a single loss among its crew members. So successful was the mission that a few months later, in 1670, King George I granted a royal charter to the Governor and Company of Adventurers of England Trading into Hudson Bay and ceded to it control of one-third of the territory of present-day Canada. Rupert's Land, as this immense tract was known, included the northern areas of Ontario and Quebec, the entirety of Manitoba, most of Saskatchewan, the southern half of Alberta and a large swatch of the Northwest Territories. Thus, the Hudson's Bay Company was born, the oldest corporation in North America and one of the oldest still-active companies in the world.

Time and advancing civilization ate into the company's monopoly. In 1857, the British Parliament deemed the "fertile belt" of Manitoba, Saskatchewan, and southern Alberta suitable for settlement. Twelve years later, by the Deed of Surrender of 1869, the Hudson's Bay Company gave up ownership of Rupert's Land in return for a hefty chunk of cash and seven million acres of the fertile plains it had formerly controlled outright. By the 1950s, when I began taking a look at the company, it was known primarily as one of Canada's largest retailers: All those old trading posts had become department stores. But it still held major stakes in Hudson's Bay Oil and Gas, Roxy Petroleum, and some other energy concerns. Plus, the company had a checkerboard of freeholds all over western Canada. It would be hard to make a major energy find anywhere out there, I figured, without involving at least a chunk of Hudson's Bay Company land.

Because the share price was set largely by the retail business, not the energy and retail holdings, I thought Hudson's Bay Company would be a good outfit to go after. Buy it at a reasonable premium over the going stock price, and you could break the company up, sell the retail stores, and either sell or hold on to the land and energy interests, depending on the market, and come out way ahead. This time, I contacted Buck Ewing at Morgan Stanley and Ed Bermingham at Dillon Reed to get both of them interested first. Then I approached Wertheim & Co. with the argument, "Here's something three firms can do!" The response was a little more positive than it had been with Franco Wyoming (it could scarcely have been worse) but after some initial fumbling around, this effort came to nothing, too.

Again, I didn't get down in the dumps about it. I was zero-for-two, but at some level, I think, I must have known that a confluence of experiences was slowly coming together that would take me on to something new. I also had other things to worry about by then. My private life was getting complicated.

———◆———

Thais hadn't been overjoyed about leaving Hingham. She was moving away from her family, and her earlier relocation to New York—to live with my parents while I was overseas during the war—hadn't gone well. This time, in addition to settling herself into a new venue and coping with my extended family, she had our year-old son Duncan to worry about.

We moved first into a house in Stamford that my father owned, a big old ark of a place on Shippan Point, looking out over Long Island Sound, with five or six bedrooms and a forty-foot-long living room. My brother Arthur and his wife had been living there with their four children, but Arthur had left some time earlier to begin working on a doctorate in marketing at Ohio State University, and the house had been sitting empty. For the three of us, one still crawling, it was more living space than was even remotely sensible. Doing the place justice would have required a staff of five or six. But we hired a nurse to help and stayed there until 1950, when I bought the home in Darien that I still own today.

Two years later, in 1952, we rented a house in Dennis, Massachusetts, out on Cape Cod for the summer. I commuted back and forth to New York, but Duncan and Thais stayed put. When it came time to leave that August, Thais balked. Soon her end-of-the-summer reluctance turned into something stronger and worse, and it became evident that the nervous disorders that had afflicted her back in 1944 and 1945 had not been anomalous. I got Thais back to Darien and to doctors in New York City, but she was on a downward slide from which she never pulled out. Finally, in 1953, Thais went off to the Austen Riggs Center, in Stockbridge, Massachusetts. Founded in 1919 on the same Main Street that Norman Rockwell made famous, Riggs was then and still is a small, not-for-profit psychiatric hospital notable for its open setting and intensive psychotherapy treatment. (Emily Fox Gordon describes her own stay there, a decade after Thais, in her memoir *Mockingbird Years*.) None of it did Thais much good.

I was determined to do everything possible to get Thais well, but I also knew, from the moment she left for Riggs, that our relationship was beyond repair, no matter the outcome of her treatment. Our divorce didn't become final until 1957. Laws were different then, especially if one of the parties had profound psychological problems, but for all practical purposes, our marriage had ended four years earlier.

Thais's collapse and departure also left me with the dilemma of what to do with Duncan. He was six when his mother entered Riggs for what was obviously going to be an extended stay, and I had a job in the city, an hour away by train. Out of desperation, I called an English couple I had met in Darien: Caroline and Frank Groves. Caroline did some catering, and Frank was a roofer and general handyman. They had a son, Graham, who was a year or two younger than Duncan. I knew they were having trouble making ends meet; so I explained my situation and made Caroline an offer: "Would you consider moving into the house? The three of you? All I want you to do is keep house for me and take care of Duncan. Frank can keep doing his other jobs."

To my great relief, Caroline said yes, which took care of the immediate problem, but larger problems were looming behind that one. The first was Duncan himself.

Especially early on in Thais's stay at Riggs, I would take Duncan up to see his mother on weekends, grim visits that always seemed to end badly. After a few such encounters, I began racking my brain for something else to do on weekends—something constructive and fun for both of us. Finally, I got the bright idea of trying winter skiing. So we went up to Tremblant, north of Montreal, where Duncan was fitted with a pair of terrible wooden skis and sent out on glare ice to learn the sport, with results predictably awful. Duncan dragged his heels the next time I tried to get him on the slopes, this time at Jiminy Peak in Hancock, Massachusetts, up in the Berkshires, but he seemed to take to the sport that day, and the next thing I knew he was hooked on skiing and obviously immensely talented at it. In time, Duncan would go on to become one of top high-school skiers in the East, a member of the U.S. Ski Team, even a pro skier for a number of years. Until recently, he was still winning races in the over-50 category, but sadly, Duncan would also end up battling mental illness.

By the time Duncan was ready for high school, I could tell that New Canaan Country School, where he had been all along, simply wasn't working out for him. Skiing was clearly what gave Duncan's life meaning, and not only was New Canaan a long way from the mountains, the school had an inane policy of allowing students to leave early on Fridays for horseback riding, but not for skiing. Holderness—a small boarding school begun in 1879 in the rugged North Country of New Hampshire, with a terrific winter sports program—seemed the ideal solution, and for a time it was. Duncan flourished on the slopes. In the classroom, he did very well in the courses he liked, but made no effort in the ones he didn't. Soon, the "F's" were mounting. Worse, his behavior was beginning to alienate teachers, coaches, and classmates.

He was asked to leave before his senior year and came down to New York City to live with me and my new wife, Dorothy, and there his behavior began to fall apart completely. I enrolled him at the Rhodes School on West Fifty-fourth Street, where he could board, and took him out to Van Cortland Park in the Bronx, where a little rope tow ran skiers up a tiny slope with about a fifty-foot drop. But the urban skiing experience didn't go over any better than the new urban school. Clearly, there was no possibility of a biological connection to Thais's illness. Nor was any mention ever made to Thais and me when we were adopting Duncan of a genetic history of mental illness, but like Yogi Berra, I had the feeling of deja vu all over again as I began to see my son disintegrating in front of me.

At McLean Hospital in Boston—the nearly 200-year-old psychiatric teaching wing of the Harvard Medical School and a part of Massachusetts General Hospital—Allen Stone, one of the finest doctors I've ever met, diagnosed Duncan with "ambulatory schizophrenia," generally defined as a schizophrenia mild enough not to require hospitalization. That was the good news. Dr. Stone also recognized that skiing was basically what held Duncan together: what kept him "ambulatory." Although hospital policy generally forbade patients from leaving, he arranged for Duncan to head off to New Hampshire every weekend during the ski season to get his practice in. But even "mild" schizophrenia is still schizophrenia, and Duncan had already begun the pattern of his life that he would never escape.

Instead of returning to us after he was ready to leave McLean, Duncan went to Littleton, New Hampshire, near Dartmouth, to finish high school and continue working on his skiing. From there, he went out West, where he joined the national team, but soon he was fighting with the coach, Bob Beattie, and thrown off the squad. More quarrels followed, and more ski teams and skiing circuits. Ambulatory schizophrenics often have severely compromised social skills, and Duncan didn't believe in medication, then or now. The skiing gave him status and prestige; the sport also introduced Duncan to Liv Sverre, part Norwegian (her father had known the great skier and 1952 Olympic gold medalist Stein Eriksen), part Mexican-Indian-American, a wonderful woman by whom he had two children as part of a common-law marriage. But finally, the disease drove everyone off, including Liv.

At the time Thais fell ill, though, that was far in the future. Later on I could afford to help Duncan with his medical bills and, more important, help Liv and her children. Back in those early days, when Thais was first hospitalized, I had few resources of my own, and the Austen Riggs Center was crushingly expensive. By 1954, I had been footing the Riggs bill for nearly a year and was nearly tapped out when my brother Edgar came to see me as the family emissary.

My father, Edgar told me, had a job waiting for me at Cullman Bros. Edgar told me what my position was going to be, what I would be paid, what the business thought I could do for it, and everything else imaginable. This wasn't a hastily conceived offer: Family councils must have been convened on my case for some time, and they obviously knew their man. After six years at Wertheim & Co., I was still peddling securities. The deals I had tried to get the company and other investment banks involved in had been an invaluable education, but the education wasn't paying any bills. I was now, effectively, a single father with a son to raise. The lawyers told me they had no idea how long it was going to take to push through my divorce. The vagaries of the statutes were such that the final split could take half a decade or more. In the meantime, as I had no desire to move Thais from the place that seemed to have the best chance of helping her, I was facing, at my current salary, a ruinous expense.

In short, I didn't see that I had any real choice. In the early summer of 1954, I gave notice at Wertheim and started hanging my hat at 161 Front Street, where Cullman Bros. had been doing business for forty or so years, in a building designed for my father by a notable architect of the time, Aymar Embry. (Embry had also designed the Far Rockaway home; much to my mother's shock, though, he neglected to include a staircase to the second floor in the original plan.)

My father, I suppose, had won. All those years of preparing us, from Collegiate and Fessenden through Yale, had finally paid off. He would finally be able to say that all four of his sons had at least tried the tobacco business, whatever the cost.

———⊷⊶———

In fact, bringing us boys into the business had already claimed one victim. Arthur and Edgar had been 4-F during the war, physically unfit for service. While Joe and I toiled for the Navy, the two middle sons had gone to work for our father. Arthur, the older of the two, had been directly under Dad and by all accounts had done an excellent job, but when the war ended and Joe mustered out of the military, Dad dropped Arthur down the pecking order and slipped his first-born son, Joe, into his place.

Dad had a typical German, Old World belief in primogeniture: He ran the business while his younger brother Howard played second fiddle, just as his father had run the business while his younger brother, Jacob, looked on from the wings. Uncle Howard compensated for his junior status at Cullman Bros. by serving as Commissioner of the Port of New York and New Jersey Authority, in which capacity he cleared the path for the construction of the World Trade Center. (I distinctly remember asking him afterwards how in the heck he could sign off on a crass commercial enterprise engineered by the Rockefellers on public lands.) Howard and his wife, Peggy, were also two of the best known and most active "angels" on Broadway, helping back such smash hits as *Life with Father*, *Mister Roberts*, *Dial M for Murder*, *Teahouse of the August Moon*, and *No Time for Sergeants*.

Joe had worked for Dad before the war and had every expectation that a good job would be waiting for him when he returned from the Pacific. Nonetheless, the shock of being demoted was so great to Arthur that he sought treatment twice at Payne Whitney, the famous psychiatric clinic at New York Presbyterian Hospital/Cornell Medical Center, not the famous Yale gym designed by John Russell Pope. My family sometimes seems to have kept the U.S. psychiatric profession going single-handedly.

Perhaps through analysis or counseling he received during his second stay at Payne Whitney, Arthur decided to leave the business altogether, rather than continue competing with Joe or suffering under our father. That's why he had vacated the sprawling Stamford house for Ohio State University before Thais and I relocated to New York. I'm sure it must have felt to Arthur at the time as if he were throwing in the towel. That's certainly how the rest of us treated it, but I can see now that it was closer to a liberation for him. Arthur was to spend the rest of his working life at the university, in a distinguished career teaching advertising and marketing. When he died in 1994, Joe established a chair in marketing at the university in his honor.

Along with me, Arthur had suffered a second insult before I ever came on board at Cullman Bros. At some point between Arthur's leaving the business and my joining it, Dad and Uncle Howard reorganized Cullman Bros. by taking back preferred stock for all the value they had in the business and creating a new common stock that had practically no value, except in the aggregate. Dad then gave huge chunks of this new common stock to Joe and Edgar, both of whom were working there, and not a share of it to Arthur and me, or to our sister, Nan. Nan, I'm sure, was taken care of some other way: That, too, would be the Old World father in Dad. But excluding Arthur and me must have been his way of punishing us—the one for not being able to cut it in the mold he had shaped for us, the other for not yet being willing to conform to it. The strange thing was that Dad cracked this whip so silently. If Edgar hadn't told me about the deal after Thais and I moved to New York, I might never have known I'd been shortchanged.

———◆———

All this I was walking into when I left Wertheim & Co. and started with Cullman Bros. in the summer of 1954, but I was also joining a business that had mushroomed in complexity since my grandfather's day. Mr. Junior was a man of great energy and restlessness, and as the decades mounted up, Cullman Bros. came to bear his stamp. As events turned out, Dad had a Midas touch.

His insistence that we purchase the Connecticut River Valley land, over his own father's objections, added tobacco growing to the portfolio. Early in 1929, he put together a closed-end investment trust, Tobacco and Allied Stocks, the first such trust to invest in a single industry. The trust was relatively tiny at its inception—capitalized at only $3 million—but Cullman Bros. took 10 percent of the stock and received warrants that eventually brought its share to 40 percent, and that 40 percent proved a gold mine.

The same year, 1929, Chase National Bank asked Dad to take over a small, troubled cigar manufacturer, Webster-Eisenlohr. To sweeten the deal, the bank offered him a large chunk of the company's preferred stock at a fire-sale price of $40 a share. Repackaged and reblended, Webster would become the best-selling high-grade cigar in the country. In the early 1940s, under pressure from Chase, which wanted to liquidate its own large investment in Webster, Cullman Bros. sold out its preferred stake at $140 a share.

Ever since the mid-1800s, when Ferdinand Kullman began rolling his apparently fetid stogies, the family had been in the cigar business. All it took was one phone call to Mr. Junior early in 1942 to change that. The setting was the Club LaSalle, a fishing enclave 50 miles square, way to heck and gone in northeastern Canada. Dad had been dipping his line that day with some other tobacco men and was enjoying his scotch back at the camp when a phone call got patched through from Richmond, Virginia. Dad apparently had no idea what he was agreeing to when he shouted "Yes!" into the receiver—the reception was scratchy and it wasn't his first scotch—but when he got back to civilization, he discovered that he had bought a sizable stake in Axton Fisher, a tiny cigarette maker that included among its inventory a brand improbably called Spud, the first menthol smoke.

Axton Fisher would soon disappear from my father's radar screen, thanks to a nasty court battle with the Bank of America, but cigarettes were there to stay. At the same time Dad was buying and dumping Axton Fisher, Tobacco and Allied Stocks purchased for $850,000 a 51 percent interest in Benson & Hedges, a small, high-end cigarette manufacturer and retailer with an elegant shop at 435 Fifth Avenue and "in season" outlets at Palm Beach, in Florida, and Newport, Rhode Island. Because Cullman Bros. controlled the investment trust, Dad controlled B&H. Mornings, he devoted to the family business; afternoons, to his new toy. B&H was where Arthur worked under him during the war, and where Joe took over from Arthur at war's end.

Benson & Hedges would never capture even one percent of the total market share for U.S. cigarettes, but its Parliament brand with the distinctive flip-top box and recessed filter ("Removes much of the tar—keeps all loose bits of tobacco from reaching your lips," went the ad) was much admired and imitated, and for a while the company had the best growth numbers in the industry. The record didn't go unnoticed. In late 1953, Philip Morris, trying to break out of its status as a mid-sized cigarette maker, offered to buy Benson & Hedges for $22.4 million in stock, nearly 370,000 shares of Philip Morris, 25 times earnings for a company whose total assets were valued at less than $6 million.

Forbes wrote that Philip Morris had paid, in effect, $16 million for a name, but my father didn't mind in the least. In 1954, just as I was coming to work for Cullman Bros., Dad liquidated Tobacco and Allied Stocks, giving the stockholders in the trust the underlying shares while Cullman Bros. took all the Philip Morris stock that was an indirect holding. Three years later, the head of Philip Morris died suddenly and my brother Joe, who had gone over to the company with Benson & Hedges and overseen the introduction of its wildly popular Marlboro brand, became the new CEO, a position he would hold for the next 21 years of spectacular growth for the company.

Joe Senior's daring nineteenth century dash back and forth across the Atlantic to purchase Sumatra leaf had brought the family out of the middle class. Joe Junior's purchase of Benson & Hedges and its subsequent sale put us seriously into the chips, but Dad didn't get to enjoy his success for long. He fell sick around Christmastime 1954 and died three months later, on March 18, 1955.

My job at Cullman Bros. was to be a financial man—the assumption being that Wertheim & Co. had at least trained me for that, while the weather business had prepared me for nothing but forecasting snow. Just as at Wertheim, though, after I learned the ropes, I found there wasn't all that much to do. Once again, I started looking for ways to make the job interesting, and once again, the pieces of my future began to fall together.

When I was still at Wertheim, Buck Ewing introduced me to a fund called Pennroad, later known as the Madison Fund. (Buck is also the one who put me on to the Franco Wyoming Oil Company.) Through Pennroad, I got Cullman Bros. involved in an outfit called Gunnar Mines Ltd., a Canadian uranium mining company that was just beginning operations on the north shore of Lake Athabasca, in the far northeastern corner of Saskatchewan—part of a brief uranium boom that flourished up there until the bottom fell out of the market in the 1960s. I was talking with one of the Pennroad people, Everett Callender, when he happened to mention that a junket was heading up to have a look at Gunnar.

"Why don't you go along?" he said. "It'll be a bunch of finance people and insurance executives."

"That would be fine, Everett," I told him, "but how can I go on this junket? No one asked me."

That was no problem, he assured me, and the next day I got a letter from a Montreal firm, Dawson Hanaford, inviting me up to Toronto, where the group was meeting with the Gunnar management, and from there out to western Canada to have a look at other energy outfits. (Toronto was a relief, I have to admit: This was February 1955. Meeting the management team on site at Gunnar would have taken us almost to the sixtieth parallel, the northern border of the Canadian provinces and just about on a line with Oslo and Leningrad.)

I showed Dad the letter. He was in his sick bed, with less than two months to live, and asked him what he thought I should do.

"Go," he told me. "You never know, you just might meet someone."

The trip had its lighter moments. We traveled by chartered DC-3, which meant we had to leap-frog our way west, from Toronto to Thunder Bay at the top of Lake Superior, and from there to Winnipeg, Regina, and finally out to Alberta Province. But we'd barely left Toronto before everyone jumped out of his seat and started talking about some kind of hot action involving a company I'd never heard of called Canadian Anaconda. By the time we got to Thunder Bay—then known simply as The Lake Head—the excitement had reached a fever pitch. No sooner had the door opened and the ladder gone down than my junket mates were rushing to the few phones available and calling New York to place their orders.

"What's this all about?" I finally asked when I could corner someone who seemed to be in the know—although I was probably the only one along who *wasn't* in the know.

"Oh, there's been this tremendous discovery—Savannah Creek Gas Field—in western Canada by Phillips Petroleum, and this tiny little company, Canadian Anaconda, has a fractional interest in the field!"

"Where's the company based?"

"Calgary."

"Well," I said, "we're heading to Calgary. Why don't we call on them?"

By now the discussion had become a general one involving most of the group, and no one was inclined to agree with me.

"Why bother?" one of them said. "We know more about this gas field than the company does."

"That may be," I said, "and I certainly wouldn't recommend taking a special trip from New York to Calgary just to see Canadian Anaconda, but as long as we're going there . . ."

No one was very enthusiastic. They had already put in their buy orders and just wanted to sit back and watch the profits roll in, but maybe just to humor me, the group agreed that we would drop in on the company if I would arrange the visit. I tried, but we were one city off: Canadian Anaconda was in Edmonton, not Calgary. Fortunately, Edmonton was the last stop on our itinerary; so I called the company, which turned out to be two guys who ran a trade school, and set up a meeting at the Canadian Pacific Hotel, right on top of the railroad station in downtown Edmonton, and off we went.

At last, we all sat down in one room—the trade school guys and our crew of hotshot financial professionals—and I opened the discussion:

"We're a group of investors that has come from New York and Toronto," I explained, "and we're interested in talking about the company."

"Oh, yeah," said the one who seemed to be the president, "me and my partner here, we noticed quite a bit of interest in our stock from you people back east; so we sold 600,000 shares of treasury stock. Do you think that was a good idea?"

Even back then, the SEC required registration in order to sell treasury shares, but Canada had no such protection. My savvy traveling companions had been buying stock diluted by more than half a million previously unissued shares.

"Well," I asked when we finally got rid of our Cheshire Cat trade school owners, "do you think it was a good idea to call on the company now?"

<hr>

I got back from the trip shortly before my father died. For me, and maybe for all my brothers, Dad's death was a complicated moment. It's hard to imagine a man more loved by his contemporaries. Dad was an avid outdoorsman and tennis player, generous to a fault, a great mixer and "party animal" before that phrase even existed. All of us boys inherited those qualities to a degree. Joe and Edgar, particularly, aren't really satisfied unless they are surrounded by people, in the middle of the action.

To his children, though, Dad was often as tight-lipped and reserved as he was loquacious and outgoing to his friends, and far more dictatorial. I'm sure he was afraid of spoiling us, afraid we would turn out "soft" now that the family fortune had done so well. If that was his goal, he succeeded, but he also distanced himself from us, or maybe I should just say from me. Still, Dad had a genius instinct for business, and he had been prophetic when I went to see him about the Canadian trip: The people I met on that DC-3 and at our stops along the way would change my life.

Gordon Jones of John Hancock, Dick Wilson of State Mutual, Dick Bowser of State Street—they were all on the trip, and once I got out on my own and starting making deals for myself, I would do business with each of them. When I flew up to Toronto to start the trip, I was greeted on the steps of the Royal York Hotel by a young guy in a raccoon coat who introduced himself as Bob Wisener. Bob was a salesman for Dawson Hanaford, the firm that sponsored the trip. Later, on the way back from Alberta, another fellow and I got curious about a company we had heard about that held shares in Canadian Anaconda. Someone on the plane told us that a firm in Toronto, Wisener and Co., had the inside story on the company; so we stopped off to see the people there once we were back on the ground. That visit came to nothing, but the Wisener we called on was the father of the Bob Wisener I had met a few weeks earlier.

The next fall, Bob invited me and a number of others who had been on the junket up to "Rose Hill," his father's lakeside compound at Sturgeon Point, 90 miles north of Toronto. That outing was the first of what became an annual fall ritual that lasted for more than fifteen years and included as many as forty or fifty people at its largest. The compound consisted of a large main house and two other houses on the property. We would arrive just after summer, when the autumn colors were spectacular. Dick Wilson of State Mutual and I fell into the habit of traveling up to the outings together, arriving first, and taking a room together. Often, Dick would borrow the private plane favored by his CEO and pick me up at La Guardia on his way to Toronto. (The plane came courtesy of H. Ladd Plumley, a remarkable name that I've never forgotten because H. Ladd's brother, Paul, was one of my masters at Fessenden School.) I would often return the favor by providing Dick with World Series tickets, and from 1954 to 1961—the years I was at Cullman Bros.—there was but a single October when at least one New York team wasn't playing in the Series.

Those outings to Sturgeon Point cemented my friendship with Dick Wilson and, of course, with our host, Bob Wisener, but they also brought me in touch with a wide range of other people, many of them Canadians, who shared my interest in finance and deal-making. Had Everett Callender never mentioned the Gunnar trip to me, had Bob Wisener not been the one who met me when I arrived in Toronto, had Dad not encouraged me in his own gruff way to go, who knows how my future might have turned out? Success is often a matter of simply opening yourself up to opportunity.

=♦=

With my father's death, Uncle Howard became head of Cullman Bros. By 1957, Joe 3rd was running Philip Morris, closely aligned with our own interests ever since the purchase of Benson & Hedges. Edgar had taken over direction of the tobacco farms in Connecticut, which put him nearest to the cigar trade where the family business had begun. My side of the enterprise, investments and finance, was a one-man shop until the end of the decade when, at Edgar's suggestion, we brought aboard Bill Leach, who had been at Fidelity, to work with me. Bill was as bright as he was difficult—and he was plenty of both. But we hit it off well enough, and maybe because we had so little to do otherwise, we began sketching out an investment philosophy that I had come to think of as "incubation."

I was just starting to write down some incubation guidelines, a first step toward formalizing a philosophy of pursuing unrecognized equities, when out of the blue my phone rang and the Canadian connection struck again.

"My name's Gordon Smith," the caller said. "I'm with the Monarch Life Assurance Company, in Winnipeg, and I'm calling you on Bob Wisener's recommendation. I'd asked Bob if he knew anybody in New York who knew something about unusual securities, instead of the same junk that I get normally...."

Until that moment, I'm not sure what I really had planned to do with this incubation philosophy. To some extent, it was an intellectual exercise. I had begun showing up at Sturgeon Point each fall with some new security that fit the incubation criteria and tossing it out to the group for discussion. I suppose I could have field-tested the philosophy with Cullman Bros. investments, but unrecognized securities weren't what the family was interested in. Gordon Smith's call and his enthusiastic response as I outlined my thinking seemed to hold a kind of promise: If he was interested in my ideas, why not others? And if others, why couldn't I launch my own fund built around the incubation principles? The more I thought about it, the more excited I got, but there was still one large problem: I already had a job in the family business. Rod Robinson would take care of that, at least indirectly.

Rod was with Chemical Bank; I had known him for some time. One day in the fall of 1961, he stopped by the office and mentioned that his bank was representing a fellow named Jake Hain, over in Lebanon, Pennsylvania, right on the edge of the Amish tobacco growing area. Hain had amassed 35 percent of the the stock in the General Cigar Company, a controlling interest, and he was ready to sell. Was Cullman Bros. interested? Not in the least as far as I was concerned, I told Rod, but I suggested he talk with Edgar, who was the one most involved in the cigar end of the business. Edgar, it turned out, was indeed interested, as was Uncle Howard, and before I knew it, the excitement had come to a boil and Cullman Bros. was on the edge of buying control of General Cigar.

To me, the deal made no sense. The stock was way overpriced. (And remember, the reason I was at Cullman Bros. in the first place was that I was supposed to know something about these matters.) I told my brother and uncle as much, time and again.

"I think it's outrageous. The price is crazy," I would say, whenever they asked my opinion.

"Well, you don't know anything about the tobacco business," they would shoot back, invoking their many years of experience while I dallied in weather maps.

"I guess you're right," I would answer. "I don't know anything about the tobacco business, but I can't possibly see how this can make any sense."

So it went on, day after day. My brother and uncle, though, were not to be deterred. Along with a few outside investors, including the Haas family in San Francisco (makers of Levi Strauss), Cullman Bros. bought General Cigar in 1961, paying about $25 million for a company with $30 million or so in annual sales. Those figures still don't make any sense, but Edgar, to his great credit, proved as big a success at branding and marketing cigars as our brother Joe had been at launching Marlboro, Virginia Slims, and other blockbuster cigarettes.

When Edgar took over General Cigar, it was a high-volume maker of such low-end brands as White Owl, William Penn, and Robert Burns. Gradually, Edgar picked up several small high-end manufacturers—Gradiaz Anis and Temple Hall—as well as the American Sumatra farms, one of the larger tobacco growers. By the 1970s, he was introducing (and in some cases reintroducing) quality brands, many of them wrapped in our own Connecticut leaf. In the mid-1990s, when the cigar boom hit and no respectable Wall Street wizard would be photographed without a Macanudo in his fist, Edgar and his son, Edgar Jr., were sitting on top of some of the classiest hand-rolled brands in the business: not only Macanudo but Partagas, Temple Hall, and Ramon Allones as well as the machine-made Garcia y Vegas and American rights to Bolivar, Cifuentes and Cohiba cigars. For a while, the company even operated cigar bars, before the craze broke along with Nasdaq and the rest of the market indexes.

Edgar called me maybe half a decade after the purchase to ask if a company I had just bought could help him find a sleek, new name for General Cigar. I put them to work on the subject—the company specialized in corporate branding—and they came up with Culbro, just what the old family tobacco farming operation had been called. But names aside, the General Cigar purchase effectively spelled the end of the Cullman family business. General Cigar bought the Connecticut farms, and with that Cullman Bros. was out of the tobacco business. Then our portfolio of securities, all that was left, was exchanged for shares in one of the earliest swap funds: Federal Street, later State Street Growth. (Goldman Sachs, which created the fund, was located on Federal Street.) When that transaction was completed, Cullman Bros. simply ceased to exist. Today, even Culbro is gone: Edgar and his son took the company private and sold it off in 1999 to Swedish Match, the Stockholm-based niche marketer of everything from cigars to chewing tobacco, snuff, and lighters.

I'm not sure that I felt insulted when Edgar and Uncle Howard went ahead with the General Cigar purchase, but I certainly felt slighted. What was my role with the company if my advice, especially such strongly felt opposition, was going to be brushed aside so easily? But if that's what pushed me toward the door, it wasn't what opened it wide and sent me packing. The larger issue was that Edgar and I couldn't get along under the same roof. Maybe the problem was that we were so close in age—a year apart, the tail end of five children. Certainly, we were both headstrong, a quality we inherited from our father.

Whatever the cause, the simple fact is that we were always having arguments about what to do, circling each other like a couple of wary middleweights. General Cigar was just the biggest and newest in a running series of battles. From his perch at Philip Morris, Joe, the oldest of us, had been watching and fretting. Finally, just about the time the cigar company purchase was coming to head—and not long after Gordon Smith had popped into the picture—Joe suggested that maybe it was time for me to go. By then, I was a highly motivated listener.

FIVE

FROM INVESTOR TO OWNER

In late 1961, I left Cullman Bros. for good, taking Bill Leach with me. A month later, at the start of 1962, I opened my own investment advisory business, Lewis B. Cullman, Inc., at 120 Broadway, and very soon after that I began setting up what I had decided to call The Incubation Fund, Inc. To let potential investors know what they were in for, I drew up a formal four-part statement of its "investment philosophy," a distillation and codification of theories and notes that I had been tinkering with for half a decade. The statement reads as follows:

A. Objective. The principal objective of the Incubation investment philosophy is to maximize gain by the transition, or "incubation," of unrecognized securities to a recognized status. The high standards of the incubation investment policy demand quality in addition to unusual opportunities for profit. Confidence must be established in a company's competitive position, growth prospects, and integrity. A high average of success, not ownership of specific industries or fashionable stocks, determines profitability.

B. Incubation. It is our experience that the safest and most rewarding profit stems from the transition, or "incubation," of an unrecognized security that has a low price–earnings ratio into an institutionally recognized security with a high price–earnings ratio. As stocks become recognized, they are replaced with securities not yet widely held by institutions. Stocks of secondary quality or those without prospects for institutional recognition are avoided no matter how alluring.

C. Application. The application of our standards requires skill, judgment, and individual research beyond those exercised for standard securities investments. Our pattern of operation includes continuous, direct, personal contact with management. Such contact is vital to the continuance and success of our program.

D. Selection. Casual selection and insufficient commitments hamper results. While essential, diversification ceases to be prudent when it involves more stocks than can be managed intelligently. Information, though obtained from reliable sources, requires interpretation and judgment. Selections are made independent of public opinion and management estimates. Companies with simply defined business and prospects are preferred for several reasons. Judgment is easier, developments are understandable, and risks are reduced. Each purchase is made for a clear, attractive reason. Fulfillment or disappearance of this reason justifies sales.

More than 40 years down the pike, that philosophy still sounds just about right to me. A lot of misery could have been avoided in the collapse of the dot.com market if investors had shied away from "public opinion and management estimates," and stuck with companies that had "simply defined business and prospects." Apparently, the Incubation philosophy impressed the powers that be in the early sixties, too. By June 1962, the *New York Herald Tribune* was referring to me as one of the Street's "top analysts" even though I had hung out my shingle only six months earlier and the fund itself was still in its gestation period. (Admittedly, this was before "analysts" had begun multiplying like fruit flies.)

My intention from the beginning had been to register The Incubation Fund with the Securities & Exchange Commission and set it up as an American entity. I couldn't see any reason to do otherwise, but the Canadian connection came riding to the rescue yet again. Gordon Smith, who continued to have a great interest in the fund and the philosophy behind it, had had an earlier taste of the molasses-like pace of the SEC and didn't much like the experience.

"What's happening?" he finally asked me in frustration, after months of waiting for the fund to be approved.

"Well," I told him, "the SEC just isn't acting."

"I told you the SEC was bad news," Gordon shot back. "I'm getting sort of sick of this thing. Why do we bother with the SEC?"

That took me by complete surprise. "What do you mean?" I asked.

"Why don't we found this thing in Canada?"

"Well, Gordon," I said, "Canada sounds all right with me, but I don't know anything about Canada. I'm not a Canadian. How could I do that?"

"Don't worry about that," he said. "I'll take care of it."

Gordon Smith was as good as his word. Soon, he and Bob Wisener were setting up venues in Toronto, Winnipeg, Calgary, and Vancouver for me to talk with groups about this bizarre philosophy of investing in nothing but unrecognized securities. Alfred Ruys de Perez, a Dutch Canadian who worked with Bob at Wisener & Co., helped me refine my thinking about the fund and its philosophy and was among its original investors. So were two other Canadians: Michael Koerner and Brian Benitz. By myself, I doubt that I could have gotten to first base with those private audiences in Toronto and elsewhere, but Gordon Smith in particular was a golden passport north of the border: a very prominent Canadian, a director of the Bank of Nova Scotia, one of those men whose leads others naturally follow.

Thus, instead of launching The Incubation Fund sometime in 1962 as I had planned, in April 1963 I launched The Incubation

Group Ltd., a Canadian-registered entity, even though the underlying assets were all U.S. securities. Thus, too, the early investors who provided our original million-dollar stake turned out to be an extraordinarily classy group for such an outré investment strategy: Noranda Mines Pension Fund, the Bank of Nova Scotia Pension Fund, and Monarch Life Pension funds, among others, as well as directors or executives from many of them.

Two months after launching the fund, Herb Weiner and I were discussing its holdings over lunch at the Wall Street Club when he mentioned the idea of buying the incubation companies themselves rather than stock in them, and with that everything began to change one more time. By then, too, my private life had taken a decided turn for the better.

⟞—◆—⟝

In the winter of 1961–1962, I went down to Key Biscayne, Florida, where Gordon Smith was vacationing, to visit him and ask if he would serve as a director of The Incubation Fund. Gordon agreed after I assured him (wrongly) that registering with the SEC would be a breeze, and of course he saved the day when the SEC wouldn't—or couldn't—get off its duff. But Gordon was older than I, and more old-fashioned by far, and what he couldn't get over was that I had showed up at Key Biscayne accompanied by a woman who was not my wife.

Dorothy Freedman Benenson and I met through the United States Committee of the World Federation for Mental Health. Founded in 1948, the federation worked with groups like UNESCO and the World Health Organization to promote better diagnosis and treatment of mental disorders around the globe. The committee we had both signed up for was a fund-raising arm, a vehicle that allowed donors to take a U.S. tax deduction for gifts to an international charity. I might have been influenced to join the committee by Thais's problems and by Duncan's emerging ones. He was hitting his mid-teens by then, a rebellious time for most kids and just a few years before schizophrenia commonly begins to manifest itself. But I had been talking with a psychiatrist myself, to see if there might be some emotional basis for the asthma I was then suffering from, and he had encouraged me to get involved with the federation.

I recognized Dorothy's face at one of the committee meetings. She and her then husband Charles B. Benenson, who was in the real-estate business in New York, had been part of some dinner party Thais and I had attended a decade earlier. Dorothy had been divorced for about a year when we remet, and it wasn't long before we were going out together. I found Dorothy to be a person of wonderful contradictions and broad interests. A native New Yorker, she had done modeling for Saks and studied drama with Madame Ouspenskaya. *Always* referred to as "Madame," Maria Ouspenskaya had come to America in the 1920s with the Moscow Art Theater and stayed behind to act and coach. Her school was the predecessor of the Actors' Studio and its famous "method." One of Dorothy's drama-school classmates was Ardis Ankerson, later Mrs. William Holden.

Born to a father who considered Franklin Roosevelt the devil incarnate and Democrats generally the scum of the earth, Dorothy campaigned for Adlai Stevenson in the 1950s and was already opposing the American presence in Vietnam when I got to know her. In the late 1930s, she had picked Rollins College—in Winter Park, Florida, just on the north side of Orlando—over the far better known Bennington because Rollins had no math requirement, but she stayed only two years, worn down by the red-neck culture of Central Florida and distracted by a dating schedule that was, by her own admission, way too ambitious. (Rollins was her first co-ed school.) Filled with literary and intellectual interests, Dorothy returned to New York and married Charlie Benenson after a whirlwind six-month courtship. The fact that she had chosen a Jew of Russian descent led Dorothy's German-Jewish mother, already prone to breakdowns, to threaten never to leave bed again. Her mother recovered from the shock, but Dorothy soon found herself living in Scarsdale and raising two sons. In effect, she had traded one form of parochialism for another, but it would take her another decade and a half to free herself from the arrangement.

Dorothy and I were married June 6, 1963, at my brother Edgar's home in North Stamford—only a year or so later than Gordon Smith thought proper. She had an apartment at 29 East Sixty-fourth Street, where we lived during the winter; I kept my house in Darien for the summer. Dorothy's two sons, Billy and Freddy, were in their mid-teens when we married. Billy, the older, was at Berwick Academy in Maine. He would later go on to become a TV and movie producer. Freddy was at the Lawrenceville School in New Jersey, already showing signs of the academic he would become. (Freddy has taught the philosophy of science for many years at the University of Birmingham, in England.) Both of my new stepsons couldn't have been more different than Duncan if you had ordered them from Central Casting, but the three boys' lives rarely crossed. Freddy and Billy stayed with their father when they were home from school in those early days. Duncan seemed always to be passing through whatever address he occupied, and in later years, even an address was hard to come by. Amazingly, a generation later, Freddy's and Duncan's children would become friends and summertime playmates, but back then, I couldn't have predicted anything like that.

Charlie Benenson and Dorothy might have been incompatible in marriage, but Charlie was close to the ideal ex-spouse. From the beginning, he and I had plenty of interests in common, Yale among them—Charlie had been eight years ahead of me at New Haven, just two years in front of my brother Joe. Eventually, we would serve on a number of charitable boards together. My ex was another story. By the time Dorothy and I got to know each other, Thais had moved to Florida and was living with a fellow patient she had come to know at Austen Riggs, but she would continue to contact me for years afterward—sometimes when she was short on money or, often, after Duncan and she had tried yet another reconciliation. He never dressed to her standards, or acted appropriately or affectionately enough, or probably even made enough sense. Every meeting between them was a preordained disaster.

An ardent skier then and now, I talked Dorothy, who had never skied, into coming with me to Portillo, Chile, where Duncan and I had been going annually since 1959 to ski during the North American summer. Dorothy survived the experience but almost succumbed to her mother, who kept fretting that her daughter was going to be swept away by an avalanche—unlikely on the bunny slopes Dorothy practiced on. Fortunately, her mother didn't know about the first trip Duncan and I had taken to Portillo, when it snowed something like fourteen feet in three days. Avalanches weren't a problem, but finding a doctor to tend to the woman who had been impaled with a ski pole in her groin definitely was. Normally, the hotel rotated medical personnel in and out, but the doc who had been there got out before the big snow hit, and the one who was coming couldn't get in. Finally, several Austrians who had come to ski made a daring foray overland through the Andes into Argentina, found a doctor, and brought him back in time to save the woman's life. In the meantime, helicopters were dropping food to the rest of us.

Dorothy and I had been back in New York about six months when she extracted her revenge for our skiing expedition.

"Now look!" she said to me one day out of the blue, "I've been darn good about your sport. I've gone skiing. I think it's high time you did something that I like to do, and I like to play golf."

I had never played a hole of golf in my life and couldn't really imagine ever doing so, but because it was February, I readily agreed. Surely, I could find some way to talk myself out of the commitment before golf weather came to the upper Middle Atlantic States. Alas, Dorothy was far, far ahead of me.

"Fine," she said, "we'll go over to Walter Reveley's place, and you can take lessons."

Walter Reveley ran an indoor facility, complete with practice tees, and I was trapped. While one other customer, a woman, stroked golf balls beautifully from a nearby rubber mat, Walter set out to teach me the subtleties of the game. He assured me that I had a natural swing, was going to be a great golfer (if only I took dozens of lessons from him), and was the next Hogan in the making—all the usual baloney. When we were through, Dorothy joined us and asked how the lesson had gone.

"It was okay," I said.

"Well," she responded, "at least you have to admit that when you take a golf lesson, you don't have to worry about breaking your leg the way you do when you take a ski lesson."

At that exact moment came a tremendous crash. When the woman who had been practicing beside me stepped off the rubber mat onto the painted floor in her spikes, her feet had gone out from under her. Now, she was lying on the floor with a compound spiral fracture of her leg. Who knows what the odds of that happening at that precise instant might be—one in a million? one in a billion?—but I took the poor woman's suffering as a sign of divine intervention.

"Gee, Dorothy," I said, "this sport's too tough for me." And that was the end of my golf career. I never picked up a club again.

—————◆◆◆—————

In retrospect, the Orkin buyout colors so much about Dorothy's and my first years together, but once the dust had settled on that, I had my day job at Lewis B. Cullman, Inc., to tend to and a fund to watch over. For tax purposes, the investment decisions of The Incubation Group, Ltd., had to be run through my Canadian partners, but in effect, Gordon Smith, Bob Wisener, and the others north of the border tended to administrative functions and investor relations, and left the decision-making to me. I would sit in my office at 120 Broadway and determine what to buy and sell. Then either I or Bill Leach—at least while he worked for me, which wasn't long given his difficult personality—would call the fund's office in Canada and relay the decisions, and someone up there would call back to New York to place the order with our brokers. It sounds awkward, and it sometimes was.

In the very early days, too, the market was rough going for every-one. I can remember inviting all the investors in for the first earnings report, a half year or so after we had launched the fund. The results weren't stellar, and one of the shareholders, Doug Matthews, let me know it.

"Fine," I told him when he was through venting. "I don't want anyone in this company who's unhappy; so here's what I'll do. I'll write facedown on this piece of paper my bid for your stock; you write facedown on your own paper what you want to get for it, and then we'll compare."

Doug did, and when the results were in, I'd bid more for his stock than he was asking; so we split the difference, and he left a little happier than when he had come in—and a lot poorer than he would have been if he had just held his horses a while longer. By the spring of 1967, only four years in existence, the net asset value per share of Incubation had nearly doubled, compared to a 25 percent rise in the Dow-Jones Industrial Average over the same time.

An article on the fund in the March 28, 1967, *Home Furnishings Daily* lists its fourteen holdings as of that date. Among them are companies that are today household names but were then either just starting out or first going public: Denny's Restaurants; Samsonite, the luggage makers; Rouse, the builder, making a big new splash with its planned city at Columbia, Maryland, halfway between Baltimore and Washington. Deluxe Check Printers, now Deluxe Corporation, had begun life as a private company in 1915 in St. Paul, Minnesota, but it became publicly traded only in 1965, by which time it was the industry leader in the new MICR (magnetic ink character recognition) technology. Scot Lad Foods eventually was purchased by Roundy's, one of America's top-ten food wholesalers. Duro Pens continue to be collectors' favorites. Spencer Gifts, which ballooned from a mail-order business into a 700-unit chain of novelty-gift shops, would pass through several owners until Vivendi International finally sold the business (still profitable) in June 2003 to a group of private investors. Lin Broadcasting, another of the fund's holdings, is a nearly perfect metaphor for the wild market gyrations of the 1990s: acquired by McCaw Cellular Communications in 1990; which was acquired by AT&T in 1994; which spun off Lin's television operations as a publicly traded company, Lin Television Corporation; which was acquired in 1998 by Hicks, Muse, Tate, and Furst, a Dallas-based private investment firm; which again took the company public in 2002 as Lin TV Corp.; and so on. In the mid-1960s, though, when I added Lin to the fund, it was a start-up company.

Of course, not all that glittered in The Incubation Group's portfolio was real gold. Equity Funding had the seemingly brilliant idea of merging mutual funds and life insurance. Dividends from the fund's shares were used to pay premiums on the insurance policies, which were then sold to reinsurers. On paper, the business should have been a nice money machine. In practice, its executives began booking non-existent shareholders for the fund, issuing them false insurance policies that they then sold to reinsurers while banking the ill-earned profits for themselves. By the time the lid blew off the scam in 1973—in a scandal of Enron-like proportions—investors had lost $300 million, enough malfeasance to buy jail time for twelve Equity Funding bigwigs and their auditors. Until that time, though, the stock was a skyrocket, rising from $6 a share to over $90; and by 1973, The Incubation Group had been out of business for three years.

——◆——

When I launched The Incubation Group Ltd., I expected the fund to be my principal occupation for years to come. The investment philosophy was sound. My partners were a winning group. I still wonder how we would have done in the OPEC-inspired market crash of 1973–1974, when the DJIA gave up 48 percent of its value, almost exactly what it would lose three decades later when the dot.com bubble burst. But the truth is I could never get Herb Weiner's question out of my head: Why buy the stock of companies such as Orkin when you might be able to use creative financing to pick up the company itself? And I could never forget what Dorothy had said when we were toasting the Orkin deal and what I had been thinking at the time. What was I going to do for an encore? Well, maybe Orkin had been a fluke. Maybe Herb and I had simply lucked into an irreplicable situation. To the extent that the deal had rattled cages on Wall Street, I think that was the conventional wisdom: I'd gotten lucky. But I didn't accept that, and I was damned if I wasn't going to try it again. As 1965 was drawing on, I pulled out a list of The Incubation Group's holdings and began running down it from the top. The first company I came to, Allied Graphic Arts, seemed to pose just the right opportunity. Talk about exhaustive research!

On the surface, Orkin and Allied Graphic Arts couldn't have been more different. Orkin was a combination service and utility company; it operated like a private utility. Allied Graphic Arts, or AGA, was in the catalog agency business. Clients included some of the major New York City department stores and several trade magazines, but AGA's biggest account by far was S&H Green Stamps, the little green bonus stamps food retailers gave out at the cash register that could be redeemed for everything from lawn chairs to major appliances.

Green Stamps have disappeared from most modern supermarkets, but in their heyday, the stamps were practically as popular as the Beatles. No suburban housewife would think of not collecting them. By the 1960s, S&H was the largest purchaser of consumer products in the world. In 1964, the year before I began to look seriously at AGA, the S&H catalog became the highest volume publication in America, enough catalogs to circle the earth one and a half times. No single American printer could handle the load. By then, S&H was turning out three times as many stamps annually as the U.S. government, all at AGA's sole physical asset, a printing plant in a little Oklahoma town called Sand Springs, not far from Tulsa.

As different as they might have looked from 10,000 feet, AGA and Orkin had loads in common once I began to study them more closely. Both were old-line, family-dominated businesses. Both had gone public recently—1962, in AGA's case. And both had similar experiences as publicly traded companies: Share price had shot up initially, then sunk back down to below the issue price. As with Orkin, The Incubation Group Ltd. also owned a nice block of AGA stock: 10,000 shares, reason enough for me to go calling on the president of the company, a guy named Salie Wyker. (As if Salie's name wasn't confusing enough, his wife's name was Billie.) Maybe best of all, AGA was about one tenth the size of Orkin, small enough that we might be able to secure financing without having to give away the entire store. If I could convince Salie Wyker to sell, I thought there might be a good chance I could end up owning a nice share of a mid-size catalog company with a lovely balance sheet.

As I always did when heading into possible negotiations, I sat down beforehand with Herb Weiner to rehearse the arguments and counterarguments. Over the years, I've run into just about every negotiating trick in the book. I remember during the Orkin deal sitting in a Newark hotel room with Wayne Rollins, ironing out what we thought were going to be the final details on Wayne's share of the package. His brother and business partner, John, was supposed to join us but had been detained, Wayne told us, suggesting we go on without him. So we did until the eleventh hour, just as everything was ending, when John suddenly popped in and began undoing everything we had negotiated.

"Oh, Wayne, you didn't agree to that, did you ? And that, too? Oh, my heavens, Wayne!"

It was a stunt, of course, prearranged to the finest detail, but it forced us back to the table, where Wayne Rollins could try to pare down our take one last time.

I've used more than a few tricks myself and a fair amount of textbook psychology. Pleasure trips to Europe have become irrevocable deadlines—"Listen, we've *got* to get this done in ten days before Dorothy and I leave for Paris!"—because so many people need deadlines to get off the dime and overcome their natural inertia. While Herb was alive and helping me with negotiations, we always made sure that when one of us was talking at the table, the other was watching the people being addressed. I would handle the substantive parts; Herb stepped in when the tax ramifications got tricky. Always, the silent one would be studying the reactions across the table, the way eyes were moving or blinking, tension around the mouth, other tell-tale signs of weakness. During the breaks, we would compare notes and then go back and probe the sore spot to see what might happen. As Andy Scharps knew, poker players look for the same cues, if they want to win.

I've seen people go into rages during negotiations, people reduced nearly to tears, people make every kind of threat and imprecation and supplication imaginable, and I'm still convinced that the best strategy is to be the best prepared person at the table: to know more, to have thought more thoroughly about all the contingencies, to always have that one argument in reserve that you don't have to use. Role playing, dry runs, dress rehearsals—whatever helps you do your homework best will also leave you the most relaxed person in the room. When someone on the other side starts to boil over, you can deflect the moment with a joke because you know you have ammunition you're never going to have to use.

In any event, that's how I prepared for my meeting with Salie Wyker. As with the Orkin boys and Perry Kaye, my plan was to walk in, ask the obvious question, make an opening offer, and then we could get down to serious business. Indeed, that's almost how it went.

"Salie," I said, sitting across the table from him at AGA's office in the Fred French Building on Fifth Avenue, "how do you like being a public company?"

"Dumbest mistake I ever made in my life," he said, pretty much as I had expected.

"Why's that?"

"Well, first of all, I didn't get enough money out for myself and my family. And second, I inherited all these damn public stockholders. They're blaming me for the price of the stock, and I have nothing to do with it. I don't have any control over that."

It was the Orkin story all over again. Bache (later Prudential-Bache) had made the IPO sound like the proverbial goose that laid the golden eggs, but the money wasn't what Salie thought it would be now that the stock price had turned south, and the misery factor of public ownership was exponentially greater than what he was used to. Salie was a charmer, a natural print salesman (the business he had started in), an all-around pleasant guy; but none of that necessarily prepared him to deal with irate shareholders.

So I looked up at him and said, "Salie, I'll do for you what Bache never did."

"What do you mean?" he asked, temperature rising.

"I'll pay you $8 a share for the assets," I told him. The stock was then selling at $5; so I was offering a 60 percent premium on the share price. "But there's one proviso. You and your family have to take six and two: $6 in cash and $2 in purchase money notes."

With that, Salie Wyker jumped out of his chair, rushed around the table, shook my hand, and that was the deal. With minor technical modifications—a matter of the distribution of the purchase money notes—the agreement never changed an iota after that moment.

⊷⊶

Flushed with success and still a little stunned by it, I hustled back to 120 Broadway and caught a train under the Hudson River to Prudential headquarters in Newark. The Orkin deal was by now maybe fifteen months old. Rollins stock had performed spectacularly, and the Pru had made a tremendous amount of money on the kickers that had been built into that financing. Surely I had enough good will built up with Ray Charles and his crew to entice them into a much smaller deal—$6 million as compared to $62.4 million—with pretty much all the same advantages to the lender. Ray didn't disappoint me. I told him about the proposed acquisition, and before I left the room, he pledged the Pru to put up all the money except the purchase money notes, which the Wyker family was taking back, in return for 75 percent of the equity. The other quarter of AGA was ours, no money down. Who was I to complain?

Less than a week later, Ray called me at my office.

"Lewis," he said, "would you do me a favor? I know I agreed to that transaction, but as you know, we're in a credit crunch here. The

My brother Arthur, four years my senior, and I in Central Park, in the early 1920s. My family lived just a few blocks away; the park was our playground.

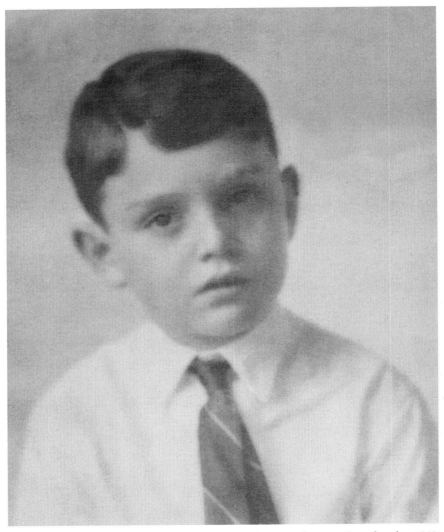

I must have been eight years old when this photograph was taken for the 1927 Collegiate School yearbook.

My grandmother, Frances Wolff, hitching a ride on my back at our summer home in North Stamford, Connecticut. The 1870 murder of Granny Wolff's father remains one of New York's great unsolved crimes.

My father, Joseph Cullman Jr., in the late 1940's. Dad expected all his sons to attend Yale University, then join him in the tobacco business. I had other ideas about how to make my living.

In 1939, after our sophomore year at Yale, Walter Gips, at right, and I set out for the West Coast. Ten weeks, 10,000 miles, and one busted Buick later, we limped back to New York. Here we are in Montana.

Brother Joe, at left, and I decked out in our Navy blues at the start of World War II. Joe went on to serve in the Pacific. I spent the war as an aerologist, making weather forecasts for the blimps that patrolled the Atlantic.

My first wife, Thais MacBride. We were married in December 1942, near the South Weymouth Naval Air Station to which I was assigned for the bulk of the war.

A quick lesson in weather forecasting, at the South Weymouth station. I'm wielding the pointer. Life at the station got far more exciting when the blimps were out and storms came in.

Want to know when to get the snow plows out? Just sign up with Weather Advisors—at least that was our message at the 1947 New England Road Builders Show.

Off the slopes at Portillo, Chile, in 1959. With me is the multi-talented Clemens "Mikki" Hutter—PhD, ski instructor, and journalist.

Still off the slopes at Portillo a half decade later, this time with my new wife, Dorothy. After I had talked Dorothy into ski lessons, she insisted I try to learn golf. Happily, the golf experiment didn't last.

Dorothy and I hosting a 1972 fundraiser for Democratic presidential candidate George McGovern, at left. Dorothy had opposed the Vietnam War before most people even knew it was underway.

For years, the ski instructors at Snowmass, in Colorado, had been holding an informal race among themselves. Then, I decided to jazz up the event with the silver Cullman Cup, from Tiffany's no less. Here I am, in 1975, with winner Walter Stoeckel and runner-up Franz Kopp.

One of my proudest moments. We poured a lot of resources into Keith Clark and the Sidney, New York, area, and Sidney wanted to say thank you. I especially like that quirky plural: "years."

Way off the slopes, at the Milk Studio in Manhattan, during our first fund-raiser for Chess-in-the-Schools. My dance partner is brother Joe's wife, Joan Cullman.

An April 2002 fundraiser for a favorite non-profit, Chess-in-the-Schools. Agnes Gund of the Museum of Modern Art, New York Giants owner Bob Tisch, and I look on as high-schooler Damion Josephs triumphs over former Giants captain Charles Way.

Federal Reserve is getting after what they call nonproductive loans, and my board is taking a different position on this. They don't look upon these acquisition loans with much favor."

"Ray," I told him, "forget it. Don't even think about it. You're off the hook. Goodbye."

I was patting myself on the back for my generosity, my ability to keep cool in the face of great disappointment, even my general sangfroid, when it dawned on me that there was still a mess of work to be done.

The financing for a corporate acquisition is always complicated, no matter what the size of the property. Corporations aren't just *things*; they're assets and obligations; employees and owners, including shareholders if the company is publicly held. Emotions play a part, too, always. But the financing for just about any leveraged buyout could fill a book if you went into enough detail. The success or failure of the package—and ultimately of the purchase—depends on a complicated interaction of parties, on very minute fractions of numbers, and on building a structure that will minimize the tax impact on everyone involved. Who's going to put up what? In what form? For what percent interest or percentage of the equity? How does each new element introduced into the equation ripple back through all the arrangements that have been made to date and the ones that still need making? Just as important, how does each new element change the human chemistry, in the present and out into the future? The process sounds miserable, I admit; in truth, it was my favorite part of the whole business. Strike the basic deal, and you could start assembling the orchestra on stage. My job ultimately was to raise the baton and get them to play together. To me, nothing could have been more fun.

With Ray Charles and Prudential out of the picture, it seemed only natural to bring Dick Wilson and State Mutual into it. Dick and I had been going back and forth to Bob Wisener's Sturgeon Point retreats for a decade by then. We had talked about everything under the sun, including the Orkin-Rollins deal and the incubation companies I had been assembling for the fund. I had never before approached

Dick as a financing partner, but State Mutual's money was as much legal tender as the Pru's.

With Dick Wilson's intercession, State Mutual and one of its partners, Paul Revere Insurance, offered to put up $2.5 million of the purchase price: $2 million as a straight loan and $500,000 as a senior subordinated security convertible into 65 percent of the equity. For sheer creativity, the financing package was quickly becoming a thing of beauty: The senior subordinated debt made it easy for a bank to come in on top with senior debt that could then be paid out of some kind of term loan. But as the Wykers pointed out—and as the Orkins had noted at about this same stage in our previous negotiations—there wasn't yet any real money on the table, any folding green they could pick up and carry home.

To satisfy the Wykers, we raised about a half a million dollars of equity from the The Incubation Group Ltd., with the full consent of the directors. We were still offering a handsome premium on the stock price, and the fund held 10,000 shares in AGA. It was to everyone's advantage to back the deal. Three of the Canadians associated with the fund came in on their own, as well. To sweeten the pot further, Herb Weiner got in touch with a woman whose tax work he had been handling—Florene May Schoenborn, one of the Mays of the May Department Store fortune—and brought her in as an equity partner. The Wykers continued to balk, though; they wanted a million dollars on the barrel head. So Dick Wilson suggested that State Mutual's $500,000 senior subordinated security be adjusted so that it converted one year later than the notes the Wykers had agreed to take back. Nobody had actually put up the missing half million, but for all intents and purposes it was the same thing, and the very essence of leveraged buyout deal-making.

Just as we had done with the Orkin-Rollins deal, Herb and I set up a buying entity, the AGA Corporation, to run the deal through, and we split the equity 50–50 between Herb's family and me. When we needed to bring in a lawyer, I trotted over to Paul Weiss's firm and was referred to someone in the corporate finance department named

Jack Massengale, who turned out to be a neighbor in Darien. I offered to pay the law firm a fee or to give it an equity stake in the AGA Corporation. When the firm opted for the latter—to my surprise, I might add—Herb and I reduced our shares to 40 percent and gave Paul Weiss the remaining 20 percent.

By the time we were through with all those machinations, we had $1 million as equity for the Wykers and $2.5 million toward the deal: $2 million in straight debt from State Mutual and Paul Revere, and $500,000 in the convertible preferred, plus a thousand dollars in equity from Herb, Jack, and me, in addition of course to the sweat equity we were accumulating. That left us with the challenge of the top-tier $2 million, but Dick Wilson said not to worry: "No problem," were his exact words, "Any bank will do it, obviously." In fact, a lot of banks wouldn't do it, but a series of contacts led us to Meadowbrook National Bank, which put up the $2 million in the form of a five-year term loan, to be amortized at $400,000 a year. The bank figured the business was good for $200,000 of the amortization annually. The other $200,000, we hoped, would come from an aggressive tax plan that Herb Weiner and I had devised. If that didn't pan out, we had the right to sell senior debt to the insurance companies to make up the shortfall.

Finally, the deal was done. We closed in July 1966. I woke up the next morning owning a graphic arts business, but the maneuvering still hadn't played out its final twists and turns. The credit crunch had eased as we were closing down negotiations; so I went back to Ray Charles to see if the Prudential would like to help us refinance by taking on the $2 million that Meadowbrook National Bank had loaned us, now reduced to $1.8 million because we had already paid off some of it. I knew my question was likely to fall on deaf ears: Insurance companies don't like to aid their competitors, and by agreeing to a favorable refinancing for us, Ray would be indirectly helping State Mutual and Paul Revere. But, still, Ray's answer floored me.

"Why didn't you force me to do this in the first place?" he said. "I'd said we would do it. If you'd leaned on me, I would have had to go through with the deal."

"What are you talking about, Ray?" I replied. "I can't believe this."

"That's right. If you had been a bastard about this thing and told me that I had given my word to do this, I would have had no recourse but to have gone through with the financing."

It's rare in my life that I've been excoriated for *not* being a bastard, but I took it in stride and went once again to State Mutual, which had the biggest stake in helping us refinance because then the insurance companies would be out from under their guarantee to make up for any shortfalls. State Mutual, in turn, sent us to Mass Mutual, which was so hungry for a deal that it loaned us the $1.8 million at 6.5 percent straight interest over thirteen years, with no amortization payments starting until the fourth year out. While all that was going on, we had AGA buy back The Incubation Group's ownership position in the company to shrink the capitalization and to generate a profit for Incubation. Simultaneously, we bought out Florene Schoenborn's interest. Throw in a few more side deals—two separate closings, one for the stock and one for assets, so that the Wykers could minimize their tax exposure—and by the fall of 1967, we had the refinancing completed at very favorable terms to us, plus IRS approval for a mongrel tax approach that worked to our advantage. Best of all, ownership of the company was left in the hands of my three Canadian friends who had put up the money for the convertible preferred, plus our little group of three, which had risked only a collective thousand dollars, just as in the Orkin-Rollins deal. This time, though, we ended up with the company, and AGA was up and humming.

⟫•⟪

I suppose that at this point I might have sat back on my laurels for at least a little while. To the extent that Wall Street thought Orkin was a fluke, Allied Graphic Arts had proved otherwise. Sure, the deal was nowhere near as large, but the principles and applications were exactly the same. We had leveraged AGA's assets to secure financing for the purchase, and everyone from the Wykers to the other shareholders to the lenders to Herb Weiner and me had come out happy. The decades ahead would show just how poisonous leveraged buyouts can be, but that hadn't been the case here or with Orkin. We were creating value all the way around.

The late 1960s, though, were a wild time. As in the late 1990s, the new-issue market was boiling, with stocks being offered at then nearly unheard of multiples of 20 and 25 times earnings. The Standard & Poor's 500 was on a roller coaster ride as well. From January to September 1966, it gave up 22 percent of its value. Then it shot upward for more than two years until November 1968, when it went into a 19-month tailspin that cut the index by a third. Everyone's adrenaline seemed to be pumping, and mine was no exception. Besides, opportunities were flying around so fast and furiously that it was hard to get out of their way.

One nice summer morning in 1967, I was sitting on the steps of Dr. McGary's office in Darien waiting for Dorothy to finish up her appointment—Dr. McGary was the local G.P.—when Jim Bowling sat down and joined me. His wife was inside as well, or maybe his daughter, and the day was too nice to wait inside.

Jim was with Philip Morris, then being run by my brother Joe; so we fell into the usual conversation about business, what we were up to, and so on. I'd just finished telling Jim about the AGA deal when he suggested I meet with someone named Perry Wolf. Wolf, he said, had bankrolled two other guys, Russ Sangren and Joe Murtha, who had opened a firm called Sangren & Murtha, at 866 Third Avenue. The firm helped corporations develop logos, packaging, typeface treatments, and other forms of corporate identification. Wolf would turn out to be one of those people I never quite felt I could trust, but Sangren and Murtha had excellent pedigrees: They had both been principals in Lippincott & Margulies, which practically invented the idea of corporate branding. (FTD, Walgreens, Betty Crocker, Weyerhaeuser, Campbell's, Xerox, Hertz, Coca-Cola, Citgo, and many others bore the Lippincott & Margulies touch by the mid-1960s.) More to the point, Jim Bowling said, Perry Wolf was anxious to get his money out of the company, and Sangren and Murtha had given him a green light to see what price the market might be willing to pay.

Herb Weiner and I figured we had nothing to lose; so we met with Perry Wolf and his accountant and heard them out. Sangren & Murtha was in the chips, Perry told us. For the year ending sometime in the fall of 1967, the business expected to show pre-tax earnings of half a million dollars and an after-tax take of $250,000. This was a private company, of course: Such audited figures as they had were of no consequence. But assuming Perry was on the up and up with us, Herb and I structured a proposal that included a very small percentage of cash at closing and a $4 million total purchase price—eight times pre-tax earnings at a time when IPOs were being introduced at more than double that ratio. With Allied Graphic Arts, we had gotten around the tax obligation on the premium we paid for the business by allocating it to two of AGA's trade publications. This time we figured we could allocate it to a copyright on a little house organ that the company put out.

That, at least, is where we began, but the plot thickened immediately. I met during the summer with both Sangren and Murtha, and it soon became apparent that Perry Wolf had lured them into testing the market by telling them he could get the three of them each $500,000 in cash, right at the front end. That was issue one. Issue two was that Perry's earnings estimate was melting away in front of our eyes. Instead of half a million, the pre-tax take for fiscal 1967 looked as if would be closer to $300,000, down a whopping 40 percent. Because Perry was the partner who most wanted this deal to go through, Herb and I met with him alone and spelled out the new realities.

"You know, it looks as if there's no deal, Perry," I told him. "The whole thing's falling apart. After all, you advertised that it was going to earn half a million dollars, and it's not possibly going to earn that. We just can't do it."

It was up to Perry, I figured, to salvage the deal, and he did just that, not to his own best advantage. We finally agreed to pay $1 million in cash, but the rest of the purchase price—$3 million, not $4 million now that earnings had slumped—came in the form of some of the most extraordinary purchase money notes I've ever known anyone to agree to: 20-year notes, with no payments of interest or principal for the first three years and with payments after that to be contingent on the performance of the business. At closing, Sangren and Murtha walked away with $500,000 in cash each, just as Perry had more or less guaranteed them. Perry Wolf himself got virtually nothing, except a bundle of notes, but as we kept telling him, "There's really no problem, Perry. If you're so bullish on the future of the business, these notes are good. You'll get paid off anyway. What difference does it make if it's now or later?" Sometimes a man can be just too good at stating his own case.

Financing the purchase was as close to beautiful as deal making can get. I showed Dick Wilson the material on Sangren & Murtha as we were flying up to Sturgeon Point that fall on the State Mutual plane, and he basically committed to $400,000 before we touched ground. Mass Mutual, which had come in as the senior lender on the Allied Graphic Arts deal, chipped in another $400,000, and we took $200,000 of excess cash out of the till. That gave us the million dollars for Perry Wolf's partners, but what was truly amazing was the equity split we were able to negotiate: 55 percent for ourselves, although we had put up nothing really but our sweat, and 45 percent to be shared between the two insurance companies. This time around, the money arrived so effortlessly that Herb and I decided to share our equity stake with the Canadians who had come in on the AGA deal—a gesture of goodwill but also a nod to all the good fortune that had flowed my way since that first flying tour north of the border, a dozen years earlier.

Oh, yes. One last mention needs to be made of the Sangren & Murtha negotiations. Closing took place on December 15, 1967, at the downtown office of the Marine Midland Bank. The LeBouef,

Lamb attorneys who served as special counsel for the two insurance companies involved were on hand. So was Perry Wolf. I was there as well, itchy to get things concluded because Dorothy and I had an evening Swiss Air flight to catch. Also on hand was our host, the Marine Midland officer who had kindly made a room available to us. There was only one problem: He was drunk as a skunk. Papers were missing. Guaranteed signatures had disappeared, along probably with the bank officer's third martini. "The Sorrows of Gin," John Cheever titled one of his most famous stories. Sitting there, counting the wasted minutes, I couldn't have agreed more.

———※———

With the purchase completed, we now had two separate companies with almost identical ownership: our group, including the Canadians, State Mutual, and Paul Revere in the case of AGA; and State Mutual and Mass Mutual in the case of Sangren & Murtha. Bringing everything under one roof seemed the reasonable thing to do; so in 1969, we formed a holding company called Cullman Ventures Inc., or CVI.

The three insurance companies agreed to exchange all of their convertible debt, of both businesses, for class-A, nonvoting stock of the newly formed Cullman Ventures Inc. Under the formula we worked out, that gave the insurers 892,549 shares in CVI. We kept the rest—316,491 shares, for a total of just over 1.2 million shares. In effect, the insurance companies owned the business, but the only circumstance under which they could vote their stock was pursuant to a registration with the SEC. (The nonvoting part was essential because insurance companies are not allowed to own more than 10 percent of a company.) Then I set out to buy back all the stock in CVI that I could lay my hands on, and to retire every last obligation remaining from the purchases under the most favorable circumstances possible.

In 1970, Herb and I drove up to Worcester, Massachusetts, to see if we could talk State Mutual and Paul Revere into selling us a million dollars worth of the CVI stock they were holding, equal to about 270,000 shares at the time. To sweeten the pot, Herb suggested that the transaction be conducted as a dividend payout. CVI would declare a dividend of a little over $1 million dollars; all the shareholders other than the two insurance companies would waive their rights to it; and then the companies out of the goodness of their hearts would donate the 270,000 shares back to the CVI treasury. Who could resist?

Sangren & Murtha, meanwhile, had gone into the toilet. Not only did it fail to earn its $300,000; it failed to earn anything at all, and prospects didn't look all that good for the future. At this rate, those famous long-term purchase money notes with all their built-in contingencies were going to be worth nothing at all; so I asked Russ Sangren and Joe Murtha to pop down to my office and made them an offer.

"Look," I said, "I think you're never going to get anything on these notes, but even so, I don't like having them hang over my head. The two of you hold two-thirds of the three million in notes we issued, something like a million-eight; so how about if Cullman Ventures buys the lot of them from you for $220,000?"

Perry Wolf, I'm sure, would have felt differently about it, at least back then. After all, he hadn't gotten any real money yet. But Sangren and Murtha had already pocketed the $500,000 each they had hoped to get out of the purchase. Even just a little more than ten cents on the dollar was found money as far they were concerned, and they jumped at it.

And so it went, piece by piece, bit by bit, year by year. The late 1960s had been one of those episodically weird moments on Wall Street when risk gets discounted and everything seems certain to go public and make its backers a fortune. That's what had lured State Mutual and the others in: not the interest they were charging us but the kickers they could exercise when CVI went public. As the 1970s rolled in, IPOs lost their luster, and insurance companies found themselves under increasing pressure by their boards to divest themselves of deals such as we had struck with them over AGA and Sangren &

Murtha. To be sure, we took advantage of the shift in sentiment, but everyone came out ahead.

It wasn't that I had lost interest in new acquisitions, far from it: We had hit upon what was clearly a novel and successful formula. But I took the position during this entire period that the best buy we could make was our own stock, to beef up our ownership of CVI, and I felt we had to keep at it until we had grabbed up as much of our stock as we could and exhausted all the possibilities. Sometimes we played hardball; sometimes we rode to the rescue. Our approach depended on the circumstances. But I tried to make certain we never took our eyes off the prize.

In the summer of 1970, at the tail end of that 19-month stock market collapse, Herb and I realized that State Mutual was nearly out of earned surplus, a growing catastrophe because when an insurance company is out of earned surplus, it can no longer write insurance policies. So we went back up to Worcester, this time to see Fred Fedeli, who had taken over from Dick Wilson. (Despite Herb Weiner's warnings, Dick had gotten in dutch over a bad tax shelter deal—the infamous Black Watch cattle scam—and had been farmed out to manage one of State Mutual's fund families.) Our offer to Fred was simple: We would buy back another 250,000 shares of our own shares for $1 million, to be paid for with a CVI note. The note's terms weren't all that good, frankly, but even though no real money would change hands, State Mutual's earned surplus would be richer by a cool million.

Fred, of course, said yes, and he said yes two years later when we went back to see him, to strike a deal on the debt of Sangren & Murtha, which by 1972 looked as if it might be headed into default. Our group had never guaranteed the debt on Sangren & Murtha— I've never believed in that—but we didn't want to stick State Mutual with it, either. So we ended up doing a package purchase of CVI stock discounted by the fair market value (something like 50 cents on the dollar) of Sangren & Murtha debt. Again, both parties won. And we both won the next day when we drove from Worcester to Springfield and made the same offer to Mass Mutual. Along the way, we bought up Perry Wolf's notes for pennies on the dollar. By then, he didn't have a leg to stand on. Sadly, I also ended up buying back Herb Weiner's interest in CVI after his sudden death in 1972.

With the close of the Allied Graphic Arts deal back in 1966, our immediate group—Herb and I and the Paul Weiss law firm—had ten percent of the equity in the company, four percent each for Herb and me and two for Paul Weiss. When we formed Cullman Ventures in 1969, the holding company had 1,209,000 shares outstanding, about 75 percent of which belonged to insurance companies. By the late 1970s, the number of outstanding shares had been pared down to 181,000 shares, and I held 62 percent of those. It was all through these internal renegotiations, all by constantly trying to better the position of our core group while keeping our insurance partners happy, all by seizing opportunity when it presented itself and sometimes making opportunity when it didn't seem to exist at all. But CVI wasn't all paper money, not by a long shot.

Back in the early seventies, Jack Massengale and I worked out an agreement that permitted the transfer of $2 million of deferred taxes up to the holding company, which then assumed the tax liability. Then, in 1976, Salie Wyker presented me with one of the most amazing (the word ridiculous pops to mind) propositions I've ever come across.

The OPEC embargo of 1973–74 and the inflationary spike that came along with it hit business hard, including the S&H Green Stamp people. With retail sales collapsing, fewer stamps were being given out at the cash register, which meant our Allied Stamp Corporation subsidiary in Oklahoma, which had been set up for the sole purpose of printing S&H stamps, had excess capacity. So Carl Willis, who ran the plant, received permission from S&H to offer the presses to other stamp companies. That brought our facility to the attention of Takashi Gamo of the Blue Chip Stamp Co. of Japan, and that relationship, in turn, led Salie Wyker to call me up one day.

"How would you like to sell Allied Stamp Corporation?" he asked.
"To whom?" I asked.

"Tack," he answered. "Takashi Gamo, the Blue Chip Stamp guy."

"Well, that depends. What would Tack be willing to pay?"

"$2.5 million."

I almost fell out of my seat. Our stamp subsidiary was then earning about $50,000 annually. In a down-market environment that didn't look as if it was going to improve anytime soon, Takashi Gamo had offered 50 times earnings to buy us out. (The insane multiple is at least partially explained by obscure Japanese currency laws that forbade citizens from transferring money out of the country into dollars but would allow them to buy foreign companies. In effect, Tack was using our printing company to turn his Japanese-based yen into American-based dollars.) In some ways, though, the best was yet to follow. Tack, it turned out, had no desire to run Allied Stamp; so he gave us a management contract to operate it for him. Not only did we get a monstrous premium on the business; we ended up doing better financially as managers of Allied Stamp than we had as its owners.

———❖———

The rest of us might disagree, but to the Internal Revenue Service there is such a thing as too much cash on hand. Along with the $2 million AGA transfer that was already sitting in our treasury, the sale of Allied Stamp on November 1, 1976, left us awash in cash, and ever more vulnerable to Section 531 of the U.S. tax code. Originally known as Section 102, 531 was a Roosevelt-era innovation designed to protect against what my father used to call "unjust enrichment." In the long-winded prose of the Internal Revenue Manual, 531 and its subsequent sections "Govern the imposition of a surtax on corporations deemed to have engaged in unreasonable (i.e., excessive) accumulations of earnings and profits for purposes including the insulation of shareholders against income taxes which they would have had to pay if the corporations had paid out (more of) their incomes in dividends." More to the point, 531 was both punitive in the extreme and specifically designed to root out tax sheltering in closely held corporations such as CVI.

Because the clearest justification for accumulating earnings is a future acquisition, corporations can try to skirt 531 by keeping minutes of their directors' meetings that reflect an active search. But if all you do is look and look and never seem to find anything, the IRS takes the not unreasonable position that maybe you weren't really looking very seriously. Corporations can also deplete their accumulated earnings by paying them out as dividends—clearly the intent of 531, as dividends would then be taxed at the highest rate possible. The easiest way to get out from under 531, of course, is to use excess earnings to actually make an acquisition; and given our tremendous amount of excess as 1976 drew to a close, that seemed the only feasible route.

For a time we flirted with the idea of getting involved in an equity group that was putting together $220 million to finance a drilling platform Mobil was erecting in the North Sea. I never much liked the idea. The platform was a passive investment, with almost no opportunity for all the little twists and turns of deal making that had come to so interest me. Happily, the IRS put the kibosh on the whole concept before we committed ourselves. Then, in May 1977, a small item in the *Wall Street Journal* noted that Arcata National had agreed in principle to acquire Keith Clark, a calendar manufacturer, for something like $14 million. I knew that Mass Mutual had been trying to unload its convertible debt in Keith Clark for several years; so I called up one of my friends there.

"Gee, congratulations," I said. "I'm glad you finally found a home for your converts."

"Don't be so sure," he answered. "There's many a slip between the cup and the lip."

Indeed there was.

SIX

BUILDING A BUSINESS

By 1977, the leadership of CVI consisted of myself and Jack Massengale, who retained his position as a partner in the corporate finance department of the Paul Weiss law firm. (For a corporate attorney, Jack had a wonderfully droll sense of humor. We were out at a lunch club after one of our board meetings when Michael Koerner, who took pride in having the inside track on almost everything, began talking about a remarkable, completely unknown vineyard he had discovered in France. "You go two miles due east from Lyons," he explained, "then two miles due north, then turn east again, drive for four miles, and turn right into the vineyard just after a clump of trees." Jack hadn't said a word during the entire account, but as Michael reached the end of his tale, Jack held up a hand to stop him. "No, Michael," he explained in a dead-pan voice. "at the clump of trees, you turn *left*." When I related that story at Jack's memorial service, it brought the house down.)

Also on the CVI board were two other Paul Weiss partners, Peter Haje and Howard Seitz, who were rarely seen except at directors' meetings; two Canadians, Michael Koerner and Angus McKee, who had bought out Brian Benitz's stake; and the two newest directors: a long-time New York friend of mine with the imposing name of Worthington Mayo-Smith, known as Bill, who was then with Tucker Anthony R.L. Day; and another Canadian, Lorne Webster, who had been involved with The Incubation Group.

Alfie Ruys de Perez, one of our original directors and stockholders, had gotten himself into an awful mess back in 1970, engaging in securities transactions that ran afoul of both U.S. and Canadian regulations. Although the deals had nothing to do with us, Alfie was president of

The Incubation Group at the time, and his problems inevitably threatened to smear us. Worse, he failed to level with me when I confronted him about the charges. CVI went to bat for him only to find ourselves twisting in the wind when the truth came out. By the time it was all over, Alfie had been kicked out of Wisener & Co. and barred from the securities business. Angus McKee bought his stock in CVI, and that was the end of him.

Bob Wisener, who used to put together our fall retreats at Sturgeon Point, had disappeared as well—literally. During the time I knew him, Bob divorced his first wife and married his secretary. Then one day, he suddenly ran off to Alberta with some new woman and seemed to just drop off the face of the earth. I never heard from him again. Dick Wilson of State Mutual had also been among our directors at one time, but like Herb Weiner, Dick had died suddenly, and I had convinced his widow to sell back his stock to the company.

Jack and I did the lion's share of the CVI work and, of course, I had the largest stake in the business; but the other directors were neither shrinking violets nor yes-men. Angus McKee attended every meeting, and at almost every one he argued that we should be paying dividends. None of the rest of us agreed, but Angus and his dividends became a standing joke among us all. Acquisitions were another point of contention, especially as the treasury swelled and our exposure to Section 531 mounted: Why couldn't Jack and I find one? What was wrong with the North Sea drilling platform deal? (Not everyone shared my concern that it was just too passive an investment.) At one point after the North Sea deal went sour, we looked into paying out a huge dividend that, so we hoped, would have been construed as a return of capital and thus treated as capital gains for tax purposes. Angus was elated at the prospect...until we discovered that the IRS was unlikely to agree with our logic.

But if we were of many opinions on the finer points of how to proceed, we were of a single mind on the type of companies we were most interested in acquiring. Bill Mayo-Smith, who had a fondness for football metaphors, put it best: "We like businesses that make about three yards off tackle every play. We're not looking for ones that can throw the bomb or kick a 64-yard field goal." That was the model we all agreed upon. We just couldn't find one that fit the bill. Then Keith Clark came along.

The beauty of desk calendars, Keith Clark's special niche, is that every year everyone needs a new one, and often multiple ones: for the office, for home, for school. TVs and refrigerators last for a decade or more. You can always try to stretch another year out of the family sedan. But on December 31, precisely at midnight, every calendar from the previous year is suddenly obsolete. Keith Clark's business, in short, was highly predictable, and from our perspective, that was about as good as it gets. For one thing, a predictable business is much simpler to manage. You don't have a lot of unexpected surprises, nor are you likely to have any serious technological problems. Sure, competition will always crop up. Printing presses improve. Hot type becomes cold type. Photography goes digital. But Keith Clark had nowhere near the ups and downs found in a typical business. And that leads to the second and greater advantage: Predictable businesses produce predictable earnings, and predictable earnings are much easier to leverage.

Businesses that shoot for the moon, that throw the bomb on every play in Bill Mayo-Smith's metaphor, get all the headlines, but the best and most serious lenders read the headlines just for fun. The more predictable your earning power, the greater your chances of borrowing a larger proportion of the purchase price, and that was Keith Clark to a tee. The earning power was there. The cash generation was tremendous. At the end of the fiscal year, the company collected its receivables and had nothing but cash left. Then it would print another calendar with all the dates moved forward by one slot (except in leap years), and the cycle would start all over again. And because the capital investment was minimal—presses and a physical plant—we would be able to use a good portion of the earnings, if not all, to service the debt that we incurred to make the purchase.

I already knew quite a bit about Keith Clark. Fred Fedeli at State Mutual had suggested we might be interested in the company way back in 1967. We declined: This was just after we had completed the Allied Graphic Arts purchase, and I thought this would be too much to bite off under the circumstances. State Mutual and Mass Mutual had gone ahead and provided the financing for another purchaser with senior subordinated debt, just as they had with us and AGA, and the insurers now held about 35 percent of the equity in the company. Another third, in the form of some 300,000 shares, was held by the public as a result of a 1967 underwriting by Bear Stearns, and the final third was held by company insiders.

In the mid-1970s, Don Wheeler of Mass Mutual had come back to us again on Keith Clark, to see if we wanted to buy its position. I was certainly more interested this time, but not just in owning Mass Mutual's stake.

"What would we do with your convertible debt position in the company if you can't do anything with it yourself?" I asked. "I've got a better idea. I'll negotiate a stock equivalent price with you, and if we agree, then you can recommend that price to management, and we'll make the same offer to everybody."

We did hammer out a price with Mass Mutual, and we even carried it up to Sidney, New York, to present it to Jim O'Neill, Keith Clark's CEO—a place and a man I would become intimately familiar with in years to come. But at that time, neither Jim nor his group was interested in selling, and I was still intent on using our resources wherever possible to buy back our own stock.

——≫◆≪——

That's where things stood in May 1977 when I read the *Wall Street Journal* item about Arcata National's agreeing in principle to acquire Keith Clark and picked up the phone to call my insurance pal to congratulate him.

"What do you mean?" I asked when he told me the deal was nowhere as certain as the *Journal* made it sound.

"I mean I'm not convinced that this thing is going to go through."

"And if it doesn't, do you want us to take another look at it?"

"Sure."

Two weeks later a follow-up piece in the *Journal* noted that negotiations between Keith Clark and Arcata had indeed broken down, and this time we were off and running. For starters, I suggested to Jack Massengale that we pick up 4.9 percent of the stock of Keith Clark in the open market. The number was so exact for a good reason: Once you get to five percent, you have to file a form 13-D with the Securities and Exchange Commission—a disclosure statement that would tell the world we were interested. I wasn't ready to tip our hand that far, but things were bound to heat up soon. If we were to start serious negotiations only to have the deal plucked out of our hands, the share price was likely to rise enough to give us something for our efforts.

When the stock purchase was complete, I called up the insurance companies to let them know we were in the game.

"What do we do now?" I asked.

Before long, I was sitting in my office with Steve Wyman of State Mutual and Don Wheeler of Mass Mutual. I had worked closely with Don before but knew Steve Wyman only casually. Our position wasn't quite as strong as it might have been because only a short time earlier we had used $800,000 to prepay what remained of the $1 million CVI note with which we had bought back 250,000 of our shares from State Mutual. The expenditure seemed to make sense at the moment: We were cash heavy, and the note was costing us 8.25 percent in interest. Now we were out an important bargaining chip, but none of it seemed to matter. In a relatively short time, the three of us hammered out a very simple deal to purchase both companies' positions in Keith Clark, stipulating how much cash we would have to raise on our own, how large a CVI note they would have to take back, the usual back-and-forth of a first round. To me, the terms were highly advantageous to us, less so to them: a sign of just how anxious they were to shed their positions. Then, as always happens in these negotiations, just at the point when things seemed easiest, they finally got interesting.

"Guess what," Steve Wyman told me by phone not long after our meeting, "Arcata is back in the game." He and a junior guy at Mass Mutual, Dave Marks, were coming down to New York the next morning to meet with the Arcata people; so I said, "Fine, when you're through with your meeting, why don't you join Jack Massengale and me for lunch?"

Even before we sat down to lunch the next day, Jack and I could tell the Arcata meeting had gone poorly. I hadn't expected otherwise. Arcata wanted an all-or-nothing deal: the entire company or none of it. That meant they would have to corral Jim O'Neill and his crew from the get-go, and you didn't need to be a genius to see that what Arcata was proposing—subject to all sorts of tax rulings and approvals, and a host of other variables—was iffy in the extreme. Great, I figured, we're in clover. Then Dave Marks, whom I'd never met before, spoke up.

"You know," he said as if he were discussing a mild change in the weather. "Mass Mutual has another borrower that we think would like to buy Keith Clark. We're going to have to talk to them."

"What did you say?" I asked, not quite believing my ears. By the time he finished repeating himself, I was genuinely upset and angry. Negotiations are by their nature a cut-throat business, but certain protocols apply, especially when you've had a relationship as we did with Mass Mutual that went back a decade and had been beneficial to both sides.

"Well," I told Marks, "I think that's a hell of a lot of nerve. We were perfectly willing to stand by while you were dealing with Arcata because they had already come in and we were waiting to hear what happened with that. But we didn't expect you to go out and shop our deal and find somebody else."

"I'm sorry," was all he could answer, "but evidently Don Wheeler and Dick Dooley [Wheeler's boss] had been involved with Acco International in Chicago. They'd helped finance Acco, and now they want to give them a look at this."

"That's very interesting," I said. "What happens if we just decide to deal with State Mutual and forget about Mass Mutual?" I meant it as a joke, not a threat—Steve Wyman, at least, seemed to think it was funny—but either way there was very little we could do about the situation, at least at the moment. Dave Marks had virtually no authority. If we wanted our beef to be heard, we needed to go up the ladder. In truth, too, Keith Clark was not a bad match for Acco. The company had evolved out of something called the Parrott Speed Fastener Corporation, which in the late 1920s had introduced the famous Swingline stapler. By the mid-1970s, Acco had assembled through acquisitions and leveraged buyouts a broad line of office products. A desk-calendar manufacturer fit snugly into that mix.

With Arcata out of the picture and Acco suddenly in, Jack and I went back up to Springfield to finalize our own deal—a CVI note plus the amount of cash we would have to put up at closing to buy out the entire positions of Mass Mutual and State Mutual. This time, we made sure that we were talking with someone in authority at Mass Mutual: Don Wheeler. Steve Wyman was once again representing State Mutual. When we finished the detail work, I asked Don about Acco. As Marks had reported, Don was clearly under great pressure from Dick Dooley to bring Acco into play on this.

"How long is it going to take you to find out from the people at Acco whether they're really interested or not?" I asked Don.

"Oh, we should know in less than a week," he said. So I told him to keep us informed. He knew what our deal was, and he knew that State Mutual had agreed to it—or so I assumed. Turned out, I was drowning in powerless subordinates.

———⊰•⊱———

I was just resigning myself to Acco and Mass Mutual when Ned Bennett, Steve Wyman's boss at State Mutual, called me with what quickly began to sound like an ugly echo.

"We have a friend of ours up here, an attorney, who is connected with Acco," he told me. "We feel an obligation to deal with Acco."

"Wait a minute," I told him. "Your guy Wyman was up in Springfield with us and made a deal. How come you're getting in the act all of a sudden?"

"We didn't make any deal," he told me.

"What do you mean? I just said, your guy Wyman was there."

"Wyman has no authority to deal."

"This is a funny way to run things," I said, not amused at all. "Wyman comes up and negotiates with us and gets the price down to where he wants it, and now you tell us that he has no authority. If he has none, he shouldn't be there. If he is there, then what he says goes."

Ned Bennett, naturally, didn't want to hear a word of what I was saying; so I tried to call Steve Wyman, only to find out that he was vacationing on an island in Maine where there were no telephones. Finally, we found the ferry station he used, called there, and left a message. Within a few hours Wyman called back, only to confirm that, yes, he was powerless. Maybe he could at least call Ned Bennett and tell him what had happened, we suggested—that he said certain things across the negotiating table that had in effect committed State Mutual. He agreed to do that, but Bennett wasn't buying any of that either.

"Well, we have nothing in writing with you people," he told me when we next talked.

"How do you expect to do business with anybody if you send your representative up to discuss something, and then when you want to wiggle out of the thing, you claim there's nothing in writing? This is the same as a typical Wall Street trade. You don't have a written contract. You just agree to sell at such and such a price. It's your word."

That wouldn't budge him either, but the weirdness was far from over. The final day when Mass Mutual had agreed to let me know about the Acco contract, I was sitting in my office around three in the afternoon when I got a call from Douglas Chapman, president of Acco International, asking if he could come by to talk with me the next morning.

"Mr. Cullman," he said when we had settled in across each other at the table. "I've heard a great deal about you from people at Mass

Mutual. They tell me you're a very honorable person, and I just want you to know that the stock of Keith Clark that you own, I want you to make a profit on it, and for that reason alone, the price that we're going to pay for Keith Clark is going to be a price that will make sure you get a profit on your stock."

"Mr. Chapman," I told him, "I've got news for you. We're not in that business. We don't buy stocks for the sake of making a point. I'm buying Keith Clark. You're not buying Keith Clark."

"What do you mean?" I think he was honestly surprised.

"Just what I told you."

"Well, maybe you'll be interested to know that there was a meeting of the board of directors of Keith Clark today, approving the sale to Acco."

"Isn't that interesting? I've got more news for you. The board of directors at Keith Clark has nothing to do with this: 37½ percent of the company is owned by two insurance companies, and they are the ones that call the shots here. I'm buying the position of the insurance companies, and I'm buying the company."

In the end, Douglas Chapman handed me his card, scribbled his home number in Chicago on it, and assured me that he would be in residence all weekend. I was to call when, as I certainly would, I came to my senses. I thanked him for being such a swell guy to come see me, and off he went.

This all took place on a Thursday. The following Monday, Jack Massengale and I left Darien at 7:30 A.M., headed for Springfield. We weren't far up the road when I called Fred Fedeli in Worcester, knowing he always answered his own phone before his secretary got in.

"Fred," I said, "I'm on my way to Springfield to negotiate for the purchase of Keith Clark, and I want somebody there from State Mutual who has authority. If you have to go yourself, you better be there."

A few hours later, in Don Wheeler's office with Ned Bennett representing State Mutual and a few others on hand, I offered $4.5 million cash for both insurance companies' positions. Their 37½ percent, plus the 4.9 percent stock position we had bought earlier, plus a second block of stock we had bought from one of Keith Clark's directors would give us nearly 60 percent of the company, enough to get rid of Acco and anyone else Wheeler, Bennett, and their principals might want to pull out of the hat. To focus everyone's attention, I made it a David Mahoney bid, named in honor of the Norton Simon chief executive officer who gave the trustees of Avis fifteen minutes to accept or reject his offer. Our $4.5 million, I told them, was good for today only.

I was just finishing up my pitch when Don Wheeler's secretary called in to say that none other than Douglas Chapman was on the phone. Don talked with him for a while, right in front of us to my surprise, then turned to me and said, "Chapman would like to talk to you."

"Don, this is ridiculous. I'm not buying or selling anything with, from, or to Douglas Chapman."

"Look," Don told me, "he asked me if you would take the call, and I said I would tell you to do so."

I didn't want my conversation to be public; so I walked out to Don's secretary's desk to use her line.

"Mr. Cullman," Chapman said as soon as I picked up the phone, "I want to ask you a question. If I raise my bid, will you raise your bid?"

"Mr. Chapman, you've asked me an inappropriate question. Now, I'll ask you one. Do you normally peek when you play poker?"

Clearly, we were having relationship problems.

———◆———

I wrote earlier that the details of any leveraged buyout could fill a book. This one got positively Dickensian. Douglas Chapman did eventually go away, but not before hopping on a plane that very afternoon and forcing us to extend our offer for another half day. To make matters worse, a lawyer named Joel Adler of Coudert Bros. proved more tenacious than a mongoose and about as pleasant.

As soon as we bought the second block of stock in Keith Clark, I called Jim O'Neill to let him know about it. We would have to file a 13-D in any event—the purchase gave us more than 21 percent of the company—and I wanted Jim to hear about it from me, not the financial press. The next morning, Jim and another insider shareholder, Jay Nevin, came hot-footing over to my office with their counsel, the very same Joel Adler, who started to rant and rave the minute he was inside the door and wouldn't stop doing so for months on end.

"What were we going to do about the industrial tax exemption?" Adler demanded before he ever sat down. Although it was registered as a Puerto Rico corporation, Keith Clark's facilities were solely in the U.S., but its subsidiary, PR Publishing, was based in Humaco, an hour outside of San Juan, and operated under an industrial tax exemption called Operation Bootstrap, meant to build up the economy on the island. The exemption was a problem—it couldn't be transferred to new owners without permission of the governor of Puerto Rico—but it was hardly the deal-breaker Adler kept insisting it was. Nonetheless, he, I, Jack Massengale, and Jim O'Neill all had to fly down to Puerto Rico to tend to the matter, hire counsel on the island, and ultimately petition for survival of the tax exemption on behalf of Cullman Ventures as a stockholder of Keith Clark because Adler refused to let his clients cooperate with us.

No sooner had we taken care of that and flown back to New York than Adler was at it again.

"You people didn't know that there was a right of first refusal on the Mass Mutual and State Mutual stock, did you?" he told us with obvious glee. "It has to be offered to Mr. O'Neill and Mr. Nevin first, and they have 30 days to make up their minds on that one, unless they waive their right, and my client is not going to waive it."

Surprise, surprise. Because Don Wheeler had called on August 20 to officially accept our offer, we counted thirty days from then, and I set the closing for September 21, 1977. The date happened to be Yom Kippur. I was hoping religious fervor might keep Adler at home, but no such luck. Still, he wasn't done. Once we had finally agreed to pay $13 a share for the remaining stock we didn't already own—better than Arcata and Acco had offered, by the way—Adler was at it again, insisting on a "fairness letter," a typical Wall Street piece of nonsense where you pay someone like Goldman Sachs $150,000 to type under its letterhead: "In our opinion, $13 a share is a fair price." Every time Adler opened his mouth, it seemed, another gold-plated monkey wrench came popping out.

Fittingly, the financing of the Keith Clark deal proved to be every bit as bizarre as the players. This whole process got underway because State Mutual and Mass Mutual wanted to get out from under their positions in Keith Clark; so I assumed they would have no interest in footing the balance of our purchase of the same company. Instead, I went over to the Prudential to see Ray Charles, got kicked downstairs to some of his underlings, laid out the case for them, and took a crew up to Sidney to see the facility and meet with Jim O'Neill. Before long, Ray's people got back to me with a term sheet that included some thoroughly unattractive financing from our point of view: a fixed coupon of 10 percent, with an additional earned interest coupon that could bring the rate up as high as 15 percent based on earnings. The loan had yet to be approved by the Pru's full loan committee, but I decided to take it to the CVI directors' meeting anyway, warts and all. Angus McKee in particular wanted to string up the Prudential for highway robbery: The terms really were outrageous. But Keith Clark remained a beautiful little business, and the worst thing you can do in any kind of deal is have things drag on too long. It's the unforeseen developments that kill you.

Herb Weiner and I used to talk about this all the time: There really are no ground rules in these kinds of arrangements. Nobody has any set ideas or templates to go by. Half the things that take place happen just because somebody said something and no one objected, or vice versa, or somebody didn't think enough to change them. The Pru was offering an ugly bird, but at least it was a bird in the hand. I didn't want to wait for one more element of the package to unravel. Besides, Jim O'Neill and another insider were coming by for lunch after the meeting. I hoped to be able to tell them our plans, and I couldn't do that until we had some indication of financing.

In the end, the CVI directors let me have my way: Assuming the Pru's loan committee said yes, we were to borrow $10 million to complete the purchase of Keith Clark. Included in that figure was $2.4 million to retire a chunk of senior debt from the original 1967 buyout: a 7 percent loan held jointly by State Mutual and Mass Mutual. With the go-ahead in my pocket, it seemed to me the decent thing to do was call Don Wheeler and let him know that, in all likelihood, we would be prepaying the senior debt.

"You've got no right to pay me off," he said.

"What did you say?"

"You've got no right. We like the company."

I sat there trying to think what in the heck Don Wheeler was telling me. Then I decided to take a chance.

"Are you telling me you would like to lend Cullman Ventures ten million dollars to finance the purchase of Keith Clark?"

"Why not?" he said. "We know the company well. We like it."

"Wait a minute," I told him. "I've gone this far with the Prudential. Their committee is meeting."

"We can get this thing through committee by the 12th of October," he told me, less than two weeks away.

"That's too late. That's the same date as the Pru's meeting."

"Well, can you get up here tomorrow morning?"

"I've got some real problems. My stepson is getting married the next day in San Diego." This time the date was real, not a bargaining ploy, although it served the same purpose.

"Don't worry," Don assured me. "We can get you from Springfield to San Diego."

And so it was that at six in the morning on the day before Billy Benenson was married in southern California, I caught the earliest morning flight to Bradley Field in Hartford, Connecticut, where I was met by the Mass Mutual chauffeur and whisked to Springfield, Massachusetts, where Don Wheeler, on behalf of his company, offered to loan CVI for 9¾ percent straight the same $10 million that the Pru was willing to let go for as much as 15 percent. Things got so loony during the morning that when a researcher pointed out the figures weren't working, Don told her to plug in whatever numbers were needed to get the bottom line right. Why let math get in the way of a good deal? In the end, we bought Keith Clark with money lent to us by the same people who had fought tooth and nail to get top dollar for their interest in the company. Not only that, Mass Mutual was prepaying its own note. Sometimes it really is all about luck, all a fluke, all irony.

Ray Charles, of course, was furious. I'd lost all my credibility at the Prudential, he assured me. My name was mud in Newark, and on and on. Somehow Ray had forgotten that his people had tried to saddle us not just with outrageous rates but with some onerous extra terms when it looked as if the Pru was the only lender in town. Ray also seemed to have forgotten that I had personally let him off the hook a decade earlier when he reneged on his word during the AGA negotiations. Finally, I wrote him a letter, spelling out all the circumstances and telling him that I thought the strength of our relationship was accommodation. When he needed me to accommodate him, I did it; now that the shoe was on the other foot, I was surprised he wasn't willing to do the same. I never heard back from Ray until a year later, when I ran into him at a dinner at the Economic Club of New York. By then, it was all water under the bridge.

Nailing down the financing for Keith Clark put us in the backstretch, but it still seemed like the deal that would never end. For one thing, the Puerto Rican problems wouldn't go away. Bear Stearns had worked out this ingenious system whereby PR Publishing could shelter its earnings under the industrial tax exemption, then pay out a dividend to Keith Clark—an exchange between two Puerto Rico corporations that was tax exempt under the law there. Once Cullman Ventures owned Keith Clark, the magic would disappear, and any dividends paid by PR Publishing would be deemed to be foreign-source income and thus fully taxable at the CVI level.

Meanwhile, we were waiting, and waiting, and waiting for approval on our petition to the governor of Puerto Rico to have the industrial tax exemption for PR Publishing conveyed to CVI. And we were still trying to figure out how to handle the tender offer for as much of the outstanding Keith Clark stock as we could buy. Our initial thought had been that Cullman Ventures would make the offer, but that involved more financing, and nobody wanted to lend us the money in case we weren't successful in acquiring all of the company. Finally, one of the bankers had the bright idea of having Keith Clark itself make the tender offer—we already owned the majority of the company—and that broke the logjam.

At long last, on May 9, 1978, a full year after Keith Clark had reappeared on the radar screen, the directors of Cullman Ventures met to officially approve its merger with a newly formed subsidiary of CVI called something like Newco. No more outside stockholders existed. We owned 100 percent of Keith Clark. I was in the calendar business up to my ears. The question was where to go from here?

In August 1978, three months after we had completed the purchase of Keith Clark, an interviewer for the Columbia University Oral History Research Office asked me what part of my work gave me the greatest satisfaction. Readers who have stayed with me to this point won't be surprised by my answer:

"I'd have to say that the most satisfaction is when you're really in the serious negotiations, and dealing with the seller, the lender, and the tax implications and the whole structuring of the thing. That's probably where the most fun comes. The follow-up is worthwhile, but it isn't as gratifying. The dilemma is that if you go out and try to do something else just for the sake of doing it, you may get into problems."

Ten years later, another interviewer for the same oral-history project asked me a similar question, but this time I gave a very different answer:

"Up until 1978, my whole attitude and activities in buyouts was one of strictly financial transactions, with no particular interest or expertise in operations. It was my concept up to that time that this was the way things were always going to be. I think that what has happened since '78 is that we now have another dimension that very few other people who do buyouts have. The ones I see around me are always much more financially oriented; very, very few people are interested in doing what we have done. I mean, we have built a business. And we didn't build the business to try to sell it; we built it to build value."

I was 70 years old when that second interview took place. A quarter of a century had passed since Herb Weiner and I set out to buy Orkin Exterminating Company with less than a thousand bucks on the line between us. Who says you can't teach an old dog new tricks?

Part of what changed my attitude was adjusting to new realities. The ink was barely dry on Keith Clark before the Canadian directors of CVI began pushing for a new acquisition. "What are we going to do next?" Michael Koerner would ask me every chance he got. Even Dorothy got in the act: "What happened today?" she always wanted to know, breathlessly, as if excitement came in one-a-day pills. I was always sympathetic: The directors were in it for the action as much as I was, and Dorothy would have been bored silly if I had tried to tell her all the nuances of the tax minimization scheme I had spent my day working on. But I really didn't think another acquisition made sense anytime soon.

We had paid $13 million for Keith Clark: a $3 million loan from Bankers Trust against the equity we had built up in Allied Graphic Arts, plus $10 million from Mass Mutual. I didn't regret the expenditure for a moment, but the deal had left us so highly leveraged that there was precious little margin of safety. Fifteen years of deal-making had taught me that there's one way in a hundred to do these things right and 99 ways of doing them wrong. Those are poor odds in the best of circumstances. They're dangerous odds, though, when your reserves have been stripped down to skin and bones.

Instead of searching for acquisitions, I found myself concentrating on the finance and tax sides of CVI, particularly the latter, as all the directors were financial guys to some extent. In effect, we were a private bank that just happened to have three companies in its portfolio. Cullman Ventures was never meant to be an operating business in the least. To the extent that I involved myself directly in any of the three holdings, it was to figure out how to keep the guys who were running them motivated now that they had no ownership stake. Otherwise, I pretty much left them alone, or tried to.

Allied Graphic Arts was essentially on cruise control. I would have been happy to have Salie Wyker and his son Bob, who by now was running the business with him, present us with a constant diet of possible acquisitions in related fields. Who knew the territory better than they did? But that wasn't either of them. Salie and Bob (and I'm sure mother Billie, too) were convinced that their business was unique—that there was none other like it and that no one in the world could run the company as well as they could. By all the usual business school standards, they ran an appalling shop: no budgets, no long-range plans, no anything. You could have held a gun to their heads, and neither Wyker could have told you what the company's return was on invested capital. All they did was go merrily along by the seat of their pants and consistently make money year in and year out. That was good enough for me.

My stepson Freddy came up with a wonderful saying when he was still a little boy: "People have to be forced to do things voluntarily." Forcing the Wykers to modernize "voluntarily," as I certainly could have tried to do, might have compromised or even destroyed whatever it was that made the place work so well. Instead, I put together a profit-sharing plan to keep the Wykers interested, and when we formed CVI and AGA became a subsidiary company, I suggested to Salie that he put all his key people on the board. He resisted—this truly was a family dominated business—but eventually he went along with the idea, and slowly new and better approaches began to bubble up from the factory floor. All those board members were on hand in 1978, too, along with a lot of CVI's directors when we celebrated Salie Wyker's seventy-fifth birthday with a dinner-dance at the St. Regis

Hotel. The deal really never had changed since the two of us shook hands on it in 1966.

By the late 1970s, Sangren & Murtha had rechristened itself as Murtha, deSola, Finsilver & Fiore, but it was the still the runt of our acquisitions: the smallest, the only one I had undertaken perhaps as much out of a desire for a little fresh action as out of any real faith in the outfit itself. Initially, I had hired a retired officer from Chase bank named Jack Breaks to monitor the business for CVI. When Jack died, I turned the job over to my secretary. She had been Jack's girlfriend, and he had taught her about everything he was doing. We held the purse strings completely and called all the shots through her, but even then I left the day-to-day business to its principals. Despite the genius my brothers Joe and Edgar had shown in the field, what I knew about corporate branding and the like could fit on the head of a pin. I did, however, know tax benefits, and profit or not, Murtha, deSola, Finsilver & Fiore was still giving us some of those.

Keith Clark was another species altogether. Unlike the Wykers, Jim O'Neill looked into the future and saw the big picture. He was forever suggesting ways to broaden the product line, protect the franchise, and increase market share. That was great. But the more I looked into the company—now that we owned it and I wasn't on the constant prowl for something new—the more troubles I saw.

For starters, the physical plant was a mess: a clutch of mostly Quonset huts at Union and Division streets in the middle of Sidney, New York. I didn't see any sense in modernizing just for the sake of doing something new: Keith Clark was doing 70 percent of the desk calendar business in America out of that ramshackle complex. As with AGA and the Wykers, the last thing I wanted to do was tinker with whatever arcane combination made the business successful. Having incurred so much debt to buy the company, we couldn't risk wiping out earnings. What's more, I liked having room for improvement. But this facility was costing us tangible time and money. Ad specialty work, a nice chunk of Keith Clark's revenue, was being printed generically downtown, then bundled up and trucked out to a small ad specialty facility near the airport, where it was unbundled, finished off, and then bundled up yet again for shipment. You didn't need a McKinsey consultant to see that the system was nuts.

We thought briefly about relocating the whole business down South—going south was the rage in the late 1970s—but with the help of a New York State Industrial Revenue Bond and a lot of local tax exemptions, we broke ground in the fall of 1979 on a new plant out by the airport. When we finally dedicated the new facility in July 1981, the town of Sidney threw a two-day extravaganza for us: parades, floats, the whole nine yards. We had made a contribution to the town that was used to provide lights for the softball field in what was then called Riverside Park. In our honor, the site was renamed Keith Clark Park. Sidney might have had all of 5,000 residents back then, but they knew how to make us feel at home.

When we took over the company, we discovered that Keith Clark's books weren't a lot better than its old factory complex. The Puerto Rican tax exemption had done wonders for the bottom line, but it also had encouraged sloppy accounting practices that would eventually have to be rectified. The tax exemption was its own problem: It diminished year by year until, eventually, there would be no advantage to doing business on the island and plenty of disadvantages. In a low-margin business, transportation costs—of unfinished materials to Puerto Rico and of finished materials from it—make a big difference if they're not offset by other savings.

The biggest problem with Keith Clark, though, was probably Jim O'Neill himself. He was nearing his mid-sixties when we bought the company and ready to retire, but for all his experience and all his vision, he was one of those managers who had never been able to bring himself to train a successor. The people who worked under him had been rewarded more for their subservience than their leadership, bad training for the top slot. The person he finally brought in from the outside as his hand-picked heir apparent, a salesman from International Paper, was better but still not up to the task. He could move product, but he seemed to be lost on the plant floor, and not very energetic in any event.

Meanwhile, I had made my own pass at finding someone to run the company. Back when Arcata was still in the competition for Keith Clark, I had learned that if Arcata had been successful, Jim O'Neill and the others in Sidney would have been reporting to a guy named Tom Hargrove. I knew nothing about him, but Allied Graphic Arts was doing some work for another company Arcata had picked up, and the AGA people knew Tom and respected him. That was a strong recommendation for me; so I called Tom and asked him to lunch. I liked his enthusiasm immediately: He was sorry to have missed out on Keith Clark because he had lots of plans for it.

"Well," I said to him as the meal was ending, "that all sounds very good. How would you like to run Keith Clark?"

"Oh," he responded, "there isn't enough to do there, and I have a good job anyway. I don't think I want to bother with that."

That was where we left it, but a few months later Tom Hargrove called me on what seemed at first an odd fishing expedition.

"How would you like to make another acquisition?" he asked.

"What do you mean?"

"We are in the process of selling off some of the printed products divisions of Arcata," he answered and went on to describe a gift-wrap business called CPS.

I told him we weren't at all interested in that, and I'm not certain to this day exactly why Tom called. Maybe he really was just thumbing through his Rolodex of the usual suspects, but I think that at some level he wanted to reestablish contact and let me know that Arcata was shrinking and changing. Why else would it be selling off divisions it had been trying so hard to buy only a little while earlier? When I asked Tom directly, he told me that he was going to be offered an entirely different job within the company once the reorganization was complete, one that required him to move to the West Coast.

"Do you want to do that?" I asked. I knew he lived in New Canaan, Connecticut, not far from me.

"Not at all."

The upshot of our conversation was that I asked Tom to join the CVI board, even before he had left Arcata, so he could begin to familiarize himself with our activities. Half a year or so later, in 1980, Tom severed all his ties with his old employer and came on full time with us. At first, he joined the Operating Committee we had already set up to oversee the financial aspects of Keith Clark, along with myself, Bill Mayo-Smith, and one of the Paul Weiss lawyers, Howard Seitz. Tom was the one on location in Sidney—he had begun commuting weekly from Connecticut. We would go up there to meet him. He couldn't take over as CEO until we got rid of the guy Jim had brought in, but Tom's impact was immediate and lasting.

One of the first things he helped us do was get out of the price-fixing game. Keith Clark had one major competitor in the calendar refill-pad market: Columbian Artworks. Every year, it turned out, Jim O'Neill and Coleman Norris, who headed up Columbian Artworks, would meet at some place like Hawaii and determine the "traditional value," as they called it, for the next year's flip-over pads: our 717 model, produced in Puerto Rico, and their comparable Success insert, made in Milwaukee. By the time we came along, the two of them had run the traditional value up to 87 cents—the price at which we both were selling the pads to the distribution channels. (The inserts retailed for about $3.) In the short term, of course, running the price up meant more money for both companies, but by 1978, O'Neill and Norris had taken it so high that a bunch of other people were rushing into the business, and sales for both price fixers were beginning to slide backwards.

Tom put his head together with Douglas Willies, the new vice president of sales and later president and CEO of the company, and one of Jim O'Neill's few excellent hires at the top echelons. (Doug had pretty much walked through the door and asked to be hired: He'd been working for the Illinois Tool Company, but he had gone to Colgate University and his wife was from the area and wanted to get back to her roots.) Together, Tom and Doug came up with a fairly radical solution to our price-fixing dilemma: Knock the price back almost 25 percent, from 87 cents to 67 cents; absorb the pain; remove the incentive for others to get into the market; and force Columbian Artworks to do the same. Doug told me later that he was absolutely astounded when the Operating Committee bought into the scheme, but we did, and it all played out very much as expected. We took a million-dollar hit for the year, but the competition disappeared, and Doug managed to sweeten the pot by offering distributors an even deeper discount if they bought our whole product line.

Columbian Artworks followed suit, as they had to, but not with the same results. By early 1983, Coleman Norris was sitting in my office, trying to sell me his business. We might have bought it, too, if he hadn't been asking such a ridiculous price; and in fact, we eventually did buy the Success line eleven years later, by which time the companies were on completely different trajectories. When we intervened in the cozy price-fixing scheme back in 1978, the two companies were very comparable in size: We were doing maybe $15 million a year in sales; Columbian was probably doing $12 million. By 1988, Columbian was still doing about $12 million in annual sales, I would guess. We were more than eight times that size, and we didn't get there by sitting back and watching the grass grow.

——◆——

Until the late 1970s, I had focused on company acquisitions almost by default. The ins and outs of finance, how to structure a deal, tax implications and strategies—these were what I understood best, what I had an intuitive feel for. I wasn't a printer or an exterminator or a corporate brander. It made no sense for me to try to grow any of the companies we acquired because I had no real idea how to do that. With Tom Hargrove's guidance, all that began to change. Instead of going after new companies, we started to pick up small divisions and product lines, whatever would complement and expand Keith Clark's core business.

Virtually no one knows what a Standard Diary is, but almost everyone has seen one. It's the hardbound reservation book that restaurants use. Standard Diary is far from a sexy product line. Growth is inevitably slow, but businesses of that sort are extraordinarily durable. So when Tom heard that Wilson Jones, which had become a division of American Brands, wanted to dispose of Standard Diary, we went down to the plant in Elizabeth, New Jersey, to have a look. The place was a mess—badly run, archaic equipment, poor management. Standard Diary was the only dated-goods line Wilson Jones carried among a wide variety of other office products. Clearly, nobody there much cared about the diaries, and if Wilson Jones cared little, American Brands, enormous giant that it was (it once had been known as American Tobacco Company), cared even less. Basically, we bought it for a song late in 1978, produced the next year's version in Elizabeth, then closed the plant there and moved the equipment to the new facility in Sidney.

We followed that by buying the National Division of Dennison Manufacturing. National was the only other hardbound diary of any consequence, and Tom had come to know the fellow who ran it through trade shows. It wasn't a big deal, nowhere near the size of Standard Diary, but it filled out the niche for us. Again, we closed the plant, this one in Holyoke, Massachusetts—the Connecticut River Valley had once been filled with small print shops—and moved the operation to Sidney. Next in line was Time Peace, a tiny part of the dated-goods market but a good fit with us. Then we acquired the rights to the Burkhart Financial Calendar, which competed directly with the Heinz Timeteller. Again, almost no one knows the name, but if you negotiated a home mortgage before computers became so commonplace, you probably saw one. Lenders used them to calculate loan length and interest. Heinz had all the name recognition and most of the sales, but through marketing and promotion, we were able to take a big chunk out of that lead.

One of the first acquisitions Tom suggested to us was CPC, a division of Arcata that reported to him when he was still there. Initially, Arcata had a very inflated idea of CPC's worth, but I was very impressed by the guy who showed up to try to sell it to me, a fellow named Jim Moore. Arcata eventually came back down to earth, and CPC joined the fold in August 1982. Jim started working for us early the next year, and he, too, made his presence felt immediately.

Like me, Jim leaned toward the financial side of the business. He asked a thousand questions about the aggressive tax planning I had done on the Allied Graphic Arts and Sangren & Murtha deals, and he seemed to soak up everything I had to say, worthwhile or not. We were in the midst of buying Standard Diary when Jim came up with his own inspiration: "Why can't we add a million dollars to the cost just to reduce the tax liability?" It sounds counterintuitive, but in fact it was ingenious.

As always happens, success brought its own set of problems. When we opened our facility at the airport in Sidney in 1981, we expected it to fill our needs for years to come. All of us, I think, were just glad to escape that eyesore downtown. But the new acquisitions we had made plus closing down the Puerto Rican facility, once the tax advantages there had diminished to a negative return, quickly outstripped capacity. To put up a new warehouse distribution center next to the almost brand-new plant, we secured another industrial revenue bond. But it was more complicated than that. The terms of the IRB forbid us from exceeding $10 million in capital expenditures during a six-year period—three years back and three years forward. Otherwise, we would lose our tax exemption. When we secured the first bond, that seemed the least of our problems. Now that we were on a tear, the window was closing quickly.

There was a way around the problem: You can lease equipment, rather than buy it. But the banks I had traditionally dealt with—Banker's

Trust, Marine, Chemical, National Bank of North America—couldn't be bothered with such small potatoes. So I called a guy from First Union Bank of Charlotte, North Carolina, Jim Turk, who had dropped in on me out of the blue a few weeks earlier, and before I knew it, First Union had set up a lease line for us. It was much like a credit line that we could draw on at will. First Union bid on doing the IRB for us and won that, too, for the simple reason that they had done their homework better than anyone else and knew our business better than any of the big New York banks.

Of all the proposals Tom Hargrove and Jim Moore brought to me, the one I most resisted was the idea of buying out the Canadian investors in CVI. To me, Michael Koerner, Angus McKee, and the others were more than business partners. They were part of my personal history. Michael had been with us from the beginning; both he and Angus had been among the most active directors in the early days. Tom and Jim, though, saw it differently. To them, the Canadians were simply passive investors in the business, people who reaped the rewards of our success without lifting a finger to advance it. They wanted the rewards to flow to the people who were actually doing the work, and the more they argued, the more I was inclined to agree. Cullman Ventures was no longer operating as a private bank, no longer an investment type of company. We weren't prowling for acquisition across a broad frontier; we were building value in a single entity.

Finally, I opened negotiations with the Canadian group and asked Lehman Brothers to come up with a fair share price. The Canadians hired Kidder Peabody to do the same, and the results couldn't have been much more different. Lehman calculated our share price at $150. Kidder Peabody doubled that to $300. Both were trying to accommodate their clients, I'm sure, and in fairness, valuing a private company is always tough and somewhat arbitrary. Remember, too, that we had never paid a dividend; the Canadians' entire stake was in capital appreciation. In the end, we pretty much split the difference and went our separate ways, with mixed feelings on both sides.

Then we did the same thing with our law firm, but with less reluctance on my part. Paul Weiss had taken a risk on the Allied Graphic Arts acquisition. If it had fallen apart, they weren't going to charge us anything. As it was, they got a block of stock for their participation, and the value of that stock had grown very handsomely in the years since. No one was robbed on the front end of the deal, and no one was being robbed now. Besides, we were still paying the firm full dollar whenever we used its legal services.

It was about this time that I stumbled back into the company buying business, almost. Keith Clark had developed a series of wirebound calendar books that we called the Guilford line solely to compete with the far better known At-A-Glance wirebounds made by Sheaffer Eaton, which by then had become a division of Textron. Because Textron was so huge, I figured it wouldn't mind shedding one of its tiny parts for a fair price; so I made arrangements to see the company CEO, Robert Straetz, and asked him if he might consider selling the At-A-Glance portion of Sheaffer Eaton. Oh, no, he assured me. He wouldn't do that in a million years. Sheaffer Eaton was doing very well; the sky was the limit; etcetera, etcetera. I knew for a fact that he was wrong. This was another case of a huge corporation with a pipsqueak division so far off the charts that the guy ultimately in charge had no idea what was really going on. But I didn't say any of that. Instead, I thanked him for his time, told him if he changed his long-term strategy to give me a call, and went on my way. Not long thereafter came word that all of Sheaffer Eaton was on the block and Morgan Stanley was serving as auctioneer.

Tom Hargrove and I both felt the same way when he heard the news. First, it was a heck of an opportunity: Merging At-A-Glance with the Guilford line would completely solidify our hold on the wirebound market. And second, this was a lot more than we dared bite off on our own. Sheaffer Eaton included pens, the Duotang line of office products and accessories, high-quality stationery. It was, in short, far bigger than ourselves.

I contacted someone I knew at Warburg Pincus, the reigning geniuses of the moment among investment houses. Through them and our own work, we put together a consortium to bid on Sheaffer Eaton: Dennison, from whom we had bought the National Division, came in; so did Faber Castell, the privately held pen company. All of us could see parts of this we wanted. Among the three of us, we came up with the figure of $125 million—absurdly high, but worth it collectively when you broke Sheaffer Eaton apart—and submitted it to the auctioneers. After the gavel came down, Andrew Liu from Morgan Stanley called with the results:

"Well, Mr. Cullman," I can still hear him saying, "very nice bid you have made, very nice, but unfortunately you didn't buy it."

"Really?"

"Yes," he answered, "an Arab group bid $135 million for the company."

When I asked him who they were, he mentioned the name Gefinor. I had never heard of them, but we had put too much effort into this to just dump the whole thing in the ashcan. I got hold of a statement put out by the Gefinor group, which turned out to be based in Luxembourg. The board members were mainly Lebanese and Kuwaitis, but among them, to my great surprise, was my old acquaintance George Bennett, head of State Street Research and Development, the investment management arm of State Street Investment, Federal Street, and a whole tier of funds out of the Boston area. Not only had I known George back in Hingham, Massachusetts, when Thais and I lived there after the war; he and my brother Joe were both on the board of Ford Motor Company. Maybe, I thought, this is still in play.

I called George, explained our interest in At-A-Glance, and ended up meeting in New York in early 1988 with Edward Armaly, the London-based Lebanese who was in charge of Gefinor. After much negotiating back and forth, Armaly agreed to sell us the At-A-Glance business for $65 million. The figure, he explained, was based on net assets of $20 million. We were sure the net asset number was wrong, but we also saw a way to use Armaly's formulation to our advantage. So at Tom's suggestion, we counteroffered to pay $45 million plus the net assets as determined by a balance sheet the following February 11, the closing date of their fiscal year. Then we sat back and waited.

Pretty soon came word that net assets were likely to be closer to $15 million, then $12 million, then $10.6 million. When we finally got to February 11, what had been proposed as a $65 million purchase had shrunk to a little more than $55 million, down more than 15 percent. By the time we had gone over their balance sheet figures and submitted our differences to an arbitrator from Arthur Anderson, we ended up paying about $50 million dollars. The price included the Eaton paper company, which we turned around and sold for $2 million more than its stated value. Before long, we closed down the plant in Pittsfield, Massachusetts, where At-A-Glance had been produced; sold that for another $1.7 million; and further consolidated operations in Sidney. Losing the group bid for Sheaffer Eaton in the Morgan Stanley auction turned out to be one of the luckiest moments of my business life.

—◦◦—

Ten years after loading CVI down with debt to buy Keith Clark, the company was doing $100 million in sales a year. My new friends at First Union had given us a $104 million loan to complete the At-A-Glance purchase, including more than $50 million in revolving credit. Allied Graphic Arts was rolling along just fine. Sangren & Murtha had disappeared. After we had milked out all the tax benefits we could, I offered to sell it back to the principals for the grand total of $25—an amount so ridiculously small that our accountants told me just to keep the money rather than turn it over to CVI and file all the necessary paperwork. The Canadians were gone from their ownership position in Cullman Ventures. So was the Paul Weiss law firm.

On the last day of 1986, we had converted CVI to an S corporation, essentially a partnership with limited liability. The laws were changing at the time, and we wanted to get in under the wire. Under the terms, shareholders get taxed on their proportionate share of the total earnings of the company. Once those taxes are paid, the surplus (or S-surplus in IRS-speak) can be distributed tax-free to shareholders at any time you choose. Digesting At-A-Glance took a little longer than we had expected, but once we had worked it into Keith Clark, earnings began to soar. By the mid-1990s, my tax-free distribution from Cullman Ventures was $9 million a year—more money than Dorothy and I could ever spend on ourselves, more than we could ever use. We already had homes—our apartment on the Upper East Side and my house in Darien, which had become a weekend place for us. We had even added a second weekend home that Dorothy wanted, out in Sag Harbor on the north side of the south fork of Long Island. Our creature comforts had long ago been taken care of.

I was heading into my seventies with no heir to take over CVI from me. Dorothy's sons had their own careers, their own lives: Freddy was teaching in England; Billy was in the film business. Duncan had no interest in business at all, and no ability to run one. Maybe not too far down the line I would want to sell off this little empire I had constructed, and then the broad river of money I was swimming in would become an ocean of wealth. Hotchkiss and Yale had provided me all the examples I would ever need of bums and ne'er-do-wells living off inherited fortunes. The time had come to start figuring out how to give the money away, and do so in ways that might really make a difference. Doing that would be every bit as challenging as making it all.

SEVEN

GIVING AS GOOD AS I GOT

"Gee," my mother liked to say, "I'd much rather give money away when I'm alive than have somebody afterwards say, 'Isn't it nice? She left all that money to this person or that cause!' If that's what your choice is, why not get some pleasure out of it, instead of just having it be written up after you're gone?"

Dad used to tell people that he was scared to die because he knew Mother would give all his money away, and she almost got her chance. He died in 1955 at age 72. She lasted another four years, until 1959 at age 76, and by the terms of the time and their estate, she made some significant bequests in those final years.

Clearly, I've never forgotten what either of my parents had to say about philanthropy—I can still quote both of them on the subject—but early on, at least, my own inclinations toward charity had natural limitations: I didn't have much money of my own to give away. I'd gone straight from college into the Navy and for three years lived on a junior officer's pay. The weather business, which I got into after the war, hadn't made me rich. Nor had peddling stocks and bonds or working at Cullman Bros., and what I did manage to save was pretty much wiped out by Thais's long illness and treatment. I'd always given what I could to Yale—and later would give a very sizable amount—but Yale was almost a family calling. It wasn't until the 1960s that I found an outside cause that really spoke to me, and I haven't let go of it in the 40 years since.

It all came about at a Manhattan dinner party in the mid-1960s when I fell into conversation with a lawyer named Walter Fried, who happened to mention that he was involved with the American Chess

Foundation. I had played chess as a kid, and still play. (I must have gotten my interest from my mother, who used to play "postal chess" with people all over the world. Individual moves had to be mailed back and forth in that pre-Internet world, and games could last many months or even years.) I've never been all that good at the game, but the idea of a chess foundation intrigued me; so I asked Walter to tell me more. Turns out, the foundation had been set up by none other than Maurice Wertheim, my first employer after the weather business and my father's good friend. Walter, who had been Maurice Wertheim's attorney, told me that in the very early 1950s Maurice had taken an adult chess team to the Soviet Union on a self-designed goodwill mission. Afterwards, he gathered up his receipts, took them to his accountants, and told them he wanted to deduct the cost of the trip.

"You can't do that," they said.

"What do you mean? I did something for my country. Of course, I can."

"There's no provision in the tax code for that."

"There must be a way," Maurice insisted.

"Well, yes, you can set up a foundation for promoting chess."

And so Maurice Wertheim did just that. He created the American Chess Foundation for the announced purpose of developing championship chess players. Next thing I knew, Walter Fried had called and asked me to join the foundation's board, and I'd agreed. The Orkin deal had been concluded not long before; my fortunes were changing. It was time to start getting involved in something other than business.

The 1950s and 1960s were an exciting time for chess in America. In 1956, at the tender age of thirteen, Bobby Fischer became the youngest chess player ever to win the U.S. Junior Championship. Later that year, Fischer, who had learned the game growing up in Brooklyn, took on Donald Byrne, one of the top American players of any age, in the Rosenwald Memorial Tournament in New York City. Normally, chess tournaments attract all the attention of dog fights, but Fischer was a gawky, arrogant, newly minted teenager in blue jeans, and the media couldn't get enough of him. When he beat Byrne, he became the Elvis Presley of the Mensa set. His 1966 book, *Bobby Fischer Teaches Chess*, is still the best-selling chess book ever, and his 1972 match in Reykjavik, Iceland, with the reigning world champion, the Russian Boris Spassky, is the closest chess has ever come to a Cold War stand-off. (Fischer, so the story goes, refused to take Henry Kissinger's phone calls while he was breaking Spassky's spirit and claiming the crown.)

Anyone who has followed Bobby Fischer's story in the years since knows the dénouement: the descent into eccentricity, if not madness; the vicious anti-Semitic rants; and so on. Like John Nash of *A Beautiful Mind*, Fischer's genius seems to have been won at an awful price, but when I first got involved with the American Chess Foundation, the ugly downside was still waiting to be played out. Bobby Fisher was hot, and chess was suddenly an in sport. Not that you would have known any of that from the foundation's board meetings. They were, in a word, deadly. My fellow board members were far more serious chess players than I. All anyone talked about were chess moves, the major matches, and top players. There was no discussion of how to capitalize on chess's new found popularity, no talk about what the organization might do in the long run. Everyone wanted to bring in more money. That was elementary. But apart from appealing to chess players, no one had a clue how to go about it, and with very few exceptions, serious chess players don't have a spare dime among them.

I would like to write that I took the foundation, gave it a good shaking, and set it on the right path overnight, but this tale doesn't proceed so neatly. For two decades after I joined the board, the American Chess Foundation limped along, not really doing much, and I pretty much limped along with it, preoccupied by other matters. Then in 1986, one of my fellow board members, Faneuil Adams, Jr., along with chess coach and prolific chess author Bruce Pandolfini, had the inspired idea to launch a program called Chess-in-the-Schools.

As his name suggests, Fan Adams was a pure aristocrat. He was descended directly from Samuel Adams and Peter Faneuil, who built

Boston's famous Faneuil Hall, and indirectly from John Adams by way of the second president's brother. Fan had attended Exeter Academy and Harvard, both undergraduate and law—he was a blueblood all the way. But before joining Mobil and rising to become a senior executive with Mobil South, he had also served in the Army parachute infantry, in both World War II and Korea, and won a Bronze Star for his bravery. And he was a chess nut through and through. Fan had played a major role in reforming the management of the U.S. Chess Federation at a time when it was nearly bankrupt and returning it to solvency. He had been an officer of the Manhattan Chess Club for years—the premier such organization in the nation—and he served as president of our foundation in the early 1990s.

Chess-in-the-Schools began as an intuition more than anything else. Chess is a game of imagination and strategy. It involves complex rules and established principles built up over centuries of trial and error. (The game is thought to have been imported into Europe in medieval times, perhaps from Persia and India.) But chess also rewards players who are able to jump on opportunities when they present themselves. It rewards perseverance, too: The more you practice and play, the better you get. To Faneuil Adams and Bruce Pandolfini, those qualities suggested that chess could be an effective educational tool, a way to combine learning and game playing to stimulate intellectual growth. To test the theory, Fan Adams got a grant from Mobil, from which he had just retired, and his little program began teaching chess to kids in New York City's public schools, to see if the game would catch on and produce the hoped-for benefits. The initial sampling was modest: a few classes at elementary and junior-high schools in Manhattan, Harlem, and the Bronx. Then as now, all instruction and equipment was provided free to the schools.

The first evaluation of the program's success was conducted by the well-known education psychologist Dr. Stuart Marguilies. Marguilies focused on a single school district in that first round: Community School District 9, in the dismally poor South Bronx. Later, he expanded his study to other classrooms in New York City and in Los Angeles, where a similar program was underway. Collectively, the results have been pretty astounding.

Measured against a control group of their non-chess playing peers, the Chess-in-the-Schools kids have shown statistically significant gains in reading on a national standardized test. They outperform both the average student in their school district and, more tellingly given their economic disadvantages, the average student in the nation. Best of all, maybe, the lower the initial pre-chess scores on the test, the greater the gains once the children have been in the program. These aren't self-selecting students. If we go into the second grade of a school, *all* the second graders are taught chess, not just the ones who want to learn the game; and the test results are based on the entire universe of students who were taught, not just those who learned chess the quickest or best.

As to the why of such exceptional results, Marguilies interviewed scores of chess coaches and masters, as well as teachers and parents of the children involved. His conclusions, in part: Chess teaches decoding, thinking, comprehending, and analyzing—all higher order skills involved in successful reading. The best chess players have an extraordinary capacity to concentrate and superior self-control. Teachers told him that the students in the program also seemed to develop "ego strength" (self-confidence) as they increased their chess competence: The better you feel about yourself, the easier it is to learn to read well, they said. Finally, the chess participants form a pool of gifted and talented students within the school: a support group that encourages students to explore other academic interests and provides cover for them when they do so.

I'd gotten excited about Chess-in-the-Schools the moment I heard about it. The program just made sense in all the right ways. What's more, as it expanded out into more schools, it was proving amazingly cost effective: $50 a student per year for results that far more expensive government programs can't begin to match. (Inflation has pushed the in-school cost to about $75 per student, but we've added so many extras to the program that the total cost today is closer to $100 a participant.) I remember sitting at one of the early board meetings when Fan was describing the program—after so many years of listening to chess babble at these get-togethers—and thinking "I can sell this!" Then, in 1990, I got my chance to do that.

Like Bobby Fischer, Gary Kasparov had been a boy wonder on the chess circuit. In 1979, at age 16, the Armenian-born Kasparov had won the world junior championship. Five years later, he and Anatoly Karpov squared off for the world chess title in an epic 48-game match that was finally called to a halt six months after it started, with no clear winner. Kasparov won the title outright in a rematch six months later, becoming the youngest world champion in history, and defended his title successfully against Karpov in 1986 and again in 1987. In 1990, the Kasparov–Karpov show finally came to New York.

When the U.S. Chess Federation decided to hold a dinner at the Waldorf-Astoria prior to the event, Ted Field, of the Marshall Field department store family, contacted our foundation and said that if we sold any tables, one hundred percent of the proceeds would go to us. That was all the incentive I needed. Over the next week, I contacted practically everybody I knew, asking each to take a table at the dinner or to just send a contribution. By the time the big night came, we had raised close to $250,000. For years the foundation had been living off the income from a million dollar bequest from the head of Emory Industries, a major chess fan and player. Now, we had a new source of money.

The board was meeting in my office at 767 Third Avenue, discussing our new-found success when I made a radical proposal. The people I contacted hadn't bought the tables to support the American Chess Federation in general, I said. They'd bought the tables primarily to support the new chess program. The program had become our public face; it was what excited the outside world, especially those in a position to help fund us. Why didn't we put our name where our money was, and retitle the foundation Chess-in-the-Schools? (Maybe I was better at corporate branding than I realized.)

"Holy smoke! Oh, my heavens, no!" came the response. By and large, the old guard was absolutely horrified. A few years later, though, I was elected chairman of the foundation, and in 1997 we officially changed the name. As I sit here, Chess-in-the-Schools is teaching the game and much more to some 38,000 elementary and junior-high students in all five boroughs of New York City. The 160 schools we work with must qualify for the federal Title 1 lunch program. That's our criterion for going in to a school: It has to serve a severely disadvantaged neighborhood. And we don't stop at the end of the school day.

Chess-in-the-Schools now operates after-school clubs in more than 110 New York City public schools. We also provide coaching and other support for teams participating in regional and national scholastic tournaments, including intensive two- and three-day camp programs for students preparing for tournament play. We host a wide variety of tournaments on our own: 30 weekend and holiday tournaments where up to 150 Chess-in-the-Schools kids compete against each other, plus four larger tournaments, for up to 1,000 students each, open to all New York City children. We even tried to take the concept nationwide. Intel made the suggestion and provided the seed money, and for a while we thought we had hit upon the greatest thing since sliced bread. We set up the infrastructure in many other cities, found chess tutors for the schools, made all the necessary arrangements only to have Intel withdraw its financial support after the initial two years.

As our program expanded locally and the years went along, more and more of our kids were finishing up junior high school and moving on to high school, where we hadn't established the program; so I went to the Department of Education of the City of New York and was referred to one of the chancellor's assistants.

"What can we do to get chess as an elective course in high school?" I asked her after I had showed her Stuart Marguilies's evaluation. No one, by then, could deny the obvious benefits of teaching chess. I was excited by the idea.

"What department should we put it in?" she replied, in a voice that betrayed absolutely no interest in what I was saying.

"The chess department, for crissake," I answered, frustrated as always by huge bureaucracies.

The children who had moved through the Chess-in-the-Schools program wouldn't let the matter end there. "Don't drop us," they kept saying. "We want to keep this up." So we developed an alumni program, which to date has helped upward of a thousand New York City public high-schoolers. The program combines advanced chess strategy; mentoring; Scholastic Aptitude Test tutoring; internship opportunities; and cultural events, including museum trips and even Broadway shows (for so many of these students the rich, often expensive cultural life of New York is unexplored territory); as well as college workshops and visits to college campuses.

In April 2002, 42 of our alumni competed in the National High School Chess Championships in Louisville, Kentucky. That fall, a dozen of them began higher education at places such as Bowdoin, Hamilton, Temple, St. John's, St. Bonaventure, Duke, and the University of Virginia. In previous years, we've had alumni move on to the University of Michigan, Tufts, Johns Hopkins, all sorts of places, all across the college map. Who can say where they might have ended up without Chess-in-the-Schools? But these are children from environments where schools such as Duke and Bowdoin and Michigan seem almost beyond imagination.

Born on a shoestring and a powerful intuition, Chess-in-the-Schools today is a 501(c) (3) not-for-profit educational organization with an annual budget of close to $4 million, and even so, we've got nearly 100 schools on the waiting list, schools we just don't have the money and instructors to get to yet. Donors include corporations, foundations, and private individuals. In the early 1990s, I gave $1 million to the foundation myself, with the restriction that the gift had to be used in

New York City: I wanted to be as certain as I could that the money was spent as close to the school classroom as possible, and the Intel fiasco—and the flack we took in the aftermath—was still fresh in my mind. Since I've been chairman, I've tried to fill the board with like-minded people: those with the means to back Chess-in-the-Schools and with the know-how and experience to get others involved.

Forty years ago, Dorothy had gotten to know Ward Chamberlin when she was helping raise money for New York's then fledgling public TV station, WNET. Ward moved on to Washington, D.C., where he helped found the Corporation for Public Broadcasting and nurtured another public TV outlet, WETA, into maturity. Today, Ward is back in New York and vice-chairman of Chess-in-the-Schools. Just to complete the circle, I convinced Dorothy's first husband, Charlie Benenson, to join the board, too.

Robin MacNeil, the former co-host of PBS's "The MacNeil-Lehrer NewsHour," served as master of ceremonies at the fifteenth anniversary party for Chess-in-the-Schools back in April 2002 at the Sky Club in New York's MetLife Building. Lots of people were on hand to support us, in word and wallet. Wendy Kopp, who founded Teach for America, was the honoree, but the photo that made the *New York Times* shows Damion Josephs and Charles Way in the foreground, on either side of a chessboard. Damion was in high school then, a member of our Alumni Club, headed in the fall to the University of Virginia, where Charles Way had been a star running back in the early 1990s. After college, Way captained the New York Giants before bad knees ended his career and he moved on to become the team's Director of Player Programs.

In the photo, Damion—a huge smile on his face—has just declared checkmate. I'm looking on. So are Agnes Gund, then president of the Museum of Modern Art and now co-vice chair of Chess-in-the-Schools, and Bob Tisch, owner of the Giants, who had brought Charles Way to the event. You can find lots of money in that photo and a certain amount of celebrity, at least in philanthropic and not-for-profit terms, and both are important with an organization like Chess-in-the-Schools. But what really counts is the middle of the *Times* photo: the chessboard and the exuberant high-schooler who has been given a leg up in life by our program.

——◆——

Without ever really thinking about it, I seem to have applied the same principles that made me my money to the harder business of giving it away intelligently. Just as I wasn't interested in investing CVI's surplus in Mobil's North Sea platform; so I'm not interested in being a passive donor. Almost without exception, I support organizations with which I want to get involved. My gifts come with stipulations and restrictions—not many and not complicated—because I don't want them to disappear into some general money pool where I can't follow their progress. All this applies to Dorothy as well, I should add, because we operate as a team.

Between us, Dorothy and I have served in recent years on the boards of the New York Public Library, the American Museum of Natural History, the New York Botanical Garden, the Museum of Modern Art, the Metropolitan Museum of Art, the Neurosciences Institute, Human Rights Watch, and the Enterprise Foundation, among others. (The Enterprise Foundation, which works to provide low-income housing nationwide, was the brainchild of Jim Rouse, whose for-profit Rouse development company was among the earliest holdings of The Incubation Group.) All of those associations began with a smaller gift that grew larger, sometimes much larger, as our connection ripened and deepened.

Part of the impetus for sitting on so many boards, I freely admit, is the friends I've made. I have never forgotten a conversation I had back in the 1970s with a fellow I knew in Darien, Sid Boyden, who was in the executive search business. One of his clients, he told me, had called him a few days before and said, "Sid, you know, my wife and I are terribly concerned. I'm retiring next year, and we haven't got a friend in the world except our business people. Have you got any advice?" I was appalled then, and I'm still appalled, at the thought of a life that never extends beyond business and business associations. A lot of what transpires at board meetings can be dull, but an awful lot is serious business, too, on behalf of good and important causes. Every board I've served on has broadened my world.

"What would you do if you didn't participate in the cultural or the scientific life that's around you?" Dorothy once told an interviewer. "I think you would miss everything." I couldn't agree more, whether it's taking part as a volunteer or, if you have the means as we do, as a major donor. In that same interview, Dorothy cited a news item in which Ted Turner said that his hand was shaking when he wrote out a check for $200 million to donate to some cause or another. "If he had that much to give away," Dorothy said, "Lewis's hand wouldn't shake." She's right again: It wouldn't because, first, I just get a huge kick out of supporting institutions I believe in and, second, I make certain that I know the institution and what's going to happen to my money before I ever make a pledge.

That is perhaps the ultimate value of sitting on all these boards. It takes two to three years to really understand how any organization works: to see its weak and strong points, its missing links, how it can leverage its assets, and where the drain holes are that your money will disappear through if you're not careful. For a lay person, an outsider, there's no better place to learn all that than from a seat on the board.

In a sense, I have the New York Public Library to thank for all these lessons. Sometime back in the 1980s, I got a letter from Bethuel M. Webster, another elegant name. Beth Webster, as he was known, was a very prominent New York lawyer, but he was almost equally famous for being John Lindsay's best friend and closest adviser, back when Lindsay was mayor of the city. I had known Beth since the early 1960s because we both served on the board of General American Investors, but I had no idea he was one of the directors of the New York

Public Library, and I was completely floored when he wrote to ask for money for it.

"What's going on here?" I remember saying to Dorothy. "How could the library be asking for money? It's public!"

By the time Dorothy joined the library board in 1989, I was wiser about the funding of the library and its history. In fact, the New York Public Library had been born as a private undertaking and sustained as one ever since. As the nineteenth century drew to a close, New York City had two notable private libraries: the Astor reference library, founded in 1849 with a $400,000 bequest from John Jacob Astor, who had begun as a fur trader and died the wealthiest man in America; and the Lenox library, at the site of the present Frick Collection, built around the personal library of James Lenox and including the first Gutenberg Bible to find its way to the New World. What the city lacked was a significant public library, but it did have a bequest for one: $2.4 million from the estate of Samuel Tilden, the one-time governor of New York and would-be president of the United States. (Tilden, a Democrat, defeated Rutherford B. Hayes by 250,000 votes in 1876 but had the presidency stolen from him by an electoral commission tilted toward Republicans.)

Noting that the Astor and Lenox libraries were struggling with dwindling endowments, John Bigelow, a trustee of the Tilden estate, proposed they be merged into a new public library, to be constructed with the Tilden funds, and thus was born the great Beaux Arts palace at Forty-second Street and Fifth Avenue with its famous guardian lions sculpted from pink Tennessee marble. (New Yorkers immediately took to calling the lions Leo Astor and Leo Lenox, although Leo Tilden might have been more appropriate.) When the New York Public Library officially opened its doors on May 24, 1911, as many as 50,000 visitors poured inside. Simultaneously, 39 branch libraries were being constructed in the Bronx, Manhattan, and Staten Island, thanks to a $5.2 million grant from the steel baron, Andrew Carnegie.

That much was easy to learn, but if I knew more about the library's past, I wasn't a whole lot smarter about the first major gift we made to it. Dorothy and I had already given a smaller sum—$100,000—at the urging of an old friend, Richard Salomon. Dick and Brooke Astor, the ageless philanthropist and socialite, were heading up what would prove to be a hugely successful drive to restore the main library. Our contribution, a relative drop in the bucket, went to the conservator's program, a catch-all for a wide variety of needs. Now that Dorothy was on the board, we determined to donate $5 million to the library, but we had no real sense of where it should go. Dorothy's first instinct was the branch libraries: By then, Andrew Carnegie's original 39 branches had grown to over 80 outposts. The branches carry the central library's mission to the people who really need it, Dorothy figured. By designating our gift for their use, we would be doing the greatest good for the most people. The trouble is, the branch libraries really are public, fully funded by the city. That had been part of Carnegie's original stipulation: He built; the city took over after that. Any private donations to them are always in danger of being treated simply as budget offsets: You give $5 million, and New York City could deduct $5 million from its outlay for the branches.

We had no compelling interest in helping the city meet its budget goals, and no immediate idea where else the money might go. For a short while, our gift was like one of those barges piled with toxic waste that roam the oceans, searching for some port of call that will let it dock and take the load, except our load was $5 million, not five tons of asbestos fibers. Eventually, the money was piecemealed out to a variety of recipients.

When Dorothy and I decided to give a second $5 million six years later, in 1995, we knew exactly where we wanted it to go: the Library for the Performing Arts. Ever since her days of studying drama with Madame Ouspenskaya, Dorothy has had a long-standing interest in the performing arts. She once produced a series on Edith Wharton for

WNET TV. She has produced other shows for WNET as well, served as chair of the board of the Film Society of Lincoln Center, and been active with the New York Shakespeare-in-the-Park, only to scratch the surface. (The highlight of Dorothy's tenure as chair of the Film Society might have come when the group honored the great Italian moviemaker Federico Fellini. The day before the ceremony, Fellini; his wife, Giulietta Masina; Marcello Mastroianni; Anouk Aimée; and assorted hanger-ons showed up at our Darien house for lunch, just as I was driving our suddenly ill cook to the hospital. Happily, the cook recovered in time to get food on the table.)

Like so many other offshoots of the main library, the Library for the Performing Arts had magnificent materials: the Jerome Robbins Dance Collection, with 30,000 books on dance, plus costumes and set designs, press clippings, recorded interviews, and thousands of films and video-tapes of live performances; the Rodgers and Hammerstein Archives of Recorded Sound with over half a million recordings; the Billy Rose Theatre Collection of over five million items related to theatrical performances; and on and on. There's nothing to match the library's holdings in the world, and there shouldn't be: Money and the per-forming arts come together in New York as nowhere else on earth.

The problem was the library building. All this fabulous memorabilia was housed in one of the last structures added to the Lincoln Center complex, when that project was running short of funds. Although it had opened only three decades earlier, in 1965 behind the Beaumont Theatre, the library had been built on the cheap and it looked it. We wanted our $5 million gift to go toward a total rehab—or rather, I should say, our $7.5 million because before the work ever got started our new pledge had ballooned by 50 percent.

Large institutions such as the New York Public Library always have what are called "posted rates"—totally arbitrary amounts that qualify donors to have their names attached to whatever it is they're supporting. In this case, the posted rate for the Performing Arts

Library was $12.5 million, but Marshall Rose, who had taken over as chairman of the library board, offered to change that to $10 million, including the $5 million we had previously given, and we accepted. When the time came for Marshall to tell the board, though, he muffed his lines and announced that our gifts amounted to a collective $12.5 million. After he realized his mistake, Marshall called me to confess.

"For godsake," I said, "don't you remember what you told me?"

He did, of course, but the damage was done.

"What can we do about this?" he asked. "I'm embarrassed."

"Well, Marshall," I told him, "the only thing I can think of—if you'll accept this—is that I'll make a bequest in my will for the additional two and a half."

I didn't have any real regrets about Marshall's mistake—these things happen in life. I even had some fun once the work got underway. The architect who oversaw the rehab had been a Navy weatherman, stationed at South Weymouth ten years after I had been there: Once a cloud watcher, always a cloud watcher. Far from offending us, the performing arts gift proved to be only the beginning of our commitment to the New York Public Library.

Marshall Rose had come to see me one day about the idea of turning part of the landmark B. Altman & Co. building into a new Science, Industry, and Business Library. (Completed in 1914, between Madison and Fifth avenues and Thirty-fourth and Thirty-fifth streets, the building served as a high-end department store until 1989, when B. Altman went out of business.) Naturally, I was intrigued by the idea. Science and business are my two main interests, and this library was going to be devoted to both of them. Even better, because its infrastructure would be built from scratch in the 1990s, not the 1960s, the library could take full advantage of the new communication tools of the Internet Age. In effect, it would be both a physical library and one without walls, accessible to Web users everywhere. To make sure no one got left out, the library even included a training center in its final form, where would-be users could learn to take full advantage of the facility's electronic resources. To me, that's what leveraging money and information should be all about.

The more I talked with Marshall about the library—and we talked frequently—the more it became apparent to me, too, that the board intended to do this right. Science, Industry, and Business not only was going to be an incredibly useful library; it was going to be a beautiful one, too, a marriage of form and function. And indeed, that's just what it has proved to be. Dorothy and I gave the library $7.5 million so things could get going, and the architectural firm of Gwathmey Siegel designed a facility that, in the words of New York Public Library president Paul LeClerc, "makes a brilliant transition from libraries as we've known them to the kind of facilities they will be in the future." I couldn't agree more. Nor could I be more in agreement with architectural critic Paul Goldberger's assessment of the facility, in the April 24, 1996, *New York Times*:

> The new Science, Industry and Business Library of the New York Public Library is every bit as grand, in its way, as the library's great main building at Fifth Avenue and 42nd Street. It is just that the grandeur is of a late-20th-century sort: less a matter of grandeur than of comfort; less of sprawling physical space than of accessible cyberspace.

Dorothy still serves on the library board fourteen years after she first joined it. We also continue to support the Library, and each gift has been more enjoyable to make than the one before because year by year we know the place better and understand its needs and opportunities more. I've also had a chance to pick the amazing brains of the people chosen to head up the library—from the Armenian-born Vartan Gregorian, who could work a crowd as well as anyone I've seen; to Father Timothy Healy, the brilliant former president of

Georgetown University and one of the world's best dinner companions; to Paul LeClerc, who somehow manages to be stately, scholarly, and innovative at the same time. (Tim Healy died on the job, a victim of his own vast love of food and drink. Dorothy remembers him saying, not long before his fatal heart attack, "Well, you know, after all there are very few pleasures left for a priest, except the table!")

We gave $10 million to establish the Dorothy and Lewis B. Cullman Center for Scholars and Writers at the Humanities and Social Sciences Library because the more Dorothy studied the institution, the more she saw the need for a facility that would link the scholarly and creative worlds with the general public through the medium of the library's immense holdings. Each year since 1999, 15 fellows—scholars, academicians, and creative writers—have been brought together at the center to pore over the library's collection, meet with each other and exchange ideas, and present a broad program of lectures, readings, and symposia. Peter Gay, the great Yale historian who was by then on emeritus status, helped us plan the center and served as its first director.

The Cullman Center, by the way, is dedicated to Brooke Astor because that's something else we learned early on in our association with the New York Public Library. That magnificent architectural pile at Forty-second and Fifth Avenue really was a desperate shambles when Brooke and Dick Salomon set out to rescue the place— almost too far gone to resuscitate. Brooke and Dick saved it, and Brooke was almost in her nineties when she started to wage that war. That, too, deserves some recognition. (Brooke's third husband was Vincent Astor, heir to John Jacob. When he died in 1959, Brooke took over the foundation that bore his name and eventually distributed nearly $200 million from it to a vast array of charitable organizations. She's now over 100 years old, a bright beacon of hope for us octogenarians.)

And, yes, Dorothy's and my names can be found on quite a number of walls and over quite a number of doors in and around New York City these days, sometimes permanently, sometimes just for the length of an exhibition. As noted, there's the Cullman Center for Scholars and Writers, but there's also the Dorothy and Lewis B. Cullman Center of the New York Public Library for the Performing Arts at Lincoln Center and the Lewis B. and Dorothy Cullman Circulating Library and Reading Room at the Science, Industry, and Business Library. And there are plenty of points beyond the library where the name pops up, too. At the Dorothy and Lewis B. Cullman Hall of the Universe—part of the new Rose Center for Earth and Space at the American Museum of Natural History—visitors can learn how galaxies evolved and kids can step on digital scales to learn how much they would weigh on Saturn or Mercury. The southern wing of Branford College at Yale, my old college, is now Lewis B. Cullman Hall; inside there's even a portrait of me, though I'm not sure my own mother would recognize me from the likeness. Our names will be on the Museum of Modern Art's new Education and Research Building when that's completed, too. (If Dorothy is the one primarily interested in the subject matter, her name goes first; if I'm the more interested party, mine is out front. The Museum of Natural History got it wrong with the Dorothy and Lewis B. Cullman Hall of the Universe—science is my baili-wick—but maybe they were just being polite.)

Dorothy and I funded "Art of the First Cities: The Third Millen-nium B.C. from the Mediterranean to the Indus" and "Egyptian Art in the Age of the Pyramids" at the Metropolitan Museum of Art. It was through our backing (and my persistence, to be honest) that the sculpture garden of the Museum of Modern Art—pieces by Giacometti, Rodin, Picasso, Moore, and others—ended up on dis-play at the Conservatory of the New York Botanical Garden while MoMA was being renovated and its paintings moved out to a tem-porary museum in Queens. Along with the LuEster T. Mertz Charitable Trust, we were the major underwriters of EGG, which began as "City Arts," focused on New York City, and grew into an award-winning twelve-part series on the arts in America produced by WNET for PBS. (LuEster Mertz's fortune came from Publisher's

Clearinghouse, creator of the famous sweepstakes.) A good deal further afield, the American Academy in Rome hands out the Dorothy and Lewis B. Cullman Pre-Doctoral Rome Prize and administers the John Guare Writer's Fund, which comes with this imposing appendage: "A gift of Dorothy and Lewis B. Cullman/American Academy of Arts and Letters Fellowship in Literature."

Dorothy has never much liked all this naming, but at least she says that she has stopped noticing her moniker splashed all over things. I've been more inclined to the idea, but not I hope from any particular vanity. If all I wanted to do was see my name on a wall, I could have simply handed someone the money and saved myself a lot of time and energy. I've come to believe that with great commitment, a little recognition is due. That's a principle worth enforcing, it seems to me, and to make sure it's not forgotten, I've had my attorney draw up the naming agreements so they will stick. Too many institutions in their greed and need—and sometimes plain obtuseness—end up being disdainful of the people who support them. Columbia University, to cite one of many egregious examples, has renamed many of its halls for a new generation of donors. If some institution wants to rip Dorothy's and my name off a wall after we're dead and gone, I want it to have to hire a damn good lawyer to break the faith.

Dorothy and I have done a little collecting on our own, works by up-and-coming artists—enough that we have long ago run out of space to display the pieces. Every now and then, I'll run across a bill that reminds me we have a painting in some warehouse, waiting for a wall to hang it on. As a donor, though, beautiful objects hold little lure for me in and of themselves. I'm interested in programs that make connections and knock down barriers. I loved seeing those sculptures from the Museum of Modern Art in the Conservatory of the Botanical Garden because they were beautiful to contemplate in a tranquil setting, but I loved seeing them there most of all because people kept telling me that it couldn't be done. Insurance would be impossible, the moving, the security, on and on the excuses went; and on and on I insisted that it could be done if only everyone would stop saying that it couldn't. Finally, they agreed—four years after I had first proposed the idea—and the relocation was a smash hit.

I was wildly enthusiastic, too, about Dorothy's idea for the Center for Scholars and Writers for many of the same reasons: Those people should be talking with each other, and they should be sharing the fruits of their creations and discoveries with all of us laypeople who will never earn a doctorate or pen a novel. And I liked the $5 million we gave to the Metropolitan Museum of Art with the stipulation that (a) it was to be used to cover ancillary, behind-the-scenes expenses for Greco-Roman or Egyptian shows and (b) that I meant this as an endowment and that only the spending rate from the fund was to be available. Initially, the Met didn't like the idea any better than MoMA had liked my suggestion of moving its sculptures to the Botanical Garden, but the Met gets money to name rooms and buildings. The people there always seem to find sponsors for specific shows, corporations, or individuals who will put up a set amount of money for this show or that. Being a sponsor didn't interest me, but as I looked around, I saw this huge gap—the side expenses that sponsorship fees never get around to covering—and that's where I insisted our money go. I've seen it time and again in business: Taking your eye off the small stuff just murders you.

(Happily, Dorothy's and my little endowment grew so handsomely during the late 1990s, along with the Met's fund, that it far outpaced the ancillary needs for which it was intended. Finally, Philippe de Montebello, the museum director, asked if the Met could use the excess funds to support some actual shows, which is how we ended up as sponsors of the "Art of the First Cities" and "Egyptian Art in the Age of the Pyramids" shows.)

As I wrote earlier, I like to leverage information, and I like to use my donations when I can to draw in other donors and to force organizations and their would-be supporters into getting serious about their fund-raising and giving. When I first got involved with the Neuro-sciences Institute in La Jolla, California, it was like one of those securities I used to buy for The Incubation Group: well-managed, clear in its objectives, and bursting with potential, but also under-recognized and undercapitalized.

The institute had been founded as an independent, not-for-profit research center where scientists could study the biological basis of higher brain functions, from memory and thought to sensory perception, behavior, and speech. To free researchers from the crippling restrictions that can come with government grants, the institute from the beginning has depended largely on private donations. Small and intentionally collegial, it stresses interdisciplinary approaches. The competition is against ignorance, not each other.

To me, all that was exciting. The brain fascinates me, and I'm always looking for places that break the bonds of the conventional. But what really hooked me on the Neurosciences Institute was its director, Gerald Edelman. Gerry was in his early forties, a faculty member at Rockefeller University, when he and Britain's Rodney Porter shared the 1972 Nobel Prize in Medicine for their work on the chemical structure of antibodies. (Gerry tells a wonderful story about stepping into a room at the university one day with a metal frame, a roll of piano wire, and a thousand white plastic Pop-It beads, and reemerging some 36 hours later with bleeding fingers and the first-ever 3-D model of the antibody molecule.) As the 1970s went along, Gerry's interests turned increasingly to the far larger arena of the biology of the brain. Simultaneously, his relationship with Rockefeller soured, and in 1981, he left the university and founded the Neuroscience Institute. (The institute operates under the aegis of the Neurosciences Research Foundation, which had been set up back in the early 1960s to fund brain-science research at the Massachusetts Institute of Technology.)

Within scientific circles, the institute has long had a stellar reputation. Oliver Sacks, the neurologist and best-selling author, once wrote that "There's no place in the world like the Neurosciences

Institute. It is, in effect, a scientific monastery, where extremely gifted and dedicated people from all over the world can do fundamental work, experimental and theoretical, undistracted by the demands of an academic or industrial setting." That's absolutely right. Others have noted that the facility itself—on leased land located on the grounds of the Scripps Research Institute—even looks like an ancient monastery, wrapped in its skin of fossil limestone. Over the years, too, the Institute has racked up an enormously impressive list of accomplishments: "learning machines" controlled by realistic nervous systems that can learn through experience, seminal studies of the differences in gene activity in the brain between sleeping and waking, the most comprehensive theory yet as to how biological functions of the brain lead to human consciousness, and much more.

Even though the Institute was little known outside the scientific community, it had a solid source of funding. Sandoz, the pharmaceutical firm later acquired by Novartis, provided between $5 million and $7 million a year in return for access to research results, under a contract that required a two-year cancellation notice. Just as the dot.com economy was unraveling, Novartis pulled out, and that's when I swung into action, both to keep the Institute running at full throttle and to assure that its future support would be more broad-based.

In August 2000, Dorothy and I announced what I called a "drop-dead charity challenge": a $10 million gift that was contingent upon the Institute's raising $15 million in additional contributions from its trustees, key people, and other private sources by June 2005. (The gift was the kick-off to a $100 million capital campaign.) Because organizations, like individuals, tend to put off unpleasant tasks, we made our challenge grant a phased one: We would pay out our pledge at $2 million a year, contingent upon the institute's raising $3 million. The annual aspect of the challenge not only concentrated the Institute's attention; it also served as a goad to donors. Dave Mitchell, the Institute's development director and one of the best fund-raisers I know, told me later that one foundation had changed its long-standing rules on the spot when he explained that if it didn't give, the challenge was not going to be met. To me, that's making our $10 million work about as hard it can, in all the most useful ways.

To our pleasant surprise, the Institute thanked Dorothy and me by naming two endowed chairs for us—positions for senior fellows on the scientific staff, out on the edge of the unknown, just where I enjoy being.

———※⋄※———

It's no secret: I like science, I like supporting seminal research, and I like giving money away. (In truth, I liked making it, too.) I also like finding (and sometimes imposing) new avenues of communication that will get people looking at old issues in fresh ways. That's what the leveraged buyout was all about: a fresh way of approaching the old dilemma of how to raise capital. As I get older, I also take great pleasure in forcing people to rethink how my peers get pigeonholed in our society. I was on the far side of 70 when the Museum of Modern Art sent me notice that I had been selected to be an honorary trustee of the institution—a title reserved for those of us who could claim six decades plus. Such status, I was informed, would entitle me to attend the museum's annual meeting, nothing more. No thanks, I replied, not quite that politely. If I was going to support MoMA, I would need to know a lot more about it than I could learn from a single get-together, once a year. What's the point of that? MoMA apparently agreed because it changed its rules so that I and others my age could sit on the board itself, not its creaky, "honorary" adjunct. Maybe most of all, I like leaving myself open to serendipity, chance encounters, the shock of the new, as the art critic Robert Hughes once put it. After all, it was a chance encounter raising money for the U.S. Committee of the World Federation for Mental Health that brought Dorothy and me together more than 40 years ago.

To a greater or lesser extent, all those elements pulled together in one of the most satisfying charitable forays Dorothy and I have ever undertaken: the Lewis B. and Dorothy Cullman Program for Molecular Systematics Studies. Here's how it came about:

In the early 1990s, Dorothy and I took a combination Mediterranean cruise and art trip to Turkey that had been arranged by the American Museum of Natural History. The trip was forgettable except for a series of lectures delivered aboard the *Sea Cloud* by Malcolm McKenna, a paleontologist with the museum. Strangely, the talks had almost nothing to do with Turkey. McKenna lectured on plate tectonics, the Gobi, and the like, but he was fascinating all the same, and during the course of the cruise we got to know him and his wife quite well.

Not long after we got back, during a board meeting at General American Investors, I mentioned to Bill Golden what an impressive guy Malcolm McKenna was. Bill was on the board of the Natural History Museum as well, and sensing a giving opportunity, he set up a lunch at the museum with himself; Ellen Futter, the museum president; Malcolm and one or two others from the senior staff; and Dorothy and me. (The General American board was also my connection with Bethuel Webster, who got me involved with the public library. I'm lucky serving on that board didn't send me to the poorhouse!)

That's the first leg of the triangle. The second leg requires a brief digression. Gregory Long had been the head of development at the New York Public Library back when Dorothy and I were first starting to support it in a big way. Gregory eventually moved on to become president of the New York Botanical Garden, but he kept up contact with those of us who had been major backers of the library. Soon, Dorothy and I had a very nice letter from one of his people, soliciting a donation. We gave, not much, but enough that we began receiving invitations to the endless stream of fund-raising parties they give. We went to a few of those, too, and soon enough Gregory Long came calling and asked Dorothy to go on the board of the Botanical Garden.

Fine, I figured: It's a good cause even if Dorothy might not like the garden-club aspect. Her response, though, surprised me: "Why doesn't Lewis do it?" Thus when she and I showed up for the previously mentioned luncheon with Ellen Futter and the others at the American Museum of Natural History, I happened to be on the board of managers of the New York Botanical Garden.

The third leg of the triangle, and the one that brings the other two together, is the Harvard professor and author Edward O. Wilson. Intriguingly, at least to me, Wilson and Gerald Edelman of the Neurosciences Institute were born in the same year, 1929, and have taken similar intellectual journeys. Both began with tightly focused research—antibodies in Edelman's case, ants in Wilson's—and both migrated from there into asking far larger questions. In his 1991 book, *The Ants*, co-authored with Bert Hölldobler, Wilson wrote about the interdependence of ant cultures: Disrupt one part and the disruption echoes through the the entire ant system. (The book won Wilson his second Pulitzer Prize for General Nonfiction.) A year later, in *The Diversity of Life*, Wilson was applying those lessons to the biosphere itself: Disrupt the tropical rainforests, for instance, and you disrupt all of animal and plant life.

The Diversity of Life was much on my mind as we gathered for our luncheon at the Museum of Natural History one day in 1994. I'd just finished reading Wilson's book and had been overwhelmed by what he had to say. That and the place we were meeting and the fact that I sat on the Botanical Garden board all suddenly conspired to suggest a powerful opportunity, the chance to do something really interesting.

"How about a joint project with the American Museum and the New York Botanical Garden, studying the biodiversity of life?" I asked, and from that question, and that moment, was born the Program for Molecular Systematics Studies.

As Dorothy's and my donations go, the commitment to the program wasn't all that great: $2 million to the Botanical Garden, $1 million to the Museum. Thanks in part to this gift, Dorothy would join the board of the Natural History Museum, and from that would flow the far larger gift to fund the Cullman Hall of the Universe. (Dorothy says the real reason she was asked to join the board is because she survived one of the museum's 30-day, 22-stop round-the-world tours. If you're alive on the morning of the thirty-first day, she claims, the board seat is yours.) But what I really like about this donation is that it took advantage of existing strengths and, for so relatively little money, has made so much happen.

The Museum of Natural History already had a $2 million DNA sequencer. We didn't have to spend a dime for that. For over a century the Botanical Garden had been honing its expertise in whole plants and their place and role in nature. That expertise was free, as well. By combining the two, though, we could help the whole-plant people see life at the molecular level and the molecular people appreciate life at the macro level. By spreading the wealth through partnerships—with New York University, Cold Spring Harbor Laboratory, the Yale Environmental Science/Forestry School, and Cornell—we could also make the variety of perspectives broaden almost exponentially. Just as significant and satisfying, the connections fostered by the program have added immeasurably to the prestige of the Botanical Garden. For decades, the place had drifted along as a second-tier institution. Its plant collection was first-rate, but with no capacity for molecular analysis, it was falling further and further behind the times. Today, now that it is aligned with the Natural History museum, the New York Botanical Garden is the preeminent botanical scientific institution in the world.

Smaller, innovative gifts have a way of attracting bigger money, and ours did that, too. Seven years after Dorothy and I had given our $3 million, the Starr Foundation came in with $25 million to endow a new Institute for Comparative Genomics at the American Museum of Natural History. As we had with the Neurosciences Institute, we leveraged our money into something much bigger. What I'm most pleased about, though, is that this little inspiration of mine broke down such formidable barriers.

Bill Golden told me later that back in 1890, the American Museum of Natural History and the New York Botanical Garden had struck a treaty: The former shall take care of fauna, the later of flora, and never the twain shall meet. I had a vision of an article in the "Science Times" section of the *New York Times*, under the headline "1890 Treaty Breached!" but we never could fully substantiate the story. Nonetheless, the Program for Molecular Systematics Studies did just that, and did so in the service of a vital cause. My muse in this matter, Ed Wilson, serves as an adviser to both institutions. If there's one lesson to be learned from his books and scholarship, it is that plants and people, the air we breathe, the water we drink, and the soil we grow things in are all in this together. That my wife and I can have a hand in advancing such knowledge is about as gratifying as giving gets.

⎯⎯⎯✦⎯⎯⎯

I was at a Botanical Garden meeting on planned giving when Tom Rogerson of State Street Growth, an expert in the field, talked about going to see some ancient curmudgeon in Boston who was sitting on $25 million like a hen waiting for her egg to hatch. Tom, who is now with Mellon, was trying to convince the ancient of the merits of donating his money to philanthropy instead of donating it by default to the government after he was gone.

"Hell, no," came the answer. "I wouldn't give a dime to any goddamn charity. People ought to take care of themselves. Why don't they make their own money instead of hitting me up for it?"

"Do you know that when you are dead, 55 percent of your estate is going to go to the government?" Tom responded. "Have you made provisions for how much of that you want to go do defense? How much to education?"

"You can't do that, for crissake."

"Well, we'll show you how you *can* make an allocation."

It was the right answer, mind you, but it did little good in this instance.

I simply don't get curmudgeons like that. And I don't get the truly super-rich—the ones worth billions of dollars—who insist on holding on to most of what they have. Why? What can you possibly do with $15 billion that you couldn't do with $1 billion? The interest on $15 billion alone is more than anybody could possibly spend. And I really don't get the tax laws that allow the wealthy to deduct the money they give to create private foundations yet *never* require those foundations to pay out the principal that earned the deduction. (When I write *never*, I mean it.) To me, that's just wrong: bad tax policy, bad social policy, and morally indefensible in the bargain.

Let's start with the last of those first as it's the least complex to remedy. Under what's known as the five-percent rule, the IRS requires that private foundations spend five percent of their assets annually, but the expenditures don't have to all be in the form of contributions. A typical large foundation might pay out about three percent of its assets each year in grants and consume another two percent in administrative expenses and the like. Because even a mediocre money manager should be able to average a five-percent return on principal, the IRS is effectively requiring that only the increment—income plus capital gains—be spent. The principal, the corpus that earned the deduction, might never find its way to a charity of any sort. What's more, because there's no sunset provision governing private foundations, the original gift can survive into perpetuity.

In reality, of course, five percent is significantly lower than the average historical return on investment of most large foundations; so instead of their size holding constant—or, perish the thought, diminishing—large foundations tend to get larger and larger. To eat up their excess, they move into sumptuous offices, produce voluminous reports, build large bureaucracies, and still they can't spend it all.

In 1909, Milton Hershey, founder of the Hershey Foods empire, created a private foundation to support a school for "poor, healthy, white male orphans between the ages of 8 through 18 years of age." The Milton Hershey School has been in existence ever since, a fine place, even a noble one. But the foundation's assets have grown over the last 90-plus years from an initial $60 million to over $5 billion, infinitely more than it could ever spend in fulfillment of its original purpose. The school enrolls about 1,000 students, or one student for every $5 million of endowment. Yale, by comparison, has about twice the endowment and eleven times more students. The good that could be done, the lives that could be helped by freeing up even a tenth of the Hershey foundation's assets is mind-boggling.

I happen to know all this for not entirely philanthropic reasons. Back in the 1970s, I tried to do a leveraged buyout of Hershey Foods. Because the foundation owned the majority of the stock in the company, it was an early port of call. Our pitch involved a recent court decision, in the Girard case, that upheld the right to break a will if it was clearly out of touch with the times. Milton Hershey's will was demonstrably that; so we argued that the foundation could be in real trouble with the courts unless it diversified, and what better way to diversify than sell the company to us! (It was a short visit.)

What's the solution to foundations that hog their wealth? The easiest remedy would be to require that the entire five-percent threshold be met with donations to organized charities. According to the National Committee for Responsive Philanthropy, that would add $4.3 billion annually to the philanthropic pool, no small potatoes considering that the total annual yield from private foundations is now slightly under $20 billion. But I don't think that goes far enough. Foundations should be required to spend down their assets, *all* of them, within 50 years of their founding. Sure, the average life of private foundations would be reduced accordingly, but would the wealthy be less likely to create and fund them? I don't see why. Even if the Ford

Foundation had lasted barely into the 1960s, it still would have saved Henry Ford's heirs over $300 million in federal inheritance taxes.

Already, too many private foundations sit on far too much sterile money, and that pile is just going to grow in the years ahead. Trillions of dollars will be undergoing generational transfer over the next decade or two. Without a legislative remedy, far too much of it will end up moldering in foundation vaults instead of out in the sunshine where the money can do the most good. I was talking about all this not long ago with Vartan Gregorian, who moved on from the New York Public Library to become president of Brown University and in 1997 was made head of the Carnegie Foundation. When I got to my sunset provision, Vartan almost dropped his glass.

"My God," he said, "you'll put me out of business."

Exactly, but slowly and with a soft landing.

Vartan, I should add, had plenty of horrified company among his fellow nonprofit leaders when I put together my thoughts on private foundations for an article that appeared in the September 25, 2003, issue of the *The New York Review of Books*.

⎯⎯⎯➤•◆•⎯⎯⎯

Like businesses—and business buyers—private foundations simply take advantage of what the tax law allows them. Change the law and you change the behavior. The behavior of individuals can be far harder to modify, and at least where philanthropy is concerned, it's a far more critical issue because the amount of money donated by foundations to organized charities of all sorts, from churches to museums to issues and welfare groups, amounts to only about one-tenth of all private giving.

I enjoy raising money for causes I believe in. The hunt, the courtship, the kill—all of it is fun for me, a way to use for the public good the same skills I developed for my own good and for the good of my employees and those who had invested in Cullman Ventures Inc.

But I sometimes find myself frustrated almost to the breaking (or boiling) point by what I hear when I'm trying to find an extra million or two for one of the institutions that Dorothy and I work so hard to support.

Why can't we follow the European model, someone will say to me? The state supports the arts over there, and everything seems to work just fine. Well, that's true, I'll answer, but France and Italy and Germany and the other European nations support arts and cultural institutions with taxpayers' money. The genius of our system is that the tax code is constructed so that individuals get to use their deductions to make the choices that the state makes for taxpayers in most other advanced industrial economies. Here, philanthropy is—or should be—participatory, just as our democracy is (or should be).

Sometimes, too, I'll have Europeans try to turn that argument on me when I call on them for a little support. Sure, they'll say, it's easy for you to give. You get a deduction; I don't. Fine, I'll respond, assume U.S. taxes are 50 percent, then give half of what I gave. That usually silences them.

The problem isn't the charitable tax deduction, at least as far it applies to individuals; and it's not the lack of state support for cultural institutions. If I can't stand opera, I shouldn't have to pay for it with my taxes. If you can't stand modern art, you shouldn't have to pay for it with yours. But someone has to—and that gets us to the flaws in human nature, not the ones in the tax code: Too many of the people who really have the money to give away don't do so.

In part, I fault the media. The annual *Forbes* cover story ranking the 400 richest Americans and all the other attention paid in the press and on TV to similar bilge serves as a huge disincentive to the people who appear on such lists to give their money away—and no one has more to give away than they do. To return to Ted Turner just for a moment, I remember reading a Maureen Dowd column in the *Times* in which Turner worried aloud that if he gave too much money away, he might lose his place as the third or fourth richest person on the

Forbes list. Maybe, he suggested, *Forbes* should run a derby not on how much wealth people have, but on how much money they give away. A brilliant idea! I wrote Turner immediately and told him I was ready to climb on the bandwagon. What good does it do to be wealthy if you don't use the money for something constructive?

The media, though, can't modify what's in the heart's deep core, at least with any speed, and that's where the real change needs to occur. Dorothy and I were having dinner the other day with some people we've known for years when the question came up of how much a couple would need annually to support themselves in the style to which they would like to become accustomed. Twenty million dollars, the husband answered, barely blinking an eye. I was flabbergasted. Think what would happen if all the couples making do on $20 million annually decided they could scrape by on $10 million and donated the rest to charity. Or if everyone sitting on a $25 million nest egg like the Boston curmudgeon decided he or she could be just as comfortable on a $5 million nest egg and did the same with the excess. Or if all those multibillionaires on the annual *Forbes* list of the 400 richest Americans decided they could rest easy with just, say, a billion each in the bank. (The top 25 richest on the 2002 *Forbes* list had a collective wealth of about $345 billion—half the annual gross domestic product of Canada!)

Tens of billions of dollars, maybe hundreds of billions, would be added to the philanthropic pool. Museums and the performing arts would flourish as never before. Medical and scientific research would leap forward. The poor would be taken care of even as the government abandons them. All of our lives would be enriched beyond measure.

—◆—

You really can't take it with you, and Dorothy and I had all the "it" two people (or two dozen people) could ever need. I held 90,000 shares of Cullman Ventures Inc. Each year, each of those shares paid an after-tax distribution of $100. I'd take my $9 million, and Dorothy and I would figure out where to donate what wasn't already spoken for. (Major gifts are commonly paid out over multiple years, and the sequencing can get tricky if you're not careful.) What else were we going to do with all the money, and still feel like we had tried to make a difference in life?

Thus we might have gone on for years—Keith Clark was an absolute cash cow—except that one day in 1998 my chief financial guy popped in and said, in effect, that I had two choices: Stop giving my money away or sell the company. That was one of the easiest decisions I ever made.

EIGHT

LETTING GO

By the time we got around to putting Keith Clark on the block in late 1998, it was no longer called that. Ever since we had acquired At-A-Glance and folded it into the company a decade earlier, our people had been noticing a name recognition gap. They would introduce themselves at some function as working for Keith Clark, and unless the person they were talking with was actually in the calendar business, the next question would always be something like, "What do you do? What's your product?" "Well," they would answer, "you've heard of At-A-Glance...?" And they would need say no more. It was like Kleenex and Kimberly-Clark. The famous tissues hadn't been introduced until 1924, fifty-two years after John Kimberly, Charles Clark, and others founded the company to produce newsprint from recycled linen and cotton rags, but the Kleenex name had become far more instantly recognizable than the company that owned it.

We didn't aspire to global status like Kimberly-Clark, but sales come a lot more easily when you don't have to explain your way inside the door. In 1996, we hired a consultant to help us solve this dilemma, only to have the consultant come back with what was obvious from the beginning: If almost everyone has heard of At-A-Glance and almost no one recognizes Keith Clark, we could gain instant corporate branding by renaming ourselves after our best-known product line. (I'm always reminded of that old joke about how a consultant is someone who borrows your watch to tell you the time.) So long, Mr. Keith; goodbye, our Mr. Clark. The only question was whether we would become At-A-Glance Products or the At-A-Glance Group. In the end, "Group" won out—it seemed more dignified.

We also had a trial run at selling the company three years earlier. Back in 1995, when we were still pokey old Keith Clark, Tom Hargrove had come to me with good and bad news. The good news was that through our acquisitions, by filling in this niche here and that hole there, we had achieved near-complete market domination.

"You know," I can still hear Tom saying, "I think we've practically gobbled up everything there is to be had in the commercial calendar business. Depending on how you measure it, we probably have about 85 percent of the market."

He was right, of course. By then, we were the only ones making the 717 flip-over calendar. We'd bought out our sole competitor, merged it with our flip-over line, and were now selling 15 million of the 717s alone. Overall, Keith Clark was producing 100 million calendars annually. Stacked all on top of each other, they might have reached 1,500 miles into space—300 times taller than Mount Everest—and we rebuilt the stack every year. In our own little corner of the manufacturing world, we were Masters of the Universe, a fact well worth celebrating; but Tom got to the downside of our dominion before I even had the chance to propose a toast.

"I think our business has peaked," he said. "It's not going to get any better. It can't. There's no room to expand. This is a great opportunity to sell."

That was the first inkling I had that Tom felt this way, and I wasn't very thrilled about it, or inclined to his point of view. Selling Keith Clark would mean breaking up the sub-S corporation, and that would mean the end of my tax-paid distributions. Even if the company sold for more than I thought it could possibly be worth, I didn't see how I could ever reinvest my proceeds in such a way that the yield would leave me $9 million a year, after taxes, to give away; and by 1995, I was far more interested in distributing wealth than accumulating it.

"Selling doesn't make any sense to me," I told Tom and went on to explain my logic, but he was adamant on the subject.

"I know what your theory is," he kept saying, "but I'm younger than you are, and this is an opportunity for me."

On and on it went until finally I agreed, and we engaged Goldman Sachs to look for buyers for Keith Clark or CVI or however someone wanted to divide the pie. (Allied Graphic Arts was so far out on the edge of our core calendar business that a buyer for Keith Clark was unlikely to be interested in it as well.) I still didn't like the thought of selling—I remained bullish on the company and its growth potential—but I didn't relish a big battle, and maybe Tom was right. He was younger, he had a different perspective on where the numbers might lead, and he knew the calendar business inside and out.

Goldman Sachs looked first for a strategic buyer, someone already in our business or something close enough to it that we would be complementing and expanding its reach. We had been doing that ourselves ever since I bought Keith Clark; so we knew all the players and pointed Goldman Sachs in all the right directions, but to my great surprise, no serious buyer emerged. (Day Runner, makers of what was then a well-known daily organizer, did offer to buy us for stock, but the deal they were proposing looked as if it had been crafted by Rube Goldberg, and the company, which had been launched only fifteen years earlier in a West Hollywood, California, garage, was far smaller than ours.)

Next, Goldman Sachs turned to my former colleagues: the "financial" buyers, or leveraged buyout groups, and here the interest proved greater. Three potential purchasers came forward, and finally one, Butler Capital, signed a letter of intent to purchase Keith Clark for $325 million.

On paper, it all looked fine. There was even a due date spelled out. In practice the deal was a mess practically from Day One. Gilbert Butler and the rest of the crew over at Butler Capital kept asking for extensions on top of extensions. Finally, I told them, "Look, we'll extend the agreement, but you're going to be flying naked. We're under no obligation any longer. We can change our mind any time we want. We're not bound by anything."

Just as bad, Butler was constantly adjusting the numbers to lower the purchase price even though our business was doing better than we had told them, a strange logic that was not very promising of future relationships. Before long, I got fed up with all the futzing around and inverted mathematics, and announced to our board that the party was over. "I've decided not to sell," I told them. My message to Butler Capital was even briefer: To heck with you.

To my surprise, Tom Hargrove took the decision not to sell almost as a personal insult. He hadn't been forewarned, he complained. He had been cut out of the decision loop, left twisting in the wind, you name it. Tom seemed so upset that Bill Mayo-Smith and I met with him separately to try to iron things out, and that's when he really floored us. Spurning the Butler offer wasn't all that was bothering him. He felt we had been treating him poorly all along, undercompensating him especially considering the job he had done.

"I really feel like I'm entitled to more," he said as the three of us sat in my office.

By then, Tom Hargrove had been with Cullman Ventures fifteen years, most of that time as chief operating officer: my number two, along with the chief financial officer, Jim Moore. In addition to what I considered a handsome salary, he received liberal year-end bonuses. He and Jim Moore had both been given stock in Cullman Ventures. For a decade and a half, whenever the subject of his compensation arose, Tom would always say something like "I've never been treated as well as this. I'm just so pleased." I had full faith in him; he was part of the family as far I was concerned.

I think Bill Mayo-Smith and I said just about the same thing at the same time, with equal degrees of astonishment: "We can't understand this. We've always bent over backwards for you. Why didn't you tell us this before? We would have responded." And in fact we did respond practically right on the spot, coming back with a scheme that cut him in on a larger piece of the action. Within days, it seemed, Tom went from being a bear to being a bull. Before, he had been convinced that we had topped out in our growth potential. Now that he had a larger stake, the sky was the limit. Maybe that's why he had insisted on the sale in the first place, consciously or otherwise—to set off a chain of events that would end where this one did—but he didn't have to use Goldman Sachs to help deliver the message.

———※·※———

In August 1996, less than a year after nearly selling Keith Clark to Butler Capital, we bought Landmark General Corporation, out in Marin County, north of San Francisco. If we were going to continue to grow, we would have to move beyond the commercial calendar business, but not too far beyond. Calendars, after all, were what we knew best, and Landmark looked to be a perfect fit. The company did pictorial calendars—typical, pretty calendars of all sorts. More important, they did calendars under license for some of the biggest names going, from Disney to a number of the leading museums in America. Suddenly, we had a whole new field open in front of us.

Although there was no need to, Landmark's owner, Spencer Sokale, and his wife, Kimberly, came East for the closing. I was curious to meet Spencer. I had yet to see his name in a photo credit on any of Landmark's calendars, but I knew he traveled the world snapping pictures and writing off the trips as business expenses. At least, I figured, he and his wife must have been to some interesting places. Still, when the two of them showed up at my office at 10:30 for a lunch date, I had no idea how to fill the two hours until we could reasonably eat. Desperate, I happened to mention that I went skiing in Aspen every winter.

"You do?" Kimberly Sokale perked up.

"Yes," I said, "Why do you ask?"

"I used to be a ski instructor at Aspen!"

We had just about exhausted that subject when she noticed a copy of *Cigar Aficionado* magazine on my desk and asked if I had been to the Club Macanudo yet. The club, which had opened only a few months earlier on East Sixty-third Street, was the brainchild of my brother Edgar. What's more, the interior—a very private-club feel even though it was open to the public—had been done by Cullman & Kravis, the very chi-chi decorating firm founded in 1984 by Ellie

Cullman, my nephew Edgar Jr.'s wife, and Hedi Kravis, ex-wife of leveraged buyout ace Henry Kravis, of KKR fame. (Hedi, sadly, died in April 1997 of cancer at age 49, less than a year after the club opened.) I told Kimberly that I couldn't have avoided going to the place even if I hadn't wanted to.

"Who in the heck took you there?" I asked.

"The decorator, Hedi Kravis."

And so we went on, paring down our six degrees of separation to no more than two or one by the time we could safely head to lunch.

I expected us to do with Landmark and the pictorial calendar market just what we had with the commercial calendar one: gobble up other companies when and if they came up for sale while using our muscle to take market share away from existing competitors. In a niche dominated by little companies, we had size and volume going for us, and in the era of the superstore, size and volume are critical. Otherwise, the big stores walk all over you. We knew something about that.

Back when Office Depot and Staples were just starting to go head to head—and killing off all the small, local office suppliers in the process—we landed a contract to provide Office Depot with refill pads for flipover calendars, our 717 model and the Success model made by Success Business Industries, the old Columbian Art Works. We figured the contract was a coup, until Office Depot came in and ordered double the number of refills that we knew the market could bear.

"Uh-uh," we told them, "that's too many. You should order half that. That'll put you right about on the money."

"Don't tell us how to run our business," came the reply. And they meant it, in tone and content. If the order was too big, tough, it was going to be our problem. Office Depot would ship the excess back to us and expect us to take it and absorb the loss on production and materials. Basically—and this is the superstore business model to this day— suppliers are required to take all the risks and manage all the inventory. A sweet deal, if you can pull it off.

We printed up the number of refills Office Deport ordered, and sure enough, about four months later, they sent half of them back to us. We didn't want to get caught in that game; so we refused to accept them, and Office Deport did what superstores always do in such circumstances: went to Success Business Industries and said that if it bought the over-stock, it could have our contract. In 1994, we countered by merging with Success (in effect acquiring them as we were much larger) and sneaking into Office Depot through the back door, but with one less competitor the superstore SOBs could play us off against.

That had been pretty much our modus operandi with the superstores ever since: play tough, use our size and wide variety of products to advantage, and try to turn the rules to our favor whenever possible. And it was going to be our m.o. with Landmark and the pictorial calendar trade, too. In a dog-eat-dog world, the guy with the biggest, meanest dog has a way of coming out on top.

——◆——

Almost simultaneous with the purchase of Landmark, we acquired just about the last remaining competitor in our traditional line: Southworth Company. Like so many other older printing and paper concerns, Southworth had grown up in the mill towns that dot the Connecticut River Valley. Two brothers, Wells and Edward South-worth, started the business in 1836 along the banks of the Westfield River in what is now the Mittineague neighborhood of West Spring-field, Massachusetts. (Mittineague comes from the local Indian name for "place of falling waters.") Ever since, Southworth had been a qual-ity paper manufacturer, but over the years, it had also slipped into the commercial calendar business—wirebound books, the same things we made. (We even made the refill pads for one of their products.) It was the calendar business we were buying, not the quality paper side. Our argument to Southworth, one we had been pressing for a number of years, was that the company could never compete successfully with us in commercial calendars. We were simply too big and too omnipresent.

Instead of exhausting its resources in a losing cause, why didn't South-worth sell us the calendar division and use the proceeds to strengthen its position in the paper market, its core business? Finally, they agreed, for the fairly princely sum of $14 million: roughly $13.9 million for their customer base and brand, plus maybe $100,000 for equipment of all sorts.

Southworth, naturally, was extraordinarily happy with the terms. It got quite a lot of something for almost nothing tangible. I was thrilled, too, because we would be able to merge the division into At-A-Glance with almost no disruption of our main facility. Fourteen million dollars seems a lot to pay for a customer list, but in this instance the insubstantiality of it all was a bonus because Sidney, New York, was once again beginning to burst at the seams.

One last purchase remained. In 1997, we acquired Day Dream, Inc. out of Indianapolis, Indiana, a manufacturer of colorful wall calendars and posters. The calendars fit nicely with the Landmark line, while the posters extended our photographic and pictorial range generally. Like Landmark, Day Dream also had licenses with some of the top retail names in the world, Nike among them. Buying Day Dream also gave us added, and in some cases new, distribution channels into music, video, and book stores, and other outlets where wall posters get sold. Indeed, the deal would have been a sweetheart package except for one small twist: Despite assurances to the contrary, Day Dream's financial people had neglected to file tax returns in roughly all 50 states. An annoying detail, but not an impossible one to rectify.

=⋙⋘=

That's where matters stood with At-A-Glance by 1998. We had taken a company with fewer than 350 workers and a payroll of no more than $5 million and built it over the course of two decades into a nearly half a billion dollar business, with 1,400 factory workers and another 100 or so employees in managerial positions and an annual payroll of $56 million. In 1979, we'd broken ground on a new $5 million, 185,000-

square-foot plant. Six years later, we had added another 150,000 square feet for warehousing and distribution. By 1989, we were back in the construction business again, adding 26,000 square feet for offices and a state-of-the-art cafeteria. The new, 9,000-square-foot Dorothy and Lewis B. Cullman Child Development Center opened in January 1992. Three years later, we extended the existing warehouse and office space by another 110,000 square feet. Off on the side, Allied Graphic Arts was rolling along with about 45 employees, doing another $30–$40 million a year.

I'd bought Keith Clark as a nearly 60-year-old financial guy, an investor. Somehow, somewhere along the way, I had become a nearly 80-year-old manufacturer. And it all had worked! I was rich. The company was on a roll. But it wasn't just the numbers I was proud of. I was just as proud that all along the way, we had done things right.

Back in 1984, we had introduced an employee production bonus plan that made sure every worker in the factory shared in the economic benefits of increased production, and we had paid bonuses under that plan to each factory worker every year since.

The company was privately held; we couldn't reward management with traditional stock options because there wasn't any publicly held stock. But every one of any consequence in the management team was included in a phantom stock incentive plan based on annual operating profits and other financial yardsticks. As the 1990s wore on and I got older, I took a special trip up to Sidney, called all the key people in, and announced that I was voluntarily increasing their phantom stock units by 50 percent in the event of a sale or change of management. I didn't want anyone to worry about his welfare if I had to unload the company or if I dropped dead, but I also wanted those in authority to have a carrot dangling in front of them in case I did decide to sell. I'd heard about too many deals that were killed by innuendo because the management people didn't want them to happen. This kicker, I figured, would benefit everyone involved, and indeed, when I finally did sell the company, the deal went through almost without hitches, and the top people were rewarded with $4–$5 million each. Even relatively low-level managers came into $200,000 to $300,000.

Take a look at a map some day. Sidney sits on the shore of the Susquehanna River, an hour and a half downstream from the National Baseball Hall of Fame at Cooperstown, where the Susquehanna begins at the southern tip of Lake Ostego. Binghamton, New York, is another half an hour to 45 minutes southwest of Sidney, right on the Pennsylvania line. It's beautiful country, and for a time it even had a hint of prosperity. Sidney dates back to the early 1770s when a Reverend William Johnston built a home just about where we would eventually move our factory. By the mid-1800s, the town had three hotels, and by 1910, Sidney boasted factories for French cheese and cigars; a silk mill; a carriage works, a glass works, and a "novelty" works; and the Hatfield automobile plant, which basically stuck simple engines on modified horse buggies. Bad business luck and a series of fires and strikes in the 1920s might have ruined the town, but Scintilla, a maker of magnetos for airplane engines, relocated there from New York City in 1924, was purchased within a few years by Bendix Aviation, and somehow survived the Great Depression. Keith Clark followed Scintilla from New York to Sidney a quarter century later, in 1949, and the two became the mainstays of the town in a region generally in dire need of economic boosting. Lovely as they are, those foothills of the Catskill Mountains are a geological and economic extension of Appalachia, and the population reflects it. Average education levels are way below where they should be. People eat too much of the wrong kinds of food. The high-paying jobs are east, across the Catskills. In Sidney, women work because they have to, not out of ideological conviction, and they tend to have babies early and often because that's what their mothers did, and their mothers before them.

Anyone who has ever tried to run a manufacturing concern in such a place knows you just can't ignore the socioeconomic realities that surround you. Factories need a workforce, and the better and happier the workforce, the more efficiently the factory runs. Keith Clark was also a union shop: The Teamsters had taken over from one of the small print-ing unions before we ever bought the business. We mounted a campaign to get the union decertified and would have succeeded, I'm convinced, if the Teamsters hadn't pulled a technicality that got the vote delayed until all our momentum had dissipated. (Union busting is a little like sex in your seventies and beyond: If you miss the moment, it's hard to build up that fever pitch a second time without a little rest.) But Teamsters or not, we went way beyond what we had to do, economically and morally, and not just to avoid the dreaded union grievance sessions. We added a new cafeteria because we wanted our workers to have a bet-ter, more pleasant place to eat and at least an opportunity to select foods that weren't mostly fat and starch, and we put a workout room next to it so employees who chose to could begin to remedy years of physical neglect. I can't say that the latter was heavily used by those who needed it most, but it was there, as it should have been.

The cornerstone of everything we tried to do was the Dorothy and Lewis B. Cullman Child Development Center. (There are those names again!) No problem is greater than child care in a community where so many young mothers have to work, and nothing can do more to change the balance of the economic scales for the next generation than child care that doesn't just provide baby-sitting services but focuses on developing the brain. Obviously, it's in the kids' and parents' interest to provide that, but it was also in our economic self-interest. Unless we were going to move the plant somewhere else down the road, the kids we started training at the center were going to form the labor pool we would be hiring from in the next generation, and in the age of automation, unless your workforce gets smarter year by year, produc-tion will never keep up with the competition. Doug Willies took to calling the child development center our "farm club" and he was right.

Dorothy and I got the place rolling with a $500,000 gift. The federal government came in on top of that with what's known as an Appalachian Mountain grant, and the center opened its doors at the start of 1992 with indoor and outdoor playgrounds, a self-contained kitchen, and enough staff and space to feed and take care of a hundred children, ages six weeks to 12 years. The place was (and still is) spectacular looking, and it's right on the grounds of the factory. Instead of chasing all over creation for child care, parents could now drop their preschoolers off in the morning, right at the workplace door, knowing they would be stimulated, not just corralled in front of a television.

Gerry Edelman out at the Neurosciences Institute and other researchers have been discovering that at about two years old, kids have a tremendous neural growth spurt that, properly nourished, can make a huge difference in child development. We took that to heart: The center has drawing classes for the children once they're old enough to hold a crayon. The kids start learning the alphabet and their numbers at the earliest feasible age. They're read to. It's all basic, but the basics count. For older children, the center continues to run an after-school, latchkey program so kids won't be unsupervised until their parents get back from work—and so parents won't have to worry as they work about what the kids might be doing home alone. Again, there's plenty of stimulation on hand. Chess-in-the-Schools provided all the proof I'll ever need of the value of challenging young minds.

The center is open to the entire Sidney community—it has to be to maintain its "not-for-profit" status. Until recently, the center also received annual operating funds from the state. Governor George Pataki put an end to that as part of his statewide belt-tightening, but even when New York State still had a heart, nonemployee kids ended up being subsidized by the At-A-Glance Group because the center charges about $40 to $50 a week less than the actual cost per-child for full-day care. Employee children did even better, receiving scholarships that cover 50 percent of the cost for a first child enrolled and 25 percent of the cost for subsequent ones.

I brought the boards of directors and some of the top people from places like the New York Public Library and the Museum of Modern Art up to Sidney to see the At-A-Glance facility and especially the child development center. I liked to show off both places, and it's always good for people who work and live in such rarefied atmospheres to get their feet on the ground well outside of the crystal palaces of Manhattan. The MoMA delegation arrived just about the time Hillary Clinton, then First Lady, was heading off to France on a much-publicized tour of the supposedly superior French child-care facilities. I remember Aggie Gund, MoMA's president, looking around our child development center and exclaiming, "Goddamn it! What the hell is Hillary doing going over to France to look at these places when she's got a better one right here in her own backyard?" I'd been thinking the same thing for weeks, in pretty much those same sailor terms.

My long-time friend Bob Menschel, senior director of the Goldman Sachs Group and founder of its institutional investment department, was on that same trip. He told me afterwards that he had been to plants all over the country but had never seen anything to match what we were doing. Mike Margitich, MoMA's vice president for external affairs (the classy new name for a development chief), still talks in glowing terms about what he saw up there, especially the children's center. On another occasion, William Walker, director of the research libraries for the New York Public Library, got all excited about the total quality management program we had introduced back in 1991. Bill spent hours talking with our TQM people up in Sidney and many more hours getting the total quality process embedded in his domain back in the city.

Maybe pride does goeth before the fall, but I always loved opening eyes that way. Whether it's science or finance or management, there's so much to learn by stepping out of our own boxes, and At-A-Glance gave me a chance to do that, for myself and for lots of other people. The business was a constant education. And then came the day early in 1998 when I could see beyond any question that it was time to bring down the curtain on the show.

⸎

Building a business as we had through frequent acquisitions and constantly leveraging our assets has all sorts of advantages. You're not drafting college or even high-school basketball players, uncertain if they will be able to compete at the next level. With acquisitions, you know what the goods are, warts and all, before you buy. If you have any sense (and a lot of LBO outfits don't) you also already know where and how the company you are acquiring is going to fit into a total business strategy before you ever commit a dime. Just as important, you're making your assets work as hard as they can. In the financial world, money acts the same as a traditional lever in the physical word: Find the right fulcrum point, and a little bit of pressure on one side can cause large bodies to move on the other.

But there's a cumulative effect to what we had been doing. Loan arrangements from one deal sprawl into the next one. With each new acquisition, we had a stronger market position, but we also had less flexibility until we could clear the debt away. I hadn't really realized it, but with the purchase of Day Dream in 1997, we had just about reached our limits. It took the proposed purchase of Day Runner to drive the point home.

Doug Willies, who had been running the company since 1987, was the one behind the idea. Three years earlier, when we were on the block, the Day Runner people had tried to acquire us. Now Doug came down from Sidney to a meeting in my Manhattan office, loaded down with all kinds of formulas for how we could buy Day Runner and with a long list of reasons why we should do so. The "why" part was pretty straightforward. Just as Landmark and Day Dream had extended our franchise into pictorial calendars and posters, Day Runner would take it into daily organizers, a logical extension of our core calendar business and a rapidly growing field in the plan-every-minute '90s. (We did, in fact, have a very simple organizer already in our product line, but we had added it mostly so we could tell our customers it was there.)

When Doug got to the "how" part of his presentation, things got trickier. As always, we would borrow the money for the purchase: Borrowing is integral to leveraging assets. Ever since the company had been pulled back from the brink of being sold, though, we had been buying and borrowing at a furious clip. I never had a moment's doubt about our ability to meet our obligations, but the more a company owes, the more control its lenders get over its cash flow. The next series of questions seemed obvious; so I got things started:

"Wait a minute," I said, "this may be an interesting idea, but how do you plan to finance this?"

"We have the borrowing capacity," someone piped up.

"Well, assuming we go ahead with this acquisition, what will be the extent of the restrictions because of covenants from the debt?"

"There can't be any distributions for the next three years," came the answer.

"Look," I said, "this is totally unsatisfactory. As far as I'm concerned, we just have to sell the business." This time I meant it. I didn't need the distributions for my own material well-being, but I did need them if I was going to both hold on to the company and keep giving money away at a rate I found satisfactory. If At-A-Glance had to acquire Day Runner to stay dynamic, then I was the wrong person with the wrong priorities at the wrong point in life to be owning the company. Besides, I was 80 years old. It was time to start concentrating on what I really liked doing best.

History proved to be on my side, by the way. It wasn't long after Doug Willies proposed acquiring Day Runner that Palm Pilots and other electronic organizers stole the market out from under the old paper-and-print ones. Day Runner responded by picking up a British competitor, File-O-Fax, for a price so astronomical that the debt dragged both companies under. But I wasn't reading tea leaves when I turned thumbs down on Day Runner and saved us from buying into a dying business; I was just following my heart.

———◦◦◦———

In 1995, Goldman Sachs had had to beat the bushes to turn up buyers. This time, when we went back to them to find another purchaser, they practically had one waiting in the lobby: Mead Corporation, the

$3.8 billion paper and forest-products giant with more than 14,000 employees and operations in 32 nations around the world. Negotiations opened in early 1999, and on November 2, Mead announced that it was acquiring At-A-Glance for its school and office products division.

As I had expected, Mead didn't want Allied Graphic Arts; so we spun that off into a separate corporation, continued to run it—or more accurately, continued to let it run itself—and in January 2002, we sold the whole thing back to AGA's top management for $3 million, a steal for them and a proper reward in the bargain.

Inevitably, as with any deal, other and greater complications arose. Mead was so concerned over liability protection that it insisted $55 million be placed in an escrow account and added the further, more draconian provision that the principals in the sale—myself, Bill Mayo-Smith, Tom Hargrove, Doug Willies, and Jim Moore—be joint and severally liable for any claims over and above the $55 million. That, in turn, so alarmed Bill Mayo-Smith that I ended up creating a separate $55-million principal seller's escrow account, so that the burden of any claims in excess of the first $55 million would fall largely on my shoulders. "Gee, Lewis," I remember Bill saying before I hit upon the idea of a second escrow account, "if you go broke, we have to pick up your share! I can't live with that." He was theoretically right, of course. Even Bill Gates *could* go broke, and I was a long, long way from that exalted territory. But with the sale of At-A-Glance, the odds of a liability judgment bringing me down were increasingly minimal.

Bill Mayo-Smith's greatest concern, though, was that our tax returns were going to be audited as a result of the sale and that the IRS might come along and say we had been noncompliant with some of the sub-S corporation provisions. Again, all things are possible in love, war, and tax codes. We'd bought plenty of companies whose tax paperwork looked as if it had been handled by a kennel of not very bright dogs, but that wasn't us. I had made absolutely certain over the years that we had all the necessary documentation, and I offered it all up to Bill, his lawyer, his accountant, and any other counselor whose comfort he might seek.

On the big issue—price—Mead quibbled hardly at all. Less than four years earlier, Butler Capital had offered a very shaky package that would have paid $325 million for the company. This time, when it counted, Mead agreed to pay $550 million for CVI. To be sure, the business had done well in the interim and grown through acquisition. Still, by refusing to sell the first time around, I had run the value of the company up by $225 million. Sometimes in life, the big wins are just blind luck.

In mid-November, 1999, I went up to Sidney to take part in a celebration of my years of owning At-A-Glance, a company we had bought for $13 million back in 1978. My brother Joe offered to go with me, and the two of us met Bill Mayo-Smith that morning at the Thirty-fourth Street heliport and flew up together in the Philip Morris copter. (Being chairman emeritus of a large corporation has its privileges!)

As I walked around the factory and child development center, the warehouse and distribution facilities—so much of it new within the last decade—I couldn't help but think of the Quonset hut and cinder-block buildings we had picked up for a song 21 years earlier. We hadn't grown into Sidney's biggest employer. Amphenol Aerospace (the former Bendix) still held that distinction, by a few hundred employees. But we had been her best corporate citizen. I was elected a lifetime member of the Sidney Chamber of Commerce, complete with framed certificate. So far as I know, I'm also the only out-of-towner ever to be named Sidney's annual "Citizen of the Years," an honorific I love not least of all for the quirky plural.

Because of us, 1,500 people in and around Sidney had secure, well-paying jobs. Their small children had a daycare center where they could get a leg up on life; their grade-schoolers, a secure and welcoming place to come to until mom or dad got off work. Some of the At-A-Glance workers were healthier than they would have been otherwise because of our cafeteria and gym. Among the upper ranks of management, some had even been made rich by what we had built the company into and sold it for. The employees had given a lot to us, and we had given a lot back to them. That, to me, is what good corporate ownership is about, and as I walked up and down the assembly lines, shaking hands with all 1,400 employees on the factory floor, I really felt that they understood that: We had tried our best, and they had tried theirs. The day was touching beyond words, an experience I'll never forget.

Maybe the greatest advantage of making it into my mid-eighties in such excellent health is that I've gotten to live so many lives and learn so much from each of them.

I grew up with plenty of opportunity and attended the sort of schools that are supposed to guarantee success, but to me, every step along the way seemed to be leading to an adult life I didn't want—the one my father had laid out for all us boys. Cecil Driver, my senior adviser at Yale, and my own early interest in meteorology saved me from that. Amazingly, or so it seemed to me then, Cecil was willing to take my secret ambition seriously; even more amazingly, I was willing to tell him what it was. Sometimes great things happen when we don't hold back—great *and* lucky ones. I got to be a Navy weatherman when it really mattered, when "homeland security" had a daily immediacy that even this post 9/11 world lacks; and being a weatherman, sending those Navy blimps out to search for U-boats every day, gave me a chance to use what I had learned in graduate school for the public good. All those English majors plodding along as foot soldiers couldn't make the same claim.

My career as a civilian weather forecaster and entrepreneur didn't last long, but trying to convince road-crew bosses to buy my services taught me much about sales. I was CEO of the company and chief cook and bottle washer, and I learned something in both roles and in all the roles I had to fill in between, including the role of business partner for as long as that lasted.

I didn't set any longevity records at Wertheim & Co., either, and I wasn't a very enthusiastic security salesman. But even though Maurice Wertheim died not long after I arrived at the company, I found in him a sort of absent role model. I, too, would much rather shoot one or two ducks a year than plod away hour after hour, day after day at some desk job. A decade would pass before I bagged my own first duck—Orkin Exterminating—but after all that waiting, it was a dilly.

I also found at Wertheim & Co. a wise and willing mentor in Andy Scharps. Andy was a firm believer in the permanence of human nature, and he made me one, too. Whether it's poker or negotiations, a boom market or a bear one, people behave pretty much the same way from one generation to the next. "You know, every time you hear it's a new era, fasten your seat belt," Andy used to say. I thought of that often in the rah-rah economy of the 1990s as paradigm piled on paradigm and the media gurus kept declaring that things would never be what they used to be again. The buzzwords change; yesterday's sage becomes tomorrow's fool; but it really is so often the same old song.

Dad, of course, did get his clutches on me eventually. More accurately, sad circumstances drove me into his arms. But as much as I had resisted going to work at Cullman Bros. and fulfilling the family destiny, I wouldn't trade the time for anything. I got to know my Canadian friends there; they became my first investors; and together, we found the right crease in time.

The Incubation Group could not have worked today—I'm sure of that—but back in the 1950s and early 1960s, the number of institutions that bought equities was minimal. If you could get a stock on the approved purchase list of a large bank's trust department, you were almost assured a dramatic change in the multiple. The goal was simple—find an unrecognized stock and hold on to it until the trust officers found it, too—and the playing field for stock-pickers such as I was almost empty. No more.

Last I looked, there were something like 8,000 mutual funds in America, all of them with purportedly professional managers. God alone knows how many chartered financial analysts there might be. If there's a truly "undiscovered" stock anywhere in the world, I would be surprised. All the analysts talk to each other all the time. They have conventions. They compare notes. The professional managers have computers trained to kick out anything the least unusual, the most minutely promising. Infinitesimal market vibrations are parsed as if they were pulsar transmissions from some extraterrestrial life form. For that matter, any Average Joe can log on to the Internet, consult beta averages and every other form of statistical nonsense, then use a cyber bulletin board to pile his own bad advice on the flawed conventional wisdom the paid experts are kicking back and forth. In truth, I've come to think it's all bunk, or nearly so—that indexing might be the only answer. Figures don't lie, as the old saying goes, but liars figure. Always have, always will. There are just more of them now.

The same thing happened with leveraged buyouts. When Herb Weiner and I first got into the business, the field was wide open in front of us. But the idea was too good to resist, and soon the sheer volume of the deals began to overwhelm anything approaching common sense. First the innovators, then the imitators, then the swarming incompetents: So it was with LBOs. As the competition got greater, the prices went up; and as the prices rose, the margins of safety disappeared. With leveraged buyout firms multiplying like fruit flies, so-so deals started to look good, and terrible deals, tolerable. Finally, Henry Kravis, who seemed to love a hostile takeover more than life itself, bought RJR Nabisco and established the negative sine qua non of this particular financial art form: that beyond which nothing could be more stupid.

As the deals multiplied and began to outstrip the resources (and in some cases, the imaginations) of the traditional lenders we had used—insurance companies and banks—Michael Milken helped usher in the era of the junk bond. Like LBOs, junk bonds began as a good innovation, a way to make capital do double and triple duty; but like KKR, Milken and his imitators and swarming incompetents couldn't resist the excesses. A reasonable risk in pursuit of a sweet reward became an insane risk in pursuit of a crazy reward until the last sucker was found and the whole Ponzi scheme began to collapse in on itself.

Worse than the illegalities and the idiocies, the con games and the delusions, was the mentality that came to rule the roost in the leveraged buyout business. Cullman Ventures began, in effect, as a holding outfit for companies we had purchased through LBOs. Once we acquired Keith Clark, we began to use the same technique to build an individual business into something far larger, but either way, we were looking long term. Our obligation was to the businesses we had acquired and to the people who worked for them because our bottom line depended on the companies' profitability. At so many other buyout houses, the first question asked was always "What will the exit price be?" Even before the ink was dry on the sale contract, the plotting had begun to sell the business, to a new buyer or to the public via an initial public offering. There was no other choice really: To build up the record that would allow them to raise more money for the next purchase, the LBO houses had to print a profit; and to do that, they had to keep their money in motion. The churn was what mattered, not the business, not the workers.

That's exactly the fix we would have found ourselves in if we had succeeded in buying At-A-Glance back in 1988. To dress our offer up for the financial markets, we brought Warburg Pincus in as a partner. We really had no choice in the matter if we wanted to be taken seriously, but had we won the bidding war, Warburg would have been asking about the exit price almost from day one. My best guess is that we would have been forced into selling the business no more than five years out at a price I can't imagine would have exceeded $200 million. Warburg wouldn't have tolerated any longer than that. Instead, we picked up At-A-Glance from the Arab group that had purchased it; continued to add more pieces to the puzzle; treated our people right; and sold the whole megillah (minus AGA) to Mead in 1999 for almost three times what we might have received six years earlier.

I admit it: I'm one of many, many people who helped crown finance and make it king. Herb Weiner and I turned the bootstrap technique into a global LBO orgy. Thanks to me and my ilk, the economy of the late twentieth century found itself driven by profit, not production. The Rust Belt, the places that made things, withered away. The investment bankers, the people who made deals, became the new strutting gods of the economic pantheon. IPOs flourished, in spite of reality: Half of the companies that were being taken public seemed to be trying to take off on gossamer wings. Creative accounting flourished, too, far more so than creative engineering. Profit, not product, drove everything it seemed. *Mea culpa.* At last, though, I saw the light.

In early 1990, I donated a million dollars to establish what a *New York Times* reporter speculated might be the nation's first ever professorship of manufacturing management. My motivation was simple. According to one survey I had seen, nearly four in five CEOs came out of marketing or financing, while only 21 percent came out of production. That didn't make any sense to me. Sure, a chief executive officer needs a basic grasp of the principles of finance, but ultimately, a business has to make something. CEOs ought to know something about that, too, and they ought to have top people reporting to them who really understand manufacturing. Instead, having come up through finance themselves, so many CEOs surround themselves with flunkies who know everything about numbers and almost nothing about equipment, warehousing, distribution, production, and all their variables. No wonder so many companies have made such bad decisions during the downsizing of recent years: The people making the calls could think in only one dimension. I wanted to use the endowed chair to start changing that: to begin producing a new generation of top managers who were jacks of all trades, people who could look at a business in its full dimensionality. Financing had about played itself out, I told the *Times* reporter. The future belonged to factories, and that meant the future of management belonged to those who were at home on the factory floor. I was, the *Times* noted, a "reformed" buyout artist.

The choice of a business school at which to endow the chair was a little more complicated. The Yale School of Management was the obvious choice, but I got a copy of the current curriculum and found it so full of finance courses that I decided to use Yale as the negative example of what I was searching for.

At my next stop, the hyper-famous Harvard Business School, I mentioned to the dean that I thought institutions such as his were neglecting the manufacturing component of the economy.

"Not us," he replied. "We use the case method to study manufacturing."

"Oh, come on," I told him, "how can you use a case method for learning how to run a factory? You've got to get your fingernails dirty to do that."

Finally, to the consternation of Yale, Harvard, and other such well-pedigreed institutions, I endowed my little chair at Purdue University. I liked the fact that Purdue had a large and well-respected engineering school. Engineers know grit. Maybe most of all, I loved the nickname for the school's athletic teams: the Boilermakers. Nothing says "factory floor" more clearly than that. A professor at the Columbia University Graduate School of Business told the *Times* reporter that I'd chosen a school that lacked innovative research in manufacturing and production programs. "If you're not able to leapfrog or move ahead in this area, you're nowhere," the aggrieved academic sniffed. "Purdue is not a leapfrogger." Oh, horrors.

To be sure, the endowment didn't go smoothly. I gave the money all in one fell swoop, a big mistake that I never repeated again. Because I had retained no leverage over the gift, Purdue could dawdle while it searched for the right candidate, and dawdle it did, maybe intentionally. Finally, the business school nominated one of its own for the post, and my money ended up financing an existing situation, not at all what

I expected. Almost worst of all, I had to sit for another damn portrait and endure its unveiling in a deadly ceremony at the Yale Club in New York. To top off the event, my endowee gave a speech that would have tried the merits of a far more patient man than me.

The *Times* article on the gift, by the way, referred to me as "irascible." Now, where do you think *that* came from?

———◆———

No life is without regrets, and mine is no exception. But I find that for every regret, I've had more than my share of compensation. I'm sorry that Thais has had such a difficult lot in life, but our divorce led to Dorothy, and 40 years so far of happiness. She's had plenty of cause, but the only time in recent memory that Dorothy has threatened to send me packing was when I popped out on the stage at a Chess-in-the-Schools event, all set to deliver comments in my downhill ski-racing suit, complete with goggles. The Spiderman look, Dorothy seemed to feel, was better left to a younger generation.

For his sake, I wish Duncan had more control over his brain chemistry and behavior, but his children—my grandchildren—are a delight. Mia, of whom I see too little, skies for the University of Colorado. Nikken, the oldest, has worked four summers at Goldman Sachs and is entering his senior year at Yale as I write. After all these years, I have someone close to me, family, interested in what I've learned in my six-plus decades of business.

Of my four siblings, Arthur died first, followed by Nan, the oldest. None of the three of us who remain is exactly a spring chicken, but for a bunch of octogenarians and up, we get around just fine. Joe, the senior of us boys, has always been there when I needed him, as friend, brother, comforter, and tennis foe. Joe stopped playing a few years back, but even in his mid-eighties, he was still a tough guy to hit a ball past. Edgar has been there for me, too. We were the closest in age and we competed tooth and nail. But the years sometimes sweep the difficult moments away and leave the good behind. That's the case with Edgar and me.

Someone asked me not long ago if I could think of any deals I was sorry not to have been a part of, any fields I would like to have gotten a foothold in. The question sent me ransacking memory—so many years, so many deals—but finally, the answer was no. Within the limited game I chose to play, I had all the action I could ever want, and the tighter I drew the circle, the more fun it all became. A commercial calendar is just a commercial calendar, not a semiconductor or a circuit board, but we turned out a hundred million of them annually, and as I wrote earlier, they all became obsolete at the stroke of midnight on December 31.

Focusing allowed me to concentrate on Keith Clark, and as that happened, my own internal reward structure began to shift. I became less interested in the art of the deal—like seduction, it grows repetitive—and more interested in business building and all the good vibes that flow from that. And, of course, the better my business did and the more money I made from it, the more I discovered that what I enjoyed most was not amassing money but giving it away.

In his *Gospel of Wealth*, published in 1889, Andrew Carnegie advised the rich to spend the first half of their lives accumulating wealth and the second half distributing the surplus to those causes "best calculated to produce the most beneficial results for the community." Carnegie lived his advice, doling out some $350 million during his lifetime, roughly $7 billion in current dollars, mostly to universities and to build public libraries. I got started later than Andrew Carnegie, both at making significant money and at donating large chunks of it. What's more, I never had, nor ever will have, his kind of wealth: My money came from print and paper products, not a steel cartel. And I could never, ever rise to Carnegie's level of Scottish rectitude. Still, I don't think Dorothy and I have done too badly, by Andrew Carnegie's lights or by our own.

To date, we've given away roughly $100 million, and I hope there's more to come. About $18 million remains in the first escrow account set up to satisfy Mead's liability concerns. Another $55 million sits in the second account, created to back up the first and ease my partners' concerns. The majority of that money is mine. The escrow accounts are due to be released in 2004, and Dorothy and I are plotting where the money might go and how it might be best used: neglected programs, initiatives that make connections across disciplines, ways to leverage our money to bring in much more for some worthy museum or research institute. Only recently, I was inducted into the American Academy of Arts & Sciences, in recognition of my philanthropic efforts. Founded in Cambridge, Massachusetts, in 1780 by John Adams and others, the academy puts me in some pretty heady company. (Adams, so the story goes, was playing catch-up with Benjamin Franklin, who had launched the American Philosophical Society in Philadelphia more than 35 years earlier.) With a little luck, Dorothy and I can top the $200 million mark in our lifetime. I think we can honestly say we've done our share.

I've never taken a vow of poverty, and I'm not about to take one now that I'm almost 85. Dorothy and I live well. I ski when I want and where. Sometimes I even put on my downhill racing suit and say to hell with caution, fashion, and maybe even good sense. We've got a time-share in a private jet to carry us in comfort whenever we travel. Our giving hasn't been an exercise in self-denial or doing without. We have everything we could want. To us, giving has always been a pleasure, a chance to do some good with the success of my business career. For the opportunities that have made this all possible, for the people who have helped me out along the way, for the times I've lived through, I remain deeply thankful; but I'm also enthusiastically curious about the future. After all, every phase of my life has brought something new and exciting. Who knows what the next decades might hold.

INDEX

Index

Index